Richard Boleslavsky
His Life and Work in the Theatre

Theater and Dramatic Studies, No. 7

Bernard Beckerman, Series Editor

Brander Matthews Professor of Dramatic Literature
Columbia University in the City of New York

Other Titles in This Series

Richard Boleslavsky
His Life and Work in the Theatre

by
J. W. Roberts

UMI RESEARCH PRESS
Ann Arbor, Michigan

Produced and distributed by
UMI Research Press
an imprint of
University Microfilms International
Ann Arbor, Michigan 48106

Library of Congress Cataloging in Publication Data

Roberts, J. W.
  Richard Boleslavsky, his life and work in the
theatre.

  (Theater and dramatic studies ; no. 7)
  Revision of thesis (Ph.D.)—Kent State University, 1977.
  Bibliography: p.
  Includes index.
  1. Boleslavsky, Richard, 1889-1937. 2. Theatrical
producers and directors—United States—Biography.
3. Actors—Poland—Biography. 4. Stanislavsky methods.
I. Title. II. Series.
PN2287.B484R6 1981   792'.0233'0924 [B]   81-16411
ISBN 0-8357-1250-8   AACR2

Frontispiece.   Richard Boleslavsky ca. 1923.
                Photographer unknown.
                Courtesy of Natasha Boleslavsky.

Contents

Preface

As a first biography of Richard Boleslavsky, this book does not presume to be definitive. Its scope has been limited to Boleslavsky's work in the theatre in Russia, Poland, and the United States and it offers only a summary of his work in Hollywood as a film director.

Some attention has been given to Boleslavsky's lessons in theatre, particularly as he presented his ideas at the American Laboratory Theatre in New York from 1923 to 1929. Here again, there can be no final statement. Boleslavsky's earliest known lectures have been preserved in manuscript as "The Creative Theatre," but that manuscript is apparently incomplete, missing the final lectures. Only a handful of the several hundred lectures Boleslavsky gave at the Laboratory Theatre are known to survive. His published book on theatre, *Acting: The First Six Lessons,* as even the title suggests, is also incomplete. Ten lessons were projected, but only six were written. One may still hope for the possible discovery of further materials that are presently lost to us. Readers wishing a more detailed examination of what is presently known of Boleslavsky's theory are referred to my Ph.D. dissertation: "The Theatre Theory and Practice of Richard Boleslavsky" (Kent State University, 1977).

This biography draws extensively on materials contained in the dissertation, but it is not simply the dissertation revised. Somewhat over half the material contained in the dissertation has found its way more or less intact into these pages, but this biography contains a great deal of material that is not to be found in my earlier work.

Unless otherwise attributed, translations from the Russian are by the author, working in consultation with students of the language. Translations from German and Polish were made for me by others. Play titles that are reasonably familiar to English readers have been given in their most usual form, though in a few cases common variant translations have been noted. At the first reference to works that are lesser known, my translation is followed parenthetically by the original title.

A great many individuals and institutions have given special help in the research and composition of this study, and that help is gratefully acknowledged. Special thanks should be extended to: Mr. Paul Myers and the staff of The Library and Museum of the Performing Arts at Lincoln Center; the staff of the Slavic Collection of the New York Public Library; Columbia University and New York University, for access to their Russian-language materials; Stella Adler, who supplied me with materials from her private collection; Dr. Ronald A. Willis, for giving me access to the files of the American Laboratory Theatre and numerous taped interviews he conducted with former members of the Lab; and Elfreda Lang, Curator of Manuscripts, and the staff of the Lilly Library, Indiana University, who supplied copies of several hundred items of Boleslavsky's correspondence from the Bobbs-Merrill Collection.

For help in translation, I must thank Ann Lowendahl, Irina L. Belodedova, Timothy Perrin, Stephen Mazurek, Ove Brusendorff, and Alexander Struve.

An expression of gratitude here is inadequate to express my personal debt to my good friends, John Erdwurm, for his many helpful suggestions; and Robert F. Decker, whose patient encouragement and frequent scoldings went a long way toward bringing this work to print.

A final word of warm appreciation must be reserved for Natasha Boleslavsky. Thank you, Natasha, for the friendship we shared and for the many long hours of informal conversation which provided a uniquely personal view of the man you knew and loved so well.

The research that has gone into this book has continued for some ten years now. During that time I have come to feel that I almost know Boleslavsky in a personal way, though he died before I was born. Tomorrow I leave for my first trip to Moscow, where Boleslavsky worked and learned over half a century ago. I have no doubt that once in Moscow I will continue to search for traces of the path he took.

JWR
July 6, 1981

Part I: 1889–1915

The Vistula River Region and Imperial Russia

But then my other half started to speak, and that other half spoke deep from the first memories of childhood: the first words of my mother; the first lullaby songs; the first secret lessons in history, lessons which were barred from books by law; my first feeble efforts, with pen and primer. "Pole, Polish, Poland,"—at home, before I went to school, where Poland was reduced to a nonentity and known as the Vistula River Region. As one might call the United States the Mississippi River Region.

—Richard Boleslavsky
Lances Down, p. 40.

1

The Polish Hearth

Richard Boleslavsky was the stage name taken by Bolesław Ryszard Srzednicki. He was born Polish at a time when, politically, there was no Poland. Forever homeless, he was adopted by the theatres of Moscow, Warsaw, and New York, and he finished his days in the Hollywood film studios.

Very little is known at present about his family background, in large part because of Boleslavsky's curious attitude toward his family. His wife of ten years, Natasha,—a Russian of Lithuanian extraction—retains remarkable memories of her years with Boleslavsky. Well into her eighties, she could still recall the month and year that certain of his productions opened and could name at least the important actors in the casts; but about Boleslavsky's family—almost nothing. "I never knew them, and he never talked about such things." She did not even know he spoke fluent Polish until 1920, when they fled Russia for Poland. Nor did she know he was descended from members of the land-holding Polish gentry until after they reached New York in 1922. Shortly after arriving in America, Boleslavsky spent a day at the public library locating a book on Polish heraldry. Having found his family crest, he had a small signet made, then put it away among his private papers and never spoke of it again.

Perhaps Boleslavsky hoarded his memories of family and earliest years because they were too intensely personal—or painful. In none of his extant writing does he mention the name of his father, mother, brother (he had at least one), or other relation, and as an adult, he rarely spoke of them. Curiously, while he never discussed such matters with American friends, he was eager to write at length about them in two published autobiographical books, *Way of the Lancer* and *Lances Down*. His correspondence with Helen Woodward, who served as a kind of editor and corrected grammatical errors in the manuscripts, reveals that time and again she excised lengthy passages describing his family and early life in Poland, on the grounds that such material was either irrelevant to the books' themes or too "sentimental." Woodward, a novelist (her husband, William Woodward, was also a writer), was both Boleslavsky's collaborator and close personal friend, and he always took her advice seriously, though he did not always follow it. In this instance, however, he agreed to the deletions, provided that the material was set aside for a proposed third book dealing with his early life and first experiences at the Moscow Art Theatre. That book was never written, and the material is presumably lost.

In an undated letter, Woodward, exasperated that Boleslavsky had again restored material she had already struck out in two or three previous drafts of a chapter, pondered at length the importance Poland held for him:

> Your eternal longing for a Poland that did not exist is profoundly moving. If I were a psycho-analyst I think I would be inclined to explain it rather as a longing for a childhood that can never come back. Since that childhood took place in Poland and Poland is also reactionally non-existent for you, you have transposed the two in your mind. I may be wrong, but nearly all of us have such things in us, and an enormous amount of one's patriotism is just that. What we consider love of one's own land is not love of one's own land so much as a longing for an irresponsible and happy childhood. I am singularly without this because my childhood was not happy, and I think it is one of the reasons why people who had comfortable and personally prosperous childhoods often seem more patriotic than people who were poor.[1]

Boleslavsky responded to this analysis with some fervor:

> . . . In the second book [*Lances Down*] I am a cold reporter who actually hates the things which happened. And you know no good ever comes out of hate. Another thing that strikes my mind is that the second book, being a continuation of the first, should at the same time be a book, clear and understandable by itself. How are you going to overcome that trouble without showing where my psychology sprang from and where I got that passive attitude towards the Russians; Russians who after all befriended me and were very kind to me, if I don't have in my blood what you call "recollections of childhood"? You see, Helen, you can say whatever you want about Poland, but you cannot remake me, being a Pole. And whatever I did in those days was tinted very strongly by that only passion in me—passion for Poland.

Near the end of the letter he added: "Inside I am just a Goddamned, obstinate Pole."[2]

By cultural and national heritage, Bolesław Ryszard Srzednicki was very much a son of Poland, despite the fact that Poland had been dismembered one hundred years before his birth. The Three Partitions had divided the nation and distributed its parts among Germany, the Austro-

Hungarian Empire, and Imperial Russia. At the end of the eighteenth century, Poland had vanished from the maps of Europe. The Srzednicki family had held land near the town of Płock, located on the Vistula River some fifty or sixty miles northwest of Warsaw, for four hundred years. That heritage was not erased by the mere eradication of the Polish state. Branches of the family extended into the east, reaching even into Russia proper; its members had served the rulers of the former Kingdom of Poland and distinguished themselves as soldiers and artists, servants of the King's government and defenders of the Roman Catholic Faith.[3]

By the end of the nineteenth century, the family manor house in Płock, Dębowa Góra (Oak Mountain), was occupied by Valentine Srzednicki. Wheat grew bountifully on his land, located in Poland's most fertile district, and river transport was convenient, circumstances that had once helped the family to prosper. Now, however, the family fortune had begun to decline, evidently due to Tsar Alexander II's emancipation of the serfs in 1861. Alexander had granted Polish serfs title to all property they occupied in that year, as well as any land that had been taken from them "illegally" by Polish lords. After that, Valentine Srzednicki had to pay salaries to engage his former serfs as peasant laborers. Reduced land holdings, higher operating costs, and lower prices on the Russian grain market (Tsarist policies shut off most other markets) no doubt diminished the Srzednicki's wealth.

Valentine's son, Bolesław Ryszard Srzednicki, was born on 4 February 1889. There was at least one other son, who later became a priest and served the Catholic Church in Mława.[4] The last decade of the nineteenth century—the years of Bolesław's boyhood—saw increasingly intense efforts by the Tsar to achieve russification in the Congress Kingdom, as the Russian sector of historical Poland was known. The Polish language was banned from schools, the press, and most other public institutions; it was tolerated only in the theatre and in services of the Catholic Church (although the Church itself was repressed and conversion to Russian Orthodoxy was encouraged). In some schools Polish was permitted to be taught as a "second" language.

The resilient Poles responded by setting up an underground, secret school system; members of the gentry taught not only their own children, but the children of their former serfs as well. From about 1900, when Boleslavsky was eleven, severe administrative punishments (without trial) were decreed as the penalty for involvement in the secret school system. As Boleslavsky recounts, however, such repressive measures did not stop his getting an education, primarily from his mother, in the language, history, music, and literature of Poland:

> . . . Every Pole had in his heart the long cherished idea of the Fatherland—Poland
> above all. The Poles studied their national history, not from cold textbooks, but in
> their homes in the evenings from smuggled books, which were forbidden and there-
> fore more precious, from the talks of mothers and fathers and grandfathers who had
> taken part in the 1860 insurrection, and had suffered beatings and exile to Siberia.
> Above everything, they were attached to Poland and the idea of Polish indepen-
> dence, peasants and landowners, poor and rich alike.[5]

Later, Boleslavsky repeated some of those lessons in *Way of the
Lancer:* unlike Imperial Russia, the Kingdom of Poland had been a
republic, and not an empire. Unlike the dynastic Russian Tsars, the
kings of Poland had always been elected, and "in our whole history
there wasn't a single one who was a tyrant."[6] Boleslavsky believed that
in earlier centuries Poland had been the most libertarian country in the
world, surrounded on all sides by nations that imposed serfdom and
slavery. "In Poland," on the other hand, "there had been economic
dependence, but politically, every man was free."[7]

Lessons from "smuggled books" were supplemented by less formal
training. From earliest childhood Boleslavsky heard stories and songs
celebrating the Polish folk hero, the lancer. The lancers' endless fight for
freedom and independence embodied Polish ideals:

> As a child I was told that the Lancers defended Europe and Christianity against the
> barbarians and Mongolians. That it was a tradition which had never died, and never
> would. That whenever and wherever a fight for freedom was born, the Lancers
> participated. My first book was the life story of Prince Poniatowski, the most gallant
> Polish Lancer. The first song my mother put me to bed with was the song about
> "The Lonely Lancer in the Field." The first fairy tale I listened to was a tale about a
> Lancer who left his beloved and went to war with Napoleon.[8]

Prince Joseph Poniatowski, nephew of Stanisław August Poniatowski,
Poland's last king, had led the Polish army, some 100,000 strong, to assist
Napoleon's campaign against Russia in 1812. As a reward, Napoleon
established the short-lived but independent "Duchy of Warsaw," thus
winning a position as a particular hero to Polish nationalists. In view of
such historical lessons, Tsarist efforts to stamp out the underground
school system in the Congress Kingdom are readily comprehendible.

Whether Boleslavsky began his public education (primary school
generally lasted only four years) in Płock is not certain. If he did start his
schooling there, it was soon interrupted: Dębowa Góra and the Srzednicki estates were lost. The specific cause of this family crisis is unknown. Polish lords were sometimes deprived of their land in these
years through the courts on trumped-up charges, for purely political

reasons; but a more likely explanation is that shrinking profits had forced Valentine Srzednicki to borrow from the Imperial banks at exorbitant interest rates, until he—like many others—was bankrupted and forced to sell. Regardless of the specific causes, the consequences were inevitable: Dębowa Góra was lost and the family was forced to move. There would be no inheritance in either land or money for Boleslavsky or his brother.

The family moved to the Russian-controlled provinces of southern Bessarabia, where Valentine Srzednicki had been hired to manage a large estate called Askanya Nova. Times were hard there. Agrarian revolts were frequent and rampaging peasants often focused their hatred of absentee landlords upon the landlords' agents. With frightening frequency, managers were seized and killed, the manor houses burned to the ground.

The Srzednicki family remained there only a short time before moving to the nearby city of Odessa. The move was evidently prompted by the death of Valentine Srzednicki. Neither the cause nor the date of his death are known. Nor is the date of the move to Odessa.

Tadeus Hiż, one of Boleslavsky's boyhood friends, reports that "Pani Srzednicki" was widowed and living in the Black Sea port of Odessa by the time of "Rysiek's" sixth class, probably 1903 or 1904.[9] Hiż does not say how long the family had been there.

Boleslavsky evidently received the better part of his secondary schooling in Odessa, one of Russia's most beautiful and cosmopolitan cities. There was a large Polish community here, but his teachers were Russian and he studied textbooks in their language. These lessons most surely contradicted what he had been taught at home, but to avoid punishment for himself and his family, he was compelled to remain silent or to repeat a Russian version of history.

Hiż describes what he calls the *"embarras de richesse"* that marked Boleslavsky as a young student:

> He was a painter, moulded excellently in clay (I remember his well-formed hands), sang, played a few instruments by ear, never having studied music especially; he would not have been a son of his epoch had he not also written verses and prose-poetry. Knowing Polish literature and having a thorough feeling for the Polish language (although his accent had an Eastern lilt and he used certain russianisms at times), he even set about to do translations from Polish into Russian. He translated two or three of the "curious histories" by Kornel Makuszyński, and he attempted to translate verse from Russian to Polish, but actually very badly.[10]

During Boleslavsky's sixth class the Polish colony in Odessa organized an amateur theatrical group, the Polish Hearth (*Ognisko Polski*), and gave a presentation during Lent that year. As Hiż explains, "This was . . . the kind of epoch in social life that without an appearance at least once in the amateur theatre no young woman could be eligible for marriage; and no young man could do without such an appearance either." Boleslavsky, whom Hiż called "Ryszard" or, more familiarly, "Rysiek," appeared in the production. Hiż does not name the play, but it was given in the spring of 1903 or 1904, when Boleslavsky was fourteen or fifteen. Boleslavsky "drew general attention with his acting ability and a sort of wonderful stage presence," Hiż relates. "He felt as if he were at home on the stage. This must have been an innate gift, for he had never before come into contact with the theatre, and no one in his family had been in that line."[11]

Apparently Boleslavsky was immediately stagestruck. Before long he began studying with F. P. Gorev, the famous tragic actor, a master of the formalized declamatory style that typified Russian actors of the late nineteenth century. Barred from the crown theatres of Moscow and St. Petersburg near the end of his life, ostensibly for a touch of provincial mannerism that spoiled his acting, Gorev finished his career in various provincial theatres and worked for a time in Odessa before his death in 1910.[12] Moreover, as Hiż reports, Boleslavsky soon looked beyond the amateur theatre:

> After two or three appearances Rysiek felt an irresistible urge to become an actor, said good-bye to his mother (who gave him some of her widow's savings), and went to a nearby province to appear with a traveling troupe. It was, of course, a Russian company—the Polish theatre came to Odessa but rarely, only every few years, and then only for four to six guest performances.[13]

The date Boleslavsky joined the professional Russian troupe is not known (nor is the name of the group or its leader), but most likely it was during the summer of 1904. That fall, Boleslavsky was back in Odessa and enrolled in the Polytechnic Institute, where he was encouraged to study shipbuilding.[14] Though he had been away from the Polish Hearth for a time, he "took over the plays, or, more accurately, several one-act plays . . . was the director, and played the leading role in every respect." Hiż adds: "Charming Panna Julia, the object of all the sighs of all the high school students, was no small stimulus for his artistic work here."[15]

Julia may have been more to Boleslavsky than an inspiration for hard work in the theatre. Later, after he had joined the Moscow Art Theatre, it was rumored among the younger actors that Boleslavsky had been married in Odessa and had fathered a son. One of them, Vera

Soloviova, recounts that when she asked him about it, Boleslavsky confirmed the story, but she was never certain whether he was merely teasing or telling her the truth.[16] In any event, if Boleslavsky sired a child at this time, with or without the benefit of marriage, that event cannot be confirmed and nothing more is known about Panna Julia.

Boleslavsky's growing involvement with the theatre evidently posed a difficult personal decision. The theatre was considered a socially acceptable diversion, but to pursue it as a profession was quite another matter. It was deemed an unsuitable occupation, certainly for a young man of his birth, even if the family had fallen on hard times. As Boleslavsky wrote, members of the nobility still considered the theatre to be "an occupation for people who are buried outside the cemetery walls."[17] Very likely this social stigma was what prompted him, like many others before him, to adopt a pseudonym and thereby avoid bringing public shame to the family name. Thus, Bolesław Ryszard Srzednicki began to be known in the theatre as Richard Valentinovich Boleslavsky. The use of the patronymic was a concession to Russian custom, but the transformation of his first name into his adopted last name constituted an affirmation of his national heritage: Bolesław was the name of Polish kings.

In 1904, Boleslavsky's mother (and perhaps his brother) moved to Moscow, but Boleslavsky chose to remain in Odessa—possibly living with relatives, possibly having set up his own household with Julia. No doubt he was motivated in part by a wish to continue working with the Polish Hearth, though he continued his education as well. In the fall of 1905, he left the Polytechnic Institute and enrolled at the University of Odessa.

About this time, Boleslavsky's mother was killed in a train accident.[18] Later, he spoke of the shock he felt when he received a telegram informing him of the news of her death. He remembered "how I felt, how I put my hat on when I got the wire, how I stood on the bridge and looked at the sea. . . . " After that time, Boleslavsky added, when he needed such strong emotions for a role, he returned to this memory.[19]

Boleslavsky received his two years of higher education in Odessa at a time of great social and political upheaval. Between 1904 and 1906 student strikes were so frequent that—in one historian's phrase—they constituted a "quasi-permanent feature of the university routine."[20] Boleslavsky marvelled that in 1905 even Polish school children in Odessa struck and were whipped and punished for "refusing to say morning prayers in Russian."[21] More serious demonstrations were sparked by student members of the illegal Russian Social Democratic Party;

founded in Minsk in 1898, the party had subsequently split into Bolshevik and Menshevik factions, with Lenin heading the Bolsheviks.

Precipitated by the Russo-Japanese War, civil unrest finally grew to revolutionary proportions by 1905. Following the "Bloody Sunday" massacre in January of that year, demonstrations and workers' strikes swept Russia's major cities. Odessa remained strangely peaceful, however, until July, when incidents involving the crew of the ship *Potëmkin* culminated in shooting on the Odessa steps. The killing triggered days of rioting, looting, arson, and murder, ending finally in a bloody pogrom that continued unchecked for four days and nights. Years later, Boleslavsky published a letter from Alexander Gutchel, a school friend, in which "Alec" reminded him how they had watched the parties of prisoners being loaded on the steamer of the Voluntary Fleet to be shipped to prison in Sakhalin. Gutchel asks: "You remember [how] we used to buy white bread and blushingly push it into the thin, black, chained hands?"[22]

In his private correspondence, Boleslavsky recalls the period "from the age of about fourteen or fifteen to seventeen or eighteen" as a happy time of shared adventures with "four chums of mine." The boys organized themselves into "a sort of band or gang—very young, very innocent . . . but very gay and rowdy and adventurous in all our undertakings and lives." As for the social turmoil of that period, "I will always think that politics and the Potëmkin and pogroms are, as events in themselves, not very important." Such events might interest the political historian, but Boleslavsky was more concerned with "how the human soul acts under those circumstances." Besides, he adds, "To be able to give justice to the cataclysm, I personally believe one has to be removed from it by at least fifty or a hundred years."[23]

Boleslavsky was changed nonetheless by the events of 1905 and by the Bolshevik Revolution twelve years later. He came to view the "theorists of revolution" as "the species I hate more than the theorists of war," and believed that they "would never understand me or anything I have to say."[24] When asked by a Russian at the time of the later uprising, "What are your political beliefs?" he would answer: "I have none . . . I am a Pole."[25] But when political issues affected Poland, he felt they affected him, "in my own blood and the marrow of my own bones." Later in America, when he was writing about war and revolution, he had frequent, heated disputes with Helen Woodward, who evidently took a more favorable view of the Bolshevik government than he did. To her he wrote:

. . . You say "the world consists of classes." That is a liberal idea of what the Communists might have said but what they did say was actually, "The world consists of two classes—those who work with their hands and the rest who don't consider working at all." . . . This was actually the secret of the Communist success among the working masses. It was demigogical flattery. It was telling the pauper that he is a prince. It was a Cinderella story, and when on top of that first statement, they added, "Those who work have a right to live," the whole picture of their success is clear. And don't think it is the "white" who is speaking in me right now. In my heart I am more a Communist than anybody you ever knew, but there is nobody who hates more the way that Communism was established than I do. And the only virtue which I attach to myself at all is absolute impartiality and indifference with anything in the world. It all looks to me just as important and bewildering as a drop of stagnant water under the microscope.[26]

A few months later, Boleslavsky asked his editor, George Shively, to intercede:

Will you please, George, guard my side in this and see that I don't emerge from my second book as a little Trotski waving the Red flag. . . . The humble author of the book is White and human, and wherever he meets a Red human he gladly shakes his hand. God forbid that I would ever write a political book partial to any party! I am concerned with the human soul and with the reactions of the human soul under all conditions, and when I say human soul, I mean *all* human souls. . . . As far as the critics go, I am grateful for the good criticisms, but I don't give a whoop if they are bad. Why do people like to be labeled like medicine bottles? Could you tell me that, George?[27]

Boleslavsky's experience with Tsarist policy and politics up until 1905 had been generally disagreeable, and that background evidently prevented him from trusting the promises of any revolutionary political party, even one that promised, as the Social Democrats did, greater individual liberty and self-determination for national minorities. Clearly he could not endorse the means of revolution and it is doubtful that he was persuaded that such freedoms would be extended soon to Poles.

Boleslavsky was evidently content to express his support of social reforms from the stage rather than in the street. Revolutionary social ideas and libertarian sentiments expressed in theatrical terms were more congenial to his nature than were political parties. Hiż writes that Boleslavsky was acting at this time in the plays of Hauptmann, Ibsen, and Bjørnson, as well as the works of such Polish writers as Żuławski, Świderski, and Słowacki.[28]

Presumably, Boleslavsky—by now the director and leading actor of the Polish Hearth—was primarily responsible for selecting the repertory for the amateur group. He played the role of Andrew in Hauptmann's symbolic fantasy, *The Sunken Bell.* Hiż does not name specific plays by Ibsen, but they were likely the works of social consciousness. Bjørnson, another Norwegian dramatist, likewise explored the moral diseases of contemporary society and, like Ibsen, reflected the ideals of truth and personal freedom. The plays by Polish writers, including Żuławski's *Eros and Psyche* (in which Boleslavsky played Eros) and Świderski's one-act, *Babies (Dzieciaki),* served simultaneously to reaffirm Boleslavsky's national identity and to express his cultural idealism.

Whether or not he actually selected the play, Boleslavsky acted in Wedekind's *The Awakening of Spring* at about this time.[29] Of the plays mentioned, this was perhaps the most daring and outspoken expression of youthful yearnings for freedom. It was no doubt also the most controversial, for it contains scenes of heterosexual intercourse and homosexual longings, suicide and group masturbation. More importantly, Wedekind's drama asserts the right of all young people to discover and express their individuality. Boleslavsky played the brooding, tragic Melchoir, and in Melchoir's voice he challenged the repressive sexual ignorance and moral tyranny of Victorianism, while asserting his own personal longing for freedom.

In later years, Boleslavsky made clear his belief that the theatre, possessing a social conscience, should never become the instrument for political propaganda. As an adult he believed that the theatre can serve to enlighten the individual human spirit and that only a fundamental change in human understanding and perception—as opposed to the mere alteration of political institutions—can result in significant social progress.[30] This idea of his may well have originated in reaction to the events in Odessa in 1905. Regardless, the theatre evidently provided Boleslavsky the means to make a moral response to human conflicts without becoming entangled in Russia's partisan fighting.

Boleslavsky was always shy, almost painfully so on first meetings, but once he got past that shyness he was effusive, ebullient, a fascinating storyteller. As Helen Woodward writes:

> He seems at first a simple man. He belongs to no clubs. He abhors all social functions and at a party usually stands in a corner and says nothing. But with all this outer simplicity he is not really simple in the least. He has a most complicated mind and he needs beauty as some men need food.

She felt his wide cheek-bones, short nose, blue eyes and light brown hair made him look more like a Russian of the Ukraine than a Pole, though his "powerful broad-shouldered body and large clever hands" showed his descent from generations of wheat growers.[31] He was always "Boley" to his American friends, and they remember his great charm and gentleness, the lengths to which he went to avoid hurting anyone's feelings.They also remember him as childlike in a great many ways; Boleslavsky was not insulted by such a description:

> . . . The divine spark in our nature is so powerful [he writes] that we cannot rest and find satisfaction in things that have become clear to us—that are solved—and like children we continue to look for new possibilities that will confront us with another mystery, which will arouse in us again the eternal question "why"—something that will be better than the past or the present and that will help us in our eternal search for perfection—for an ideal.
>
> For the sake of that pursuit, man—like a child longing for a new toy—gives up his life in scientific research; founds new sects for the complete perception of God; embellishes his life with works of art and cherishes a naïve—though almost unconscious—love for the theatre, where the mystery is presented in such bright colors and life seems to be so beautiful and alluring and so unlike the actual one.[32]

Boleslavsky never lost his almost boyish love of romantic adventure, fantasy, and even sentimental tales, despite the fact that a terrible dichotomy existed in his life in Russia, one which no doubt weighed as a heavy burden at times. Once he chose a life in the theatre he committed himself to constant association with Russians, acting mostly in Russian plays in the Russian tongue for a Russian public; yet beneath all this outer show of accommodation and acceptance of all things Russian, he clung to his Polishness, cherished his national heritage, and dreamed of the day the Polish Fatherland would return as an independent nation.

Though he held fast to his Polish idealism in almost every respect, one pillar of Polish consciousness—faith in the Roman Catholic Church— was evidently shaken by the influence of liberal professors at the University of Odessa.[33] Throughout his life, both in his writing and in theatrical work, Boleslavsky demonstrated strong moral and ethical convictions, even using a kind of Christian iconography in certain of his films, but in the public record he never connected his moral sense to any particular religious belief or creed. In one of the few written references to religious faith, he noted the pagan origins of a Russian Orthodox ritual: "On Easter Eve, glowing candles [were] carried from church to home, a custom dating back to Perun, god of lightning, whose fire was kept always alive on the hearth."[34] If he had lost formal Christian faith, however, he retained his own sense of man's spiritual essence, one that was both pantheistic and mystical:

14

I also remember seeing a skeleton of one of these [religious] hermits while with a hunting party near the Black Sea before the war. In the wilderness it sat on a stone by a tiny brook which wiggled its way among the boulders, its bony fingers holding a stick whose roots had sprouted and become a young willow, its shiny skull resting on the willow's fresh bark; the natural pose of a man who rests and thinks for a long, long time. The ground around was covered with blueberries, goldenrod and daisies. They were not usual in that vicinity. In spite of the skeleton, the place was alive with bees and butterflies, and brilliantly radiant with color. Matter had died. The spirit lived. It looked as if the hermit chose this spot, sat down to meditate and forgot to eat, to sleep, to die. His soul had for ever remained present and glowed in its constant transition.[35]

2

First Steps at the Moscow Art Theatre

Not long after civil calm had returned to Odessa, Boleslavsky met Konstantin Stanislavsky. According to Hiż, the Moscow Art Theatre director was returning from treatment in the Crimea when he "strayed to Odessa," where he chanced to see a performance by the Polish Hearth. The evening included a scene from Słowacki's historical melodrama, *Mazeppa*. "Namely," Hiż writes, "the scene in the tower when Zbigniew comes to Amelia in the habit and cowl of a monk." Stanislavsky understood very little Polish, Hiż notes, but after the performance he went backstage to meet Boleslavsky, who had played Zbigniew. "The conversation was short, but it ended fortunately for Bolesławski: soon after he was engaged by the Art Theatre in Moscow. . . ."[1]

Matters were not so simple as Hiż suggests. Every year hundreds of actors applied to the Moscow Art Theatre, by that time one of the most renowned in Russia, if not the world. To gain entrance to the school of the MAT, Boleslavsky had to survive three different examinations before three different boards, the last of which was headed by the Art Theatre's co-directors, Stanislavsky and Vladimir Nemirovich-Danchenko, and made up of the theatre's entire company of actors. Boleslavsky was among the handful who made it that far in the fall of 1906. Vera Soloviova, who later became his close friend, remembers his audition:

> I had already been one year at the Moscow Art Theatre and was among those watching the examinations of the new-comers. Richard came boldly, tall, handsome, daring, and recited a monologue from *L'Aiglon*. He made a wonderful impression and was accepted at once.[2]

Boleslavsky's own account of this crucial test is at once more modest and more amusing:

> I plunged into the cheapest kind of melodrama with such a fury of sincerity that the whole assembly shouted with laughter. I gave the soliloquy of a young man despairing on the grave of his mother, who had been murdered by treachery. The laughter

did not bother me. I went on in my far from perfect Russian, made up of a combination of south Russian and Polish brogue. When I finished, dripping with perspiration, red in the face, trembling with emotion, I was almost on top of the table of the faculty. They all looked at me with wide grins.

"Well," I said, "how do you like it?"

Another explosion of laughter. One of the older actors on the faculty spoke at last, "But, my dear boy, your accent is preposterous—horrible."

"It isn't an accent," I retorted, "it's temperament."

That finished everybody. I was dismissed and the next day came to learn my fate.

"It must have been 'temperament' which carried me through," Boleslavsky finishes. Not yet eighteen years old, he was one of three actors admitted to the Art Theatre's school in the fall of 1906.[3]

Boleslavsky's admission was only provisional, however; he was placed on a year's probation, with the stipulation that he rid himself of his "preposterous accent." He evidently soon mastered the difficult "Moscow dialect"—which, as he describes it, "has a more tender, singing quality than Italian; more rumbling, manly consonants than Scotch; and at times a more speedy tempo than French"[4]—for he stayed well past that probationary year.

Boleslavsky describes the atmosphere of that first term:

Once within the Theatre our whole lives were changed. We spent our days from morning until midnight without leaving the building. There was nothing bohemian about our existence. Both men and women were taught to dress simply in dark colors, almost monastic, to wear our hair smooth and short; to behave inconspicuously and with courtesy and elegance. We were encouraged to resemble scholars rather than actors. And we worked and studied hard enough to make the resemblance easy.[5]

Personal contact with the Art Theatre's directors or its older actors was marginal during this time. As Hiż notes, Stanislavsky observed Boleslavsky's progress "from near and far—and was silent."[6] Boleslavsky elaborates:

I was assigned to various classes to learn the art of the actor. . . . After that I was left alone by directors and teachers. Entirely, as if I did not exist. That was the way of the Theatre, to find out if I had enough stamina and brains to become a part of the organization by myself.[7]

Students at the school were assigned regular classes. These were taught by the actors of the Art Theatre under the supervision and periodic inspection of Stanislavsky and Nemirovich-Danchenko. Ivan Moskvin, one of the MAT's most outstanding actors and an original member of the

company, evidently played an important role in Boleslavsky's early training, for Boleslavsky mentioned him frequently as one of his teachers. The
disciplines taught included voice training, diction, dancing, fencing, and
cultural courses, incorporating the innovations developed earlier by Danchenko at the Philharmonic School.[8] Though Stanislavsky had only
started to formulate the questions and tentative principles that would lead
to his system the summer before Boleslavsky entered the school, both he
and Nemirovich-Danchenko sought to eliminate histrionic clichés, and
both stressed the psychological depths of characterization. Their cardinal
standard was the actor's truthfulness to life, both in the inner and outer
experiencing of the character.

In addition to physical and vocal training, Boleslavsky and the other
apprentices received informal lessons in history, art, and music. They
were encouraged to read widely on their own, and to attend the opera
and ballet as well. They soon learned to economize in developing their
cultural lives, for the Art Theatre paid only a subsistence wage to apprentices (Hiż writes that Boleslavsky never earned more than 2,400 to
3,600 rubles per year at the MAT, compared to about 8,000 rubles for
such older actors as Kachalov or Knipper, who were shareholders in the
theatre).[9] Boleslavsky recounts:

> We were often absurd. One member of the Theatre was translating Oscar Wilde.
> We chipped in pennies and bought each volume as it appeared. After all had read it
> we drew lots to decide to whom it should belong.
> For a while we were all esthetes. . . .
>
> Sometimes five of us would buy one ticket to a new opera or ballet. Each would
> see one act. The others would walk around the block in the snow or sleet. The rest of
> the night, we would exchange impressions.[10]

The apprentices were also expected to participate in all phases of
the theatre's work, to attend all rehearsals, and to familiarize themselves
with the MAT's artistic and personal demands. It was evidently through
watching rehearsals that Boleslavsky gained his first clear impressions of
the Art Theatre's directors, the "two demigods whom we idolized":

> These were the living gods, whose kindness was more terrifying than anger, and
> whose anger one never saw. Stanislavsky was the soul of the theatre, Dantchenko its
> mind. We adored Stanislavsky, a white haired giant, spectacular in life as on stage.
> He was the fiery leader whom we imitated. Dantchenko, mild and unpretentious,
> appealed less to us when we were young. But as we grew older we came to worship
> him. He was quiet and seldom heard, rich in wisdom but with flaming visions; the
> arbiter of all our difficulties. Stanislavsky was a brilliant actor performing Prospero.
> Dantchenko was Prospero himself.[11]

Third-year apprentices were required to serve as "contributors"—extras or walk-ons in crowd scenes—and to take an examination. Only if they passed this final test were they considered for full membership in the MAT's acting company. Boleslavsky served his term as "contributor" during the season of 1908–09, playing his first supernumerary part in Maeterlinck's *The Blue Bird,* which opened on 30 September 1908, under Stanislavsky's direction. Boleslavsky was one of numerous extras rendered invisible (by a costume made of black velvet against a black velvet background) in order to perform the wonders required by Maeterlinck's allegorical fantasy.[12] On 22 August 1908 he was admitted into the MAT's company and, soon thereafter, assigned his first two roles: he would play Laertes in *Hamlet,* under the direction of guest artist Gordon Craig, and Belyayev, the young romantic character in Turgenev's *A Month in the Country,* to be directed by Stanislavsky.

Boleslavsky's first rehearsal in *Hamlet* was conducted by Stanislavsky on 24 February 1909.[13] Rehearsals were soon suspended because Stanislavsky fell ill and Craig's arrival in Moscow had been delayed; the production was eventually postponed for some two years. This meant that Boleslavsky's debut performance with the Moscow Art Theatre would be in *A Month in the Country.* The special circumstances surrounding the production were such that Boleslavsky's MAT debut took on more than usual significance: *A Month in the Country* signalled Stanislavsky's first coordinated effort to prove his new system of acting.

During the summer of 1906, just months before Boleslavsky was admitted to the Moscow Art Theatre's school, Konstantin Stanislavsky began formulating questions about the actor's art that would result eventually in what is now known as his system of acting. During the MAT's European tour of 1905–06 he had grown increasingly distressed by his inconsistency as an actor. While resting in Finland at the end of the tour, he examined his acting and soon formulated the goal of his work:

> What I wanted to learn was how to create a favorable condition for the appearance of inspiration by means of the will, that condition in the presence of which inspiration was most likely to descend into the actor's soul. As I learned afterward, this creative mood is that spiritual and physical mood during which it is easiest for inspiration to be born.[14]

At first Stanislavsky tried new ideas only on himself, in his own acting, without fanfare or special notice. But soon he was urging his latest discovery or some new theory on other actors in the company. Predictably, many of them, particularly the older, more established actors, resisted these untested, new-fangled ideas. Many resented being treated as "guinea pigs." In the face of their reluctance, Stanislavsky often became impatient, even exasperated, in rehearsals. As the actors' resentment increased, Stanislavsky's efforts to force his ideas on them became ever more high-handed.[15] As a student of the MAT's school, Boleslavsky was required to observe the rehearsals in which Stanislavsky attempted to impose on skeptical older actors his evolving but still only half-formulated theories, first in *The Drama of Life*, Knut Hamsun's symbolic play, then in Leonid Andreyev's "mystic" drama, *The Life of Man* (both produced in 1907). These productions drew excited but decidedly mixed reactions from the public, but Stanislavsky considered them failures, both artistically and for his new system.[16]

The phenomenal success of *The Blue Bird* ameliorated the actors' resentment toward the new approach, but soon Stanislavsky became dissatisfied with their performances—they were inconsistent. On 20 February 1909, he added his comments to a note written by his assistant, Leopold Sulerzhitsky. Addressed to the cast of *The Blue Bird*, Stanislavsky's words amounted to a manifesto to the company at large:

> The actors of our theatre and Russian actors, in general, will never be satisfied with being just competent stage hacks. For that you have to be a foreigner. The art of acting consists in living a part. Our actors must not only be able to live their parts. . . . They must know how to accomplish the act of living their parts easily, and I am ready to teach this art to anyone who will himself show a desire to learn it. For without it the theatre, in my opinion, is superfluous, harmful and stupid. . . . In future I shall refuse to work in accordance with any other principle.

The note ended with Stanislavsky's invitation to those actors who were interested to meet with him "every day at one o'clock."[17]

The uncompromising tone of this declaration so frightened the actors of the company that Stanislavsky had to select "his own small team" with which to produce his next play, *A Month in the Country*, by Ivan Turgenev.[18] The fact that Boleslavsky was chosen for the cast of Turgenev's comedy argues persuasively that he had been among the actors who accepted Stanislavsky's invitation for daily concentrated work in the developing system.

A Month in the Country was the first truly thorough test of Stanislavsky's new methods. Previously, his ideas had been applied only in part, and then with disappointing results. Accordingly, Stanislavsky selected for this cast actors who were not only suitable for the roles, but also amenable to his new experiments in acting. They included Olga Knipper, the widow of Anton Chekhov, in the leading role of Natalia Petrovna; Vassily Kachalov in the part of Rakitin (Stanislavsky alternated in the role); and Lydia Koreneva in the part of Verochka (Vera). Boleslavsky was named to play the role of Belyayev, the young tutor who falls in love with Verochka and, inadvertently, wins the heart of the older Natalia. With the exception of the child actor playing Natalia's ten-year-old son, Boleslavsky, who was now twenty, was the youngest and least experienced member of the cast. He was also the first of his peers to be chosen for such an important role at the Art Theatre.

Stanislavsky described the shadings of feelings between Natalia and Rakitin, Belyayev and Verochka, and Natalia and Belyayev as a "lace work of the psychology of love." He believed the play demanded "a special kind of acting, which would allow the spectator to admire the peculiar design of the psychology of loving, suffering, jealous male and female hearts."[19]

With the beginning of rehearsals in September of 1909, Stanislavsky took a step unprecedented in the Art Theatre's history: he withdrew to a rehearsal studio with the cast of *A Month in the Country* and worked for four months in almost total isolation from the other members of the theatre. As Magarshack reports: "No one knew what Stanislavsky and his small group of actors were doing.. . . . All that was known was that they were rehearsing *A Month in the Country* in a way that no play had ever been rehearsed before."[20] During the day, rehearsals were held in a small studio, partitioned into two or three rooms representing the setting; evening rehearsals were often held at Stanislavsky's apartment or Knipper's home. It was in Stanislavsky's quarters, for example, that Boleslavsky and Alice Koonen, who was doubling in the role of Verochka, first worked on their scenes.[21]

At these closed rehearsals Boleslavsky and the others were asked to live the inner life of the character. They were asked to communicate their feelings by use of the eyes alone, without reliance on words or language. Other experiments were tried. For a time the actors "never spoke their lines, or if they did address each other, they did not even speak in a whisper, but just moved their lips soundlessly."[22]

In October, Stanislavsky rehearsed the first two acts of *A Month in the Country* on the Art Theatre's stage. He was deeply disturbed by the results:

> With the transition to the stage, they are not rehearsals any longer, but hell. We lost everything. What was good at the table became weak here. Everyone talked quietly and could not strengthen their voices. Knipper drove me to exasperation with her obstinacy, and Koreneva did too with her stupid character.. . . . Due to inexperience, Boleslavsky turned into a blockhead. Enemies of my System crowed and said, "Boring," which depressed the tone of the rehearsal.

Not for a long time have I endured such tortures, despair, and draining of energy (not since the time of *The Drama of Life* and *The Life of Man*).[23]

Nemirovich-Danchenko had long expected the worst to come of these unorthodox procedures. On November 1, he watched a rehearsal of the first three of the play's five acts. In a letter to his wife, written on that date, he expressed his admiration for Dobuzhensky's scenery, for Koreneva's playing of Verochka, and for "the young man playing Belyayev." Beyond that, he wrote, Stanislavsky was "very acceptable" as Rakitin but Knipper's portrayal was "a void." All in all, Danchenko was fearful that the production would fail, and that failure would deal a serious, if not irreparable, blow to Stanislavsky's already shaken artistic reputation.[24]

On 9 December 1909, *A Month in the Country* opened. It was an immediate triumph. The public and critics alike applauded the production for its great warmth and simplicity, for the depth and originality of its characterizations, and for its extraordinary ensemble. As one critic put it:

A Month in the Country is produced and acted very brightly—with a simple faith in that old-fashioned life which it depicts, and without any distortion or irony. And without theatricality. These qualities are present in all the roles in this wholly unusual performance. The acting of Stanislavsky and Knipper does not resemble the manner in which Rakitin and Natalya Petrovna are generally played, and all the roles in this production are so performed. Such lucidity in the young people, in Mme Koreneva and Mr. Boleslavsky, was particularly fine.[25]

Critic Alexander Koiransky compared the Moscow Art Theatre's manner with that usually seen at the Imperial houses—at the expense of the crown theatres. He also compared Boleslavsky's performance to the more conventional interpretation:

. . . Only such a theatre could find the means for the extraordinary, artless portrayal of Belyayev (Mr. Boleslavsky) and discover such an uncommon Verochka (Mme Koreneva). The whole secret of Mr. Boleslavsky's performance lies in the fact that there is nothing of "the actor" in it (that the craftmanship is concealed), and that it is so youthful and pure.

One has to see how an actor like Mr. Khodotov, on the stage of the Aleksandrinsky Theatre, portrays Belyayev—what tricks he uses, and what a "shirtsleeve lover" he is—in order to appreciate Mr. Boleslavsky's performance and the fact that such simplicity does not come easily.[26]

Nikolai Efros wrote an enthusiastic review for the journal published by the Imperial theatres, in which he singled out Knipper, Stanislavsky,

Koreneva, and Boleslavsky for special praise. He remarked that the MAT had taken a great risk in assigning so important a role to a beginning actor, "but the theatre was rewarded by talent, sincerity, and temperament. He has quite mastered spontaneity." Efros, too, praised the "concealed craftmanship" of Boleslavsky's acting: "His performance was quite remarkable in its irreproachable simplicity, its winning ingenuousness, its truthfullness to life without any false theatricality."[27] His further comments about Boleslavsky's performance were later amplified in his history of the Art Theatre:

> Inseparably connected with my memory of Koreneva's Verochka is my recollection of Boleslavsky's Belyayev. . . . I was struck by an absolutely exceptional simplicity and a highly genuine sincerity in his acting. Youth was exultant. This was a slice of young, exuberant life, filled with joy by the open air and the sun, by mental quickness, by the grass in the meadow, the water in the sluggish pond, and a song in the canebrake. And when the time came for strong emotions, how simply and how fully Boleslavsky's Belyayev expressed his feelings; how surprised he was by the unexpected arrival of the love he felt and the love that was felt for him; how emotionally he held the refined little hands of the beautiful Islaeva in his own big hands, which still bore traces of glue! An aroused passion boiled; the frightened eyes of this "student of standards" were filled with tears; his throat was blocked. This was all as true to life as it was direct, youthful, striking, and impetuous. Of course this impression came from a great theatrical nature, not from a great mastery of the theatre. But that nature was shown to be splendid, fascinating.[28]

Eugenie Leontovich, the émigré actress who has enjoyed a long and distinguished career on the American stage, was a student of acting in St. Petersburg at the time *A Month in the Country* opened; years later she recalled the impression the production made on her:

> The Turgenev production was perfection, because of the ensemble. *A Month in the Country* is not my cup of tea, but it was one of the Moscow Art Theatre's great achievements, and it was a great event in the theatre. That valentine-like tragedy was unbelievably exciting because of the excellence of the production. The ensemble! The scenery! Boleslavsky's performance was as perfect as Knipper's.[29]

All these favorable comments lend credence to Hiż's claim: "For several years all of Moscow came to see Turgenev's comedy only for Bolesławski. His fame as an actor began at this moment."[30] While this may be an exaggeration, Boleslavsky's subsequent roles suggest that he did soon become popular as the Moscow Art Theatre's "young lover" and was in fact something of a matinee idol.

Stanislavsky's casting of Boleslavsky in *A Month in the Country*—a production so crucial to his own artistic standing in the Art Theatre—is reason enough to conclude that he considered Boleslavsky, at the beginning of his stage career, a promising young talent. Boleslavsky's outstanding success in the play evidently confirmed Stanislavsky's trust. He was subsequently cast in a great many of the Art Theatre's new productions and was added to the casts of several of the MAT's revivals, as well as plays continuing in its repertory. The frequency with which he was cast, as well as the importance of the roles he played, suggests that he continued to develop as an actor, even as he soon began dividing his attention and energies between acting and directing.

3

Founding the First Studio

At the Polish Hearth in Odessa, Boleslavsky had shown equal interest in acting and directing. Natasha Boleslavsky says that long before he came to Moscow, "Boleslavsky was always crazy to be a director."[1] His early successes as an actor with the Moscow Art Theatre did not quench that ambition. Ryszard Ordyński reports a conversation he had with Boleslavsky following a performance of *A Month in the Country,* in 1910. Impressed by Boleslavsky's "engaging manner" and "excellent play-ing," Ordyński went backstage to congratulate his fellow Pole; recalling their conversation, he wrote: "Directing, and not acting, was the goal of Bolesławski's work in the theatre, just as he told me then."[2] Some two years after that, Boleslavsky got his first opportunity to pursue this aim under the auspices of the Moscow Art Theatre.

In the spring of 1912, Stanislavsky rented the top floor of the build-ing that had once housed the Lux cinema theatre. "Here we gathered all who wanted to study the so-called Stanislavsky System," he writes,

> for this was the main purpose for the founding of the Studio. . . . I began to give a
> full course of study in the shape in which I had at that time formed it. Its aim was
> to find practical and conscious methods for the awakening of super-conscious
> creativeness.[3]

What was the "shape" of the system at this time? Markov, a histo-rian of the First Studio, believes the system was already complete in its main outlines, although many exercises necessary to develop the actor's grasp of the "elements" of his art—"concentration," "relaxation," "a sense of truth," and so on—were yet to be worked out.[4] On the other hand, Stanislavsky's biographer, David Magarshack, demonstrates that key components were introduced only later, during the work at the studio (soon to become known as the First Studio of the MAT); the system was not in fact complete in all its elements until around 1918.[5]

In beginning work at the Lux, Stanislavsky delivered a series of detailed lectures on his system, but was too busy with his regular work at the Art Theatre to conduct the practical exercises, a task he assigned to his assistant and devoted friend, Leopold Sulerzhitsky.[6] Stanislavsky's primary interest at this time was in developing the actor's ability to experience the "inner life" of the character. Early in 1912, in a brief letter to Meyerhold, he wrote: "All I believe in is emotion and, chiefly, nature itself."[7] Accordingly, the element receiving greatest emphasis in the early work at the Lux was "memory of emotion" and, suitably as an exercise, frequent use was made of improvisation.

Boleslavsky was by now familiar with both the problem of emotion and the technique of improvisation, but the new emphasis given the latter evidently roused his interest, for about this time he and one or two friends from the studio spent a summer hitchhiking to Italy in order to study *commedia dell'arte*—a model of improvisational theatre.[8] During rehearsals for *A Month in the Country,* and perhaps earlier, he had worked on the problem of memory of emotion, as well as the specific technique of affective memory (whereby the actor experiences the sensory aspects of an incident from his past in order to evoke the emotions associated with that incident).[9] Boleslavsky shared Stanislavsky's conviction that the actor's inner life is an essential part of his creative work. "Living one's part" meant, to Boleslavsky, "a complete spiritual and physical self-abandon for a definite period of time, in order to fulfill a real or fantastical problem of the theatre."[10] As he described later:

> The difference between an actor who "lives his parts" and the one who "imitates life" is the same as between a *living person* and a *mechanical puppet* [his emphasis]. No matter how precise he may be, trying to copy life, if he doesn't live through his emotions he'll never be able to get hold of the spectator, to entrance him. He might be able to astonish, even amaze him but he'll never be able to penetrate into his soul, and stir it, and leave there an impression.[11]

Boleslavsky defined acting as "the life of the human soul receiving its birth through art."[12] He described theatre as "the art of investing the spiritual emotions of man in a visible form."[13] "Emotion is God's breath in a part," he believed. "Through emotion, the author's characters stand alive and vital."[14]

When speaking of the theatre, or of the actor's art, Boleslavsky always tended to lofty, idealized, even sentimental language, a trait enhanced no doubt by his association not only with Stanislavsky, but with Sulerzhitsky as well. "Suler," as he was called by the studio actors, was a popular, romantic figure. Stanislavsky described him as "a revolutionary, a Tolstoyan, a Dukhobor; he was a novelist, a songster, an artist; he was a captain, a fisherman, a hobo, an 'American.' "[15] The short, powerfully built adventurer, who generally sported a thick beard, was a close friend of Leo Tolstoy—who called him "that sagacious child"[16]—and at Tolstoy's behest had once taken the Dukhobors, a group of religious zealots, by ship to Canada.

In a sense, the studio was heir to two great legacies: the artistic innovations of Stanislavsky and the idealized spirituality of Tolstoy, as interpreted by Sulerzhitsky. "I have always hated reason when it becomes the master of the soul," Sulerzhitsky told the studio actors, "but it can be an excellent servant and one ought to know how to use it." The art of the theatre, he insisted, should reveal the inherent goodness of mankind. He tried to make the revelation of man's innate goodness the official doctrine of the Studio. "The actor is not only an artist," he often reminded them, "but also a servant of God."[17]

In the first days of the Lux, Stanislavsky appointed "Suler" to administer the group's affairs and to watch over the members' moral development.[18] Vera Soloviova suggests something of the impact this remarkable man had on Boleslavsky: "Sulerzhitsky brought out the best in our hearts and the audience responded to it with all their hearts. He taught us how to love and understand people. Boleslavsky absorbed all this from him."[19] Later, Boleslavsky would often remark that love was the "through-line" of his life.[20]

While Stanislavsky was clearly the main inspiration of the studio—which Michael Chekhov once characterized as the "gathering place for those who confess the religion of Stanislavsky"[21]—and Sulerzhitsky served as its appointed administrator and spiritual guide, the general impression that the Lux was a kind of classroom for the young and untutored is contradicted by Stanislavsky's definition of "a studio": it is "neither a theatre nor a dramatic school for beginners, but a laboratory for the experiments of more or less trained actors"[22] Under the guidance of Stanislavsky and Sulerzhitsky, Boleslavsky and the other studio members were free to conduct experiments of their own. Whatever individual contributions they may have made to the formulation of the system cannot be isolated, but Boleslavsky soon would play an important role in solving the problem that most concerned Stanislavsky at the time—the problem of emotion—and, in so doing, would help transform the informal Lux into the First Studio of the MAT.

Boleslavsky was a charter member of the Lux studio, as were several actors who were—or soon became—close personal friends, including Gregori Khmara, Nicholai Kolin, Michael Chekhov, Vera Soloviova,

Lydia Deykun, Maria ("Marutchka") Ouspenskaya, and Nadezhda ("Hope") Bromley. (Other studio members included: Serafima Birman, Sophia Giantsintova, Vladimir Popov, Aleksei Popov, Vladimir Gotovtsev, Maria Durasova, Valentin Smuishlyayev, and Alexander Cheban.) Boleslavsky's closest friend and ally at the time was Boris Sushkevich, who, along with Boleslavsky and Eugene Vakhtangov, was to become one of the directors of the First Studio.[23] Evidently, Boleslavsky did not number Vakhtangov among his intimates; as later events were to confirm, a sense of artistic rivalry, as well as distinctly different personalities, kept the two at a polite—sometimes strained—distance.

Boleslavsky's position at the Lux was unique. Most of its members were just beginning their work at the Art Theatre. Some had not yet even appeared on the stage of the MAT, and few had played better than minor parts. Several of them, including Vakhtangov and Ouspenskaya, had come from the Adashev School, where they had been trained by Sulerzhitsky, but had yet to work closely with Stanislavsky himself. Boleslavsky, on the other hand, had already won personal acclaim as an actor at the Art Theatre and had taught the system at the Adashev school.[24] At about the time of the first Lux meetings, Boleslavsky was rehearsing the role of Laertes in Gordon Craig's *Hamlet,* as well assisting the English designer in the "model shop," where plans for the play's settings were being worked out.[25]

Boleslavsky's frequent contact with Stanislavsky and Nemirovich-Danchenko, his standing in the Art Theatre's company, and his personal accomplishments as an actor all contributed to his position as a natural leader among the Art Theatre's younger members, although he was sometimes accused of getting preferential treatment because he was "Stanislavsky's pet."[26] True, Stanislavsky was openly fond of him; but as Vera Soloviova remembers it, Stanislavsky liked him especially because "Richard was taking his teaching with all his artistic heart and using it only after he had digested it well. Boleslavsky did not just take this new way, which is now known as the Stanislavsky System, but he made it a part of himself organically."[27] Generally, Boleslavsky was both liked and respected by his associates. Following Sulerzhitsky's death, in 1916, they elected him to share (with Sushkevich, Lazarev, and Pavlov) the responsibilities of the Studio's leadership.[28]

Upon moving into the Lux, Stanislavsky posted the following notice:

> Anyone wishing to read something, to appear in a scene from a play, to submit scale-models of sets, to demonstrate the results of his researches in stage technique,

or to offer some literary material for the stage, should put down his name in a special book kept for that purpose in the hall of the Studio.[29]

Likely it was this notice that prompted Boleslavsky and Sushkevich to "get a notion that we would like to have a show of our own." Boleslavsky longed to direct and was absorbed by artistic questions, but he was also spurred by more mundane considerations:

If we could take it to the suburban theatres we would make some extra money. But we were not allowed to play except in the theatre itself. How to get around this? Perhaps if we showed our elders a carefully prepared play, they would let us perform it in the suburbs of Moscow, in the clubs and workers' theatres.[30]

With this in mind, Boleslavsky had been working on his own adaptation of a short story by the American writer, Jack London, who enjoyed great popularity in Moscow at the time. Boleslavsky called his one-act play *The Immoral Woman (Beznravstvennaya zhenshchina)*. This may have been the first project he brought in for the studio's consideration, and possibly it was even read aloud by the studio actors, but it was not performed until later.[31]

Boleslavsky persisted. Soon after, he brought in another play, *The Good Hope*, by Herman Heyermans, along with his costume sketches for it. This time he won approval. Studio actress Lydia Deykun relates:

Boleslavsky brought us a play by Heyermans, *The Good Hope*. . . . Konstantin Sergeevich [Stanislavsky] decided that we would work on *The Good Hope* under the direction of Boleslavsky. . . . Leopold Antonovich [Sulerzhitsky] often came to us, watched our rehearsals, made some short comments but tried to give us and our young director, Richard, full independence. Konstantin Sergeevich himself said that he would come to see the whole play when everything was ready—all the decorations, lighting, and sound.[32]

Heyermans' play is a powerful, realistically detailed picture of life in a remote impoverished Dutch fishing village, written, evidently, from dual passions: an intense feeling for the simple fishing folk and a burning concern for social reform. The central character is a widow named Kniertje, who, since the deaths of her husband and two of her four sons, works as a cleaning woman for Bos, the shipowner, in order to support Jo, her niece, and Barend, her youngest son. The laughing, spirited Jo is in love with Kniertje's other surviving son, Geert, who has been drummed out of the marines and imprisoned for striking an officer—and for possessing illegal revolutionary newspapers, discovered hidden in his belongings. Geert returns home more cynical and rebellious than ever and soon signs on with the crew of *The Good Hope*. Young Barend is haunted by memories of his dead father and brothers and has a consuming fear of the sea, but is persuaded by Geert's example to also sign on the ship. Just before sailing, however, Barend is told by an alcoholic old sailor that the ship's timbers are rotten and that she is "a floating coffin." The terrified boy hides but is discovered and dragged aboard. Some weeks later, in the play's last act, the women of the village gather in the shipowner's office, seeking news of the long overdue *Hope*. A hatch and Barend's decomposing body are found washed ashore, confirming finally that the ship has gone down.

The initial assignment of roles is uncertain, but the cast included Lydia Deykun in the central role of Kniertje, Alexei Diky in the part of Barend, Vera Soloviova as Jo, and Gregori Khmara as Geert. The part of Bos, the shipowner, was given to Lazarev—Boleslavsky later alternated in the role—and Serafima Birman was cast as his wife, Mathilde. Michael Chekhov played the part of the drunken sailor who warns Barend of the *Hope's* fate.[33]

Two hours a day of the studio's time were set aside for Boleslavsky's rehearsals. These were held on a tiny stage set on a level with the front row; the small auditorium's banked seats accommodated an audience of about fifty. There were no footlights (the playing area abutted the front row), the ceiling was low, and there was virtually no wing space.

Scenery for the production was evolved during the course of rehearsals by Boleslavsky and his designer, Yakov Gremislavsky. There was little if any budget for the two settings, depicting the interiors of Kniertje's small cottage and Bos's shipping office. As Giantsintova reports, Stanislavsky interceded on behalf of the Studio:

> Our relations with the Theatre were very complex. At times we needed costumes, at other times, props. All this we received from the Theatre. Konstantin Sergeevich [Stanislavsky] had to wage a constant struggle with the Theatre, since the Theatre didn't always meet us half-way.[34]

Dark green draperies, discarded by the Art Theatre, were used to form a front curtain, and others were hung to conceal the backstage. Properties were borrowed from the Art Theatre's available stock. Boleslavsky writes: "We . . . used our ingenuity to make Dutch fishermen out of scraps of make-up and costumes from the Theatre's discontinued plays." When the Art Theatre's actors finally saw the production, Boleslavsky adds, "They recognized 'Brand's' boots and the shawl of 'Fru Rosmer.' They smiled at a table from a Tolstoy play and a chair from one of Maeterlinck's."[35] These borrowed properties were painstakingly redecorated. A bed, for example, was painted in the "Dutch manner" with an intricate pattern of flowers; as there was no room for a backdrop, a Dutch landscape was painted directly onto the panes of a window hung against the draperies. For the scene in the office, in addition to the required furnishings, a miniature fleet of fishing vessels was suspended from the ceiling.

The actual labor of building and remodeling was shared equally by Boleslavsky and the actors. As Vera Soloviova remembers:

> [Another] very precious quality of Boleslavsky was his artistic love of the theatre. In the productions which he directed, he made us love and be responsible for every little part of the scenery and properties. . . . He made us proud of our sets as well as of our acting.[36]

While Soloviova, and others, responded warmly to Boleslavsky's manner and methods, some of the actors were less ardent in their support. At one point rehearsals for *The Good Hope* were very nearly halted. There was talk of giving up the proposed production and even of closing the Lux studio itself. According to Stanislavsky, this near mutiny was caused by a general unhappiness over inadequate time for rehearsals.[37] Giantsintova's account suggests that deeper rivalries may have been the cause:

> The rehearsals were sometimes before the Theatre's working hours, sometimes on free evenings. The work was very difficult. For a long time there were problems with the performers—some of them were dissatisfied with their roles and refused them. In such cases Konstantin Sergeevich took drastic action. He used to say: "They're gone—get others. By such a process of elimination we shall see who is with us."[38]

Regardless of the causes of discontent, Stanislavsky "resolutely countered" such talk in a speech to the assembled players:

> The show must go on, even if we have to do the impossible. Remember that your future depends on this production. You must have your "Pushkino" phase just as we had when we were establishing the Moscow Art Theatre. If you cannot rehearse in the day, do it at night, until daybreak.[39]

These remarks suggest that by this time Stanislavsky felt the production might well go beyond a mere classroom exercise. A final word from Giantsintova makes clear that he hinted strongly there would be more for them: "He used to tell us, 'If there is ever a performance, bear in mind that after a success an actor is not to go anywhere. He must lock himself up and examine his experiences.' He was afraid that we would go off and celebrate."[40]

In any event, the final rehearsals began around midnight, after performances at the Art Theatre, and often lasted until dawn. Members of the company were still expected to resume their regular duties at the theatre at ten o'clock the next morning.

In January of 1913, *The Good Hope* was finally ready to be shown to Stanislavsky and a select number of Art Theatre members. Boleslavsky describes the results of this presentation: "Our reception rose high above our hopes. The whole assembly applauded us, they praised us and they laughed at us good naturedly."[41] Stanislavsky's response, so crucial to the production's future, was highly favorable: "The rehearsal was exceptionally successful and clearly displayed in all those who took part in it a certain special and until that time unknown simplicity and depth in the interpretation of the life of the human spirit."[42] Nemirovich-Danchenko shared his colleague's enthusiasm. Danchenko felt, he said, as if he had been present at the "christening of a son or a daughter of the Moscow Art Theatre."[43] As Slonim put it: "The older generation of directors and actors felt that they had found their successors."[44]

From January 15 through 28, *The Good Hope* was shown before invited audiences at the Lux. On February 4, it was opened to the general public, continuing through February 17.[45] The response of these audiences was such that the Art Theatre soon decided to finance the continued operation of the First Studio as a quasi-independent theatre group, to be known as the Studio of the Moscow Art Theatre (only after the opening of a Second and Third Studio was it renamed the First Studio of the MAT). Boleslavsky writes that the directors of the MAT "kept their eyes on us steadily and we always felt the iron hand of their authority." In time the weight of that authority would grow too heavy, and Boleslavsky would join other studio members in arguing for greater independence, but for the present, "We cherished our Studio and worked our own way."[46]

Critic James Lvov hailed the appearance of the First Studio as "extraordinarily important" and found *The Good Hope* a "very interesting production . . . directed and performed with especially brilliant and profound dramatization." The theatre magazine, *The Mask* (*Maska*) reported: "The general opinion was that *The Good Hope* is the biggest event of the entire theatrical season."[47]

Despite such favorable critical response and a great public interest, *The Good Hope* was at first performed only irregularly and somewhat infrequently. On 10 January 1914, almost a full year after its premiere, the cast of *The Good Hope* celebrated its twenty-fifth performance by sending a copy of the program to Stanislavsky inscribed "Dear Konstantin Sergeevich, Thank you," and signed by Boleslavsky and the cast.[48] But the production was to last. Ten years later, in 1924, Efros would record that it had been given 429 times; it would still be in the First Studio's repertory in 1927.[49]

In August or September of 1914, the First Studio occupied new quarters in an old coach-house near the intersection of Tverskaya Street and Skobeliyev Square. The three-story structure was remodeled to house a theatre, a scene shop, a rehearsal hall, a library for study and research, and—during the Revolution—a hospital. The stage was modeled after that at the Lux, but was larger in area. It was raised a step higher than the front row of seats and footlights were again eliminated. A front curtain was hung to separate the stage from the auditorium, and seating accommodating about one hundred and fifty people was installed in steeply raked rows. A ceiling of meshed metalwork was built above the stage to hold overhead lighting instruments and suspended scenery.

A critic from *Russkoye Slovo* reviewed *The Good Hope* after it opened in the new, larger quarters. He faulted certain points of the young actors' performances, but was generous in his overall praise. He also drew a number of interesting comparisons between the Studio and its parent theatre:

> The Moscow Art Theatre has long had the reputation of being a strong training ground of young actors who draw you to them, who involve your emotions little by little until you are finally overwhelmed. This is the intention of the newly created Studio of the Moscow Art Theatre, where future Kachalovs and Lilinas [Stanislavsky's wife] are developing.
>
> The Studio is now presenting the first fruits of its labor, a production—not yet complete—which is an example of the strength of this extraordinary group of young actors, directors, and producers.

After describing the small stage and auditorium, "with its overflow crowds," he continued:

> The actors' work must be very difficult in these cramped conditions, but the arrangement nevertheless makes an altogether agreeable impression on the audience.
>
> Many of the Moscow Art Theatre's sound principles are present: its intimacy, its careful arrangement, and more; but perhaps the single most important legacy to these young people is the combination of sincerity, spontaneity, and intelligence.
>
> There is a scene in the play in which a young man named Barend, who has a deathly fear of going to sea, is forced aboard the ship, *The Good Hope*. The emotion is communicated so well by Diky that when he is seized and forced to go, there were audible sobs in the auditorium. . . .

> Overall, the production creates a most gratifying impression and forces me to think that these young players will grow and mature to rival the preeminence presently enjoyed by our favorite players at the Moscow Art Theatre.[50]

Such comparisons did not endear the Studio to the older actors of the Art Theatre. "A great deal was written and said in the newspapers, society and theatres about the new studio," Stanislavsky writes. "At times it was cited as an example to us, the older actors, and we felt that side by side with us there was growing competition. . . . " Such competition, he felt, was "the motive force behind progress." With some satisfaction, he concludes: "From that time on the actors of the Moscow Art Theatre began to pay more attention to what was said about the new approach to art. I was gradually regaining my popularity."[51]

The Good Hope had also gone a long way toward solving the basic acting problems that most interested Stanislavsky at the time—emotion and the inner life of the character. As Markov—always grudging in his appraisal of Boleslavsky's work—admits: "Insofar as the 'system' concerned itself with feelings, the problem of feelings was worked out in this play. . . . "[52]

Little is known about the specific directorial techniques Boleslavsky employed at the First Studio. Vera Soloviova, who played the part of Jo in *The Good Hope,* remembers only the most general qualities of his approach. Yes, she says, Boleslavsky followed the Art Theatre practice of reading and discussing the play "at the table" before beginning actual staging rehearsals; but he held noticeably fewer discussions than did either Stanislavsky or Danchenko. Boleslavsky was eager to get the actors on their feet.

Soloviova remembers little else about Boleslavsky's practical techniques at the Studio, except that he made frequent use of improvisation and that his method of work more closely resembled Danchenko's than Stanislavsky's. While her recollections—some sixty years after the fact—are understandably vague, Soloviova is nonetheless clear and emphatic about the atmosphere of Boleslavsky's rehearsals: they were filled with an over-riding sense of joy and love. His rehearsals were a period of creative exploration and discovery, shared equally by actor and director. Unlike Vakhtangov, who "led you on a string," she says, "Boleslavsky took you by the hand and you set off on an adventure together."[53]

Marc Slonim verifies the general picture drawn by Soloviova. He says of Boleslavsky:

> He was less fanatical about the System than some of his companions and counterbalanced their excessive "depth of emotional experience" by a vivid sense of show-

manship and by a youthful joy of creation. His zest for life and love for the stage were truly infectious.[54]

While often critical of Boleslavsky's aims, Markov nonetheless provides a more detailed understanding of Boleslavsky's directorial approach to *The Good Hope*. In his first production Boleslavsky employed a principle that he later called "the long-distance mood," a term he used to designate the overall "air" or "atmosphere" of a production, as distinct from the "spine," or central action of a play. In working out the *mise en scène* for *The Good Hope*, he chose to make the sea the "invisible ambient which dictated the style of the performance" and subsequently affected every aspect of the production. This choice was significant in a way that might not at first be evident. The playwright's concerns were about evenly divided between the dramatic situation and the social implications of the capitalistic shipowner's criminal negligence. Boleslavsky might have developed his production along the lines of a revolutionary tract, making Geert a heroic spokesman for the repressed working-class and Bos the despicable representative of the capitalistic bosses. He chose instead to make the sea the pervasive influence. It became almost a character in the play and took on somewhat symbolic overtones. The ocean was the omnipresent power that, like blind fate, could offer life-giving sustenance or exact its terrible price of sudden death.

In following through with this idea, Boleslavsky guided the actors toward acquiring the gait peculiar to men of the sea and sought to infuse their physical presence with "the weather-beaten face, the stern tenderness, the strength and rolling muscularity of the body." Beyond that, however, he sought to fill the actors with a sense of the rhythms of the life of the fishing village, as well as the internal rhythms peculiar to each character. This primal rhythmicality was reinforced—particularly in the third act, which takes place during a violent storm—by the use of music and the sounds of the sea, the ship's ropes, and other natural effects, all of which were created by the actors in the wings.

Further, Boleslavsky sought to express the many moods of the sea as appropriate to the scenes of the play. Quiet, happy moments were possessed of darker undercurrents, as when, for example, Jo "hid behind her gay laughter the awareness of the grim truth." Each scene and each act was marked by a tidal ebb and flow, as when the waiting women and old salts gather around Kniertje's fire on a stormy night, alternately soothing and alarming one another with the exchange of bittersweet memories of lost sons and husbands. The equivalent of storm-tossed waters was also expressed in human terms, as when Barend breaks away from his captors to "writhe in the anguish of death at his mother's feet." Boleslavsky also drew inspiration from the sea in such local color touches as the sailors' drinking bout celebrating the ship's departure and the haunting sea chanties played by a blind beggar.

Thus, the sea provided a potent metaphor which stimulated the actors' imaginations, unified the effects, and justified a theatrical treatment of scenic and dramatic qualities. The clarity with which Boleslavsky expressed the "primitive succession of tragedy and comedy" ebbing and flowing through the lives of the simple fisherfolk proved strikingly fresh.

All actions and emotions were deliberately stripped to their essentials and an effort was made to express them with the clarity, the pristine power, and the inexorably changing rhythms of the sea itself. For the sake of this clarity, Boleslavsky demanded that each performance be stripped of anything that did not immediately convey the soul of the character. The actors were encouraged to forsake the subtle gradations of naturalistic playing and to express laughter and joy, tears and grief, and all the intermediate emotions, with equal sharpness and precision. Emotions and feelings were allowed to burst forth with the unexpected sharpness of a snapping rope or a splintering timber. Physical behavior as well was stripped to essentials, and extraneous mannerisms were eliminated.

Every line of dialogue was explored for its psychological rather than its logical meaning in a "rigorous search for the correct subtext;" words were unexpectedly emphasized; sentences were sharply broken off and then suddenly resumed. The patterns of movement crisscrossed the small playing area, receded upstage, and then flowed abruptly forward. Everything was calculated to express the essential "kernel" (core) of the characters and their perceptions. Because these perceptions and emotions were expressed with equal vividness, Markov comments, "they might have seemed accentuated and hyperbolical, but they were neither this nor that: they were simply stripped bare."

Just as Boleslavsky sought to rid the acting of all nonessential elements, he likewise reduced the scenic and decorative elements of the production to a necessary minimum. The settings were skeletonized and reduced to essential elements and forms. The functional or practical pieces of scenery might be characterized as sketchy, but the purely decorative elements were sometimes exaggerated—contrary qualities that also marked the acting style. While one or two ship models placed on a desk or counter might just as easily have suggested the particular nature of Bos's office, Boleslavsky chose instead to suspend a fleet of tiny vessels in the space over the actors' heads. Through such devices, Boleslavsky evidently sought formal unity between the settings and the acting style of *The Good Hope*.[55]

Boleslavsky's approach to the staging of his premiere production was no doubt indebted to his two teachers. Well before Boleslavsky's production of *The Good Hope*, Stanislavsky had sought to penetrate the psychology of characters and to bring actors to the living inner reality of the roles; he also had attempted to strip the actors' gestures and outer means of expression to their essential minimum in such productions as *The Life of Man* and *The Drama of Life*, productions which Boleslavsky greatly admired, though Stanislavsky himself was displeased with them.[56] Likewise, Danchenko's use of settings for the many scenes of *The Brothers Karamazov* (suggestive and necessary set pieces played against a background of neutral cloths) may well have inspired the scenic approach to *The Good Hope*.

Although Boleslavsky was evidently influenced by his elders, his work apparently went well beyond mere imitation. If Stanislavsky's judgment is to be taken at face value, Boleslavsky achieved in *The Good Hope* psychological depths and simplicity of expression that neither of the Art Theatre's directors had previously accomplished.

4

Rising Young Actor

The young actors at the First Studio, led by Boleslavsky, had worked night and day, dividing their time between theatre and studio, to produce *The Good Hope,* thereby giving birth to what they came to consider their own theatre. This was a time of feverish activity for all of them, but perhaps Boleslavsky was busier than most, for he appeared with greater frequency at the Art Theatre.

Between 1909 and 1915, the Moscow Art Theatre presented seventeen new productions (following the outbreak of the World War and in the wake of two revolutions and a civil war, the MAT's schedule was sharply curtailed for several years after 1915). Boleslavsky appeared in fourteen of these, acting a total of sixteen roles. Half were minor or supernumerary roles, and half were leading or major supporting roles, a record matched by few, if any, of the other MAT actors his age.[1] The Art Theatre's reputation for casting all its players, without regard to individual age, fame, or standing in the company, is not well supported by its cast lists; such popular and gifted actors as Kachalov, Knipper, or Moskvin were consistently given leading or major supporting parts, and the younger players—with the exception sometimes of ingenues—were almost always confined to small parts and walk-ons, only rarely winning supporting roles. Boleslavsky's career at the MAT was, therefore, an outstanding exception.

Since the Moscow Art Theatre was a repertory company, more than one actor usually was assigned to each new part. Significantly, Boleslavsky was the first actor to appear in all but one of the eight major roles he acted for the MAT. On the other hand, he followed other actors into all but three of his minor roles. These minor roles provide little basis for judging his qualities as an actor: he was rarely, if ever, reviewed in them, and, since he most often followed other actors into them, the dates he began acting such parts cannot be determined.

Still, Boleslavsky's small parts suggest something of the variety and range of his talent. Briefly—and chronologically by Art Theatre premiere dates—he first acted as Krutitsky's servant and then Mamayeva's in Ostrovsky's comic masterpiece, *Enough Stupidity in Every Wise Man* (11 March 1910); in Nemirovich-Danchenko's adaptation of Dostoyevsky's *The Brothers Karamazov* (11 October 1910), he played a Polish character, Pan Brubalevsky (due to its length, the play was presented in two parts on consecutive nights; Boleslavsky appeared in only the busy scene that opened the second evening's performance); and in Tolstoy's *The Living Corpse* (23 September 1911), Boleslavsky again acted two different roles, opening in the part of an officer and later taking over the role of Petrushkin's lawyer. Boleslavsky's size—over six feet, he was considered quite tall by contemporary standards—was used to advantage in the role of Aslak, the blacksmith, in Ibsen's poetic *Peer Gynt* (9 October 1912); later, in something of a switch, he followed Luzhsky in the role of the governor, Andrei Fon-Lembke, in *Nikolai Stavrogin,* Danchenko's adaptation of Dostoyevsky's *The Possessed* (23 October 1913); and, finally, for an evening of short plays by Pushkin, he acted the part of Don Carlos (played earlier by Stakhovich and Khokhlov) in *The Stone Guest* (26 March 1915), Pushkin's treatment of the Don Juan legend.

Unremarkable in themselves, these roles suggest that Boleslavsky possessed sufficient range to encompass the comic lackeys of Ostrovsky, the brutish blacksmith of Ibsen, and the young lawyer in Tolstoy, that he could move from realistic characters who spoke the everyday prose of common speech to the poetically heightened language of Pushkin's Don Carlos.

Boleslavsky's larger roles provide a much firmer basis for judging his abilities and growth as an actor. His first major part after Belyayev came the following season of 1910–11, when Nemirovich-Danchenko cast him as Levka in *Miserere,* a depressing study of Jewish life in Tsarist Russia by Semyon Youshkevich. The play is a realistic drama that follows the course of an ill-fated romance, but Danchenko gave it a symbolist flavor and many viewed the production, which opened on 17 December 1910, as "a dramatized funeral for the Revolution of 1905."[2] It failed to win much public support and was withdrawn after only twenty-six performances. Despite the play's failure, Boleslavsky's Levka was generally regarded highly. Efros writes that it was in this role that Boleslavsky most completely fulfilled the expectations raised by his Belyayev; the naïve candor and simple openness of Belyayev, Efros remarks, were here transformed by Boleslavsky into "fire, vividness, and impetuousity."[3] Hiż, too, considers Levka an important milestone in Boleslavsky's career and speculates on the reasons for his success in the part:

It was, perhaps, thanks to the fact that the subject of this play was taken by the author (a Russian Jew by descent) from the Jewish settlement in Odessa, an area well known to Boleslavsky since his youth; or, maybe, thanks to the fact that the leading lady, his partner for eight scenes, was played by an actess who was at that time the object of his attentions (moreover, she was a Pole, Pani Olga Gzovskaya). But to the point: Boleslavsky reached an artistic summit in this role.[4]

Olga Gzovskaya, one of the Art Theatre's most popular young leading ladies, was only one of several MAT actresses with whom Boleslavsky would be romantically linked.

The next important role Boleslavsky played may have been Blumenschon in Knut Hamsun's *In the Claws of Life,* but that is not certain. Hamsun's tangled drama of greed, selfishness, and murky sexuality premiered on 1 March 1911, but Leonid Leonidov was the first actor to appear in the part of Blumenschon, the play's suave and sophisticated, but thoroughly corrupt, leading character. Boleslavsky was the next to play it; his name appears in a program for the fifty-fifth performance of the play, dated 17 October 1913, but he may well have acted the part before that time.

In any case, Blumenschon was for Boleslavsky both atypical and demanding. There was nothing of the innocent young lover in the central character of this study of amoral exploitation leading finally to physical and spiritual death. Blumenschon is wealthy in material things, but morally bankrupt. He wields his sexual powers to hold his rich and beautiful young fiancée (played alternately by Zhdanova and Kosminskaya); his affair with a married woman (acted by Knipper) has grown inconvenient, so he uses his knowledge of her hidden guilt to rid himself of her. His actions precipitate a series of ugly revelations and jealous rivalries that culminate in miscegenation and a bizarre murder.

Any reviews Boleslavsky may have received in the role are not presently known, but his success may be inferred from the fact that he was still playing it in 1917, some three years after his first documented appearance in the part. Moreover, the fact that Boleslavsky was chosen to take over a role created by Leonidov suggests an impressive range as an actor. Some sixteen years Boleslavsky's senior, Leonidov had joined the Art Theatre in 1903, rising soon after to the ranks of its best players. Sometimes successful in comic parts, he was essentially a tragic actor, most remarkable in dark, passionate, or strange characters; his best roles included Pepel, the thief in *The Lower Depths,* the title role in *Peer Gynt,* Soleny in *The Three Sisters,* Lopakhin in *The Cherry Orchard,* Man in *The Life of Man,* and—probably his greatest achievement— Dmitri Karamazov in *The Brothers Karamazov.*[5] For the twenty-four year old Boleslavsky to be chosen to take over a role like Blumenschon from such a splendid actor as Leonidov was remarkable indeed.

Boleslavsky was not so fortunate in his next important role—Laertes in Shakespeare's *Hamlet,* directed by the visionary English designer and theoretician, Gordon Craig (though in fact Stanislavsky was responsible for much of the staging). The production, long delayed, finally opened on 23 December 1911. Boleslavsky's Laertes won little notice from the critics. They were absorbed with Craig's unorthodox interpretation of Shakespeare's tragedy and with Kachalov's work in the part of Hamlet. Briusov found Boleslavsky's acting to be satisfactory,[6] but Koiransky was far from pleased:

> Khokhlov made nothing of the role of Horatio. Boleslavsky made even less of the role of Laertes: the young actor failed completely to find a suitable tone for the role, and, in any case, did not portray that "excellent" cavalier which Laertes ought to be.[7]

In all fairness, Boleslavsky did not entirely deserve Koiransky's harsh judgment: Craig conceived of Laertes as a "little Polonius," and Polonius was stupid, servile, and of low character.[8] Judging from Koiransky's censure, Boleslavsky evidently gave his director what was wanted. In any event, this was one of the rare times that Boleslavsky's acting provoked a negative review.

Some fifteen years after the opening of *Hamlet,* Boleslavsky would still remember the difficult but valuable lessons he learned during this time of his life. In a letter to Gordon Craig, written in 1927, he asks:

> Do you remember the so-called small stage in the Moscow Art Theatre where preparatory work for "Hamlet" was going on, and the tall, clumsy young man whom Suller trusted to prepare the huge model of the second scene of "Hamlet", from the clay? This tall, clumsy young man worked two nights without sleeping. Then the model was brought to you. Your face looked as if you had tried a sandwich with soap! The model was thrown in the corner and in a few days found its way to the garbage can, and the tall, clumsy young man was perfectly convinced that he was good for nothing. Then, he rehearsed and acted Laertes and there wasn't enough despise [sic] which he got from everybody and mainly from your eye, for his interpretation and his execution of the part. Then for the second time, he thought he was good for nothing. This young man was myself. You killed me twice already twenty years ago, but as you may see, I didn't give up and I tried to be a good loser, and I am trying to do many things which I got from the people of the theatre like you, K.S., and very few others—almost nobody.
>
> Please do not be afraid. I never say that I am somebody's pupil. All my teachers taught me in a very simple way. They all told me that I was the greatest dumbbell in the world. Now, it wouldn't be fair to call them teachers for that simple and peda-

gogical way of making a man of me. But just the same, I don't know why, I am grateful to them.[9]

During the season of 1912–13, Boleslavsky created two important roles in new plays at the MAT. The first of these was in Andreyev's sordid *Yekaterina Ivanova,* in which the playwright tried none too successfully to invest a realistic psychological drama with symbolist overtones. The production opened on 12 December 1912 (just weeks before *The Good Hope's* first showing). Maria Germanova was the poetic heroine, who, wrongly accused of infidelity by her husband (Kachalov), is driven by inexplicable psychological forces to descend into a nightmare of degradation. Boleslavsky played the artist, Teplovsky. Along with other representatives of the intelligentsia (acted by Podgorny, Massalitinov, Voronov, and Khokhlov), he contributes to Yekaterina's eventual ruin. The play's climactic scene, in which a half-naked Yekaterina is forced by the debauched company to perform Salome's dance before her husband, ends with Teplovsky dragging her away for unspecified, but obviously degrading purposes.

The next production marked a change of mood for the Art Theatre and a new challenge for Boleslavsky. The program was comprised of Molière's *The Enforced Marriage* and *The Imaginary Invalid* (27 March 1913). In *The Enforced Marriage,* Boleslavsky played Alcide, his first important comic role. Luzhsky played Sganorelle; Germanova and Koreneva alternated in the part of Doremina; and Leonidov was Pancras. The critics were not wholly enthusiastic, but Koiransky was impressed by the stylishness of Boleslavsky's playing, in at least one scene: " . . . While Pancras (Mr. Leonidov) was on the stage, when the gypsy girls made their appearance in the scene with Alcide (whom Mr. Boleslavsky plays very well), one felt the pattern of a ballet, and the action progressed as if submitting to the rhythmical directions of a conductor's invisible baton."[10] And Lvov singled out Boleslavsky for special—if dubious—praise: "Only in Boleslavsky does Molière sometimes emerge, the genuine Molière, the Molière of Stanislavsky."[11]

With Alcide, Boleslavsky showed promise as a comic actor, but his first outstanding success in a comedy was as Fabrizzio in Goldoni's *The Mistress of the Inn,* which opened on 3 February 1914. The lovely Gzovskaya, Boleslavsky's sweetheart at the time of *Miserere,* took the part of Mirandolina, Stanislavsky played the role of the woman-hating Cavalier, Burdzhalov acted the Marquise, and Vishnevsky appeared as the Count. Koiransky noted in his review that he would have preferred a Fabrizzio possessed of "genuine southern ardor," rather than the "hot-temperedness" he found in Boleslavsky's portrayal, but with that reservation, he admired the performance:

> Boleslavsky-Fabrizzio is very handsome. He is a healthy country lad in whose veins, under his bronzed skin, flow blessed chianti and olive oil. . . . All his tricks with the napkin and awkward twitching of his legs very successfully approximate the droll "*lazzi*" of the comedy of masques.[12]

Fabrizzio was a role that Markov, Efros, and others would mark as a high point in Boleslavsky's MAT acting career.

Despite his busy schedule with the Art Theatre, Boleslavsky did not neglect his work at the First Studio, where from time to time he acted Bos, the shipowner, in *The Good Hope.* Following the MAT's spring tour of 1913, he went with the company to a mountain retreat in Kiev province to pass the hot summer months of June and July, but in August he returned to Moscow and went to work with the other studio members on their new quarters on Tverskaya. The Studio's new home was a considerable improvement over the Lux, though Meyerhold once remarked that Stanislavsky's students had "put him to work in a theatre with no more room than a tram car."[13] The arrangements were clean, compact, and functional, with an air of austerity and singleness of purpose matching the members' devotion to their new theatre. In addition to acting and directing, they worked in all areas of production and the studio's day-to-day operation. They designed and built the scenery and costumes, decorated the settings, tended to the properties, served as stagehands and ushers during performances, and were assigned housekeeping chores.

While giving infrequent performances of *The Good Hope,* the studio resumed preparations, begun the previous spring, for its second production, *The Festival of Peace,* by Gerhardt Hauptmann. The play, a naturalistic drama which treats a psychopathic family's suffering under the burden of heredity, was directed by Eugene Vakhtangov, a short, slender man with an ascetically attractive face and deep-set, penetrating eyes. He had studied with Sulerzhitsky at the Adashev School before joining the MAT in March, 1911. Passionate and intolerant, Vakhtangov was a probing, perceptive teacher and a volatile director; particularly in his later work he inclined to wildly elaborate improvisations during rehearsals. The pendulum of his mood swung widely between the extremes of joy and darkest depression. An artful caricaturist, he was not a particularly gifted actor, playing relatively few roles at the Art Theatre, and those mostly minor parts. Outspoken to the point of rudeness, Vakhtangov was antagonistic to anyone who dared disagree with his artistic views. His relations with Stanislavsky were punctuated by frequent letters from Vakhtangov imploring his teacher's tolerant understanding and reiterating his devotion.

For *The Festival of Peace,* Vakhtangov cast Boleslavsky in the role of Wilhelm, the sardonic, intellectual son of a disintegrating German family who attempts a reconciliation with his father, but suffers from morbid indecision, fearful that he carries within himself the hidden venom of future insanity, Wilhelm is afraid to marry lest he pass on to his children the stigma of his heritage.

Given their personalities, it was inevitable Boleslavsky and Vakhtangov should clash. Others described Boleslavsky as exuberant, with a zest and joy for theatre and life that was truly infectious; he was full of pranks and loved to laugh; of the studio members, he was the least slavish in his use of Stanislavsky's system.[14] But Vakhtangov, who sometimes was said to have tried to "out-Stanislavsky Stanislavsky," saw his colleague in a different light:

> Always inattentive, always lightminded, always unserious, always inconsiderate of friends and partners, even in those moments that their souls are filled with great, living emotions, when it seems anyone would stop joking around out of sheer sensitivity, Boleslavsky turns out to be for all of us the most objectionable partner.[15]

Nor was Vakhtangov satisfied with Boleslavsky's work. Following the twenty-fifth rehearsal of *The Festival of Peace,* on 2 March 1913, he had made notes about one of Boleslavsky's scenes:

> The brothers haven't seen each other for six years. Listening to the brothers' dialogue is completely uninteresting right now. It is boring. I do not understand a thing. Boleslavsky is in love with himself, unconsciously he is flirting with himself. This must go. Actually, nothing is quite right with him. There is no attention to the work. Everything is dry. From a sense of duty.
>
> Something cold and unpleasant has crept into the entire tone of our good work. As kind as I am to him, it hurts me that he does not understand that I am not alone in being disturbed by his behavior.[16]

Exasperated by Boleslavsky's failure to appear at an important rehearsal with N.N. Rakhmanov, who was composing the music for the production, an irate Vakhtangov wrote to Sulerzhitsky, who had evidently urged him to register his complaints, asking "Suler" to report Boleslavsky's behavior to Stanislavsky:

Everyone was most indignant that we had to stop such an important rehearsal as today's. I cannot describe our indignation to you. The entire production is falling apart. None of the scenes that Boleslavsky is in are finished. . . .

Neither the pleas of colleagues, nor my delicate tone with him, nor the fact that he himself has directed, nor the importance of the moment—nothing guarantees me any peace for rehearsals and my work in the studio. . . .

Up to today, he has missed six rehearsals, without prior warning (although he was not busy with Molière on those days).

Everything is ready. Even the sets. Only his scenes are unfinished: how can he fail to understand that such behavior is not permissible?

He has transformed the joy of work into sheer suffering. I am suffering and so are all our colleagues. I ask you to do something.[17]

What Vakhtangov judged to be indifference can be understood as an honest misreading of Boleslavsky's attitude; possibly Vakhtangov mistook a lack of solemnity for a lack of earnestness. But there was no excuse for Boleslavsky's serious breach of theatre protocol. Did Sulerzhitsky intervene? Did Stanislavsky take Boleslavsky to task for his lapse in professionalism? Very likely they did. In any case, tension between Boleslavsky and Vakhtangov eased. That fall, Vakhtangov wrote a more positive note. He had changed the "kernel" of the characters being played by Sushkevich, Deykun, Khmara, Birman, and Popov, and he was searching for the right kernel for Boleslavsky's Wilhelm: "Regarding Boleslavsky, I wish to note that I have been gladdened by his change for the better regarding his work. Several times during intimate rehearsals he worked on his scenes thoroughly, stubbornly dissecting the details."[18] Soon after, however, *The Festival of Peace* faced a new crisis.

In staging the play Vakhtangov underscored the grim naturalism of the drama and emphasized the viciousness of the characters. When the play was finally shown to Stanislavsky, the Art Theatre's director was "white with fury," Magarshack tells us. "The actors had never seen him so angry before." The extreme pessimism of Vakhtangov's interpretation of the play so angered Stanislavsky that he refused to permit it to open. He was supported in this decision by Nemirovich-Danchenko and, surprisingly, by Sulerzhitsky, as well. Several of the MAT's older actors intervened on Vakhtangov's behalf, and the directors were persuaded to allow the play to open, on 13 October 1913.[19]

The Festival of Peace was not a critical success, though it remained in the Studio's repertory for a time. Koiransky deplored the play, but felt that the production had "succeeded in presenting that atmosphere of diseased lack of will in which, according to the author's design, the terrible powers of fate, illness, and heredity direct the action with the energy of hidden natural forces.'' He found all the performers to be "more than satisfactory," and the acting of Boleslavsky, Khmara, and Sushkevich notable for "the persuasiveness and trepidation of an inner stage life."[20]

Deeply hurt by Stanislavsky's reaction and stung by the critics' remarks, Vakhtangov—in violation of the theatre's rule against outside work—temporarily withdrew from the Studio to head a group of amateurs elsewhere in Moscow. He was later reconciled with the Studio, but he worked with increasing frequency with other young theatre groups. As a result of his extended absences, in 1918 the First Studio would threaten to drop his name from their membership roles.[21]

In Magarshack's estimation, *The Good Hope* and *The Festival of Peace* "revealed two diametrically opposed tendencies in the Russian theatre, which were to become more and more pronounced and irreconcilable as the political events in Russia moved to a crisis, culminating in the revolution: the tendency of denunciation and exposure and the tendency of artistic truth."[22] Boleslavsky always pursued the ideal of truth and deplored "propaganda" in the theatre. The quality of honesty in his acting had contributed to his rapid rise in the ranks of the Art Theatre's players. Ironically, in a few years his distaste for politicized theatre would result in his fall from grace.

5

Approach of War

Tercentenary ceremonies celebrating three hundred years of rule by the House of Romanov were held early in 1913. This year and the next were years of great change and social excitement. The Fourth Duma, which first sat in 1912, gave every sign of continuing the reforms initiated by Premier Stolypin, reforms which, to cite some of the more important measures, had already led to record-breaking agricultural productivity; the influx of foreign investment and currency; the rapid expansion of native industry and the railway system; and progressive reform measures in education and land redistribution. This Duma was undeniably more self-determining than its predecessors, raising the hope in some quarters that Russia was in fact becoming the constitutional monarchy she had theoretically been since 1905. The government's growing strength inevitably caused a corresponding decline in the fortunes of the revolutionary movement—though the Duma included among its members a handful of Bolsheviks and Mensheviks. Labor agitation and factory strikes were overshadowed by new prosperity and a growing sense of national pride. Russian nationalism, fueled by Russia's Balkan Pact with Serbia, was reborn in the guise of Pan-Slavism. Serbia's territorial expansion, the result of successful wars against Bulgaria and Turkey, increased the Pan-Slavists' eagerness to enter the fray. War was in the air.

Russia's general sense of well-being inevitably caused a lively upsurge in social life. Sleigh bells jangled through the winter's short days and long nights, as troikas made an endless round of parties, some of which lasted for two or three weeks at a time. Ladies glittered in fabulous jewelry and imported French fashions; gentlemen indulged the Russian taste for resplendent uniforms. They were gayer, their laughter louder, and their intellectual debate more voluble than at anytime since 1905. Fortunes were lost and won at the gambling table, and card players passed long hours at the newly imported games of poker and bridge. The

Emperor banned the one-step and the tango for their licentiousness. Rivers of vodka and imported champagne flowed. Endless gossip was exchanged about the topics of the day. Everyone debated the merits of the sensational trial of a young Jew accused of committing a "blood ritual" murder; and there was endless speculation about the mysterious *starets,* Gregori Rasputin, who had insinuated himself into the inner circles of the court and, it was rumored, there indulged in shameful orgies of feasting, drinking, debauchery, and Olympian sexuality.

Sometime in 1913, Boleslavsky met and became enamored of Natalia ("Natasha") Valentinovna Platonova, an actress popular in singing roles and light comedies (mostly French) at Saburov's theatre in St. Petersburg. She had come to Moscow to join the Free Theatre, recently opened by Mardzhanov and Sukhodolsky. Born in Nizhni Novgorod (now Gorky) in 1887, she was the daughter of Valentin Mikhailovich Shimkevich, son of an aristocratic family, and Natalia, a peasant girl who worked on the Shimkevich estate. Natasha and two brothers had been born out of wedlock, but when Colonel Mikhail Shimkevich, a hero of the Crimean War, who had himself married a former serf after the death of his first wife, discovered his son's affair, he compelled the two to marry and legitimize their offspring. Afterwards Valentin Shimkevich became a professor of biology at St. Petersburg University and authored an important work on Darwin's theories.

It was in St. Petersburg that Natasha and her three brothers—another son had been born after her parents' marriage—received their educations. Shimkevich, a friend of Maxim Gorky, was coldly intellectual in most matters, but given to violent outbursts of temper. He eventually divorced his peasant wife and married Ludmilla, a well-educated and genteel woman who had for years served as governess to the Shimkevich children. Desperately unhappy, Natasha and her younger brother ran away from home, but were soon found and returned to their father. At seventeen, she found escape through marriage to Gregori Platonov, an engineer twenty years her senior. Theirs was not a happy union. Platonov was frequently absent for long periods, constructing bridges and roads in the Middle East, but his young wife, who had long dreamed of becoming an actress, stayed behind in St. Petersburg to study for the stage with teachers from the Imperial Theatre School. After winning her first professional engagement at Saburov's theatre, she began seeing an attorney with important connections at the Imperial Court. On the occasion of one of his infrequent visits home, Platonov, in a jealous rage, fired a shot at her but missed. For several years Natasha sought vainly to win a divorce, which she won finally through her lawyer friend's intercession.

Natasha Platonova first saw Boleslavsky on stage in one of his performances at the Art Theatre and was struck by his handsome appearance. She soon arranged through mutual friends to be introduced to him at a party held one evening after a theatre performance. A romance developed, but Natasha was not free.[1]

Boleslavsky married not long after, but his wife was Maria Yefremova, an actress who had played minor roles at the Moscow Art Theatre. They had known each other for some three years, for Yefremova's first appearance with the MAT had been in the 1910 production of *The Brothers Karamazov,* in which Boleslavsky, it will be remembered, played Pan Brubalevsky. Yefremova was the daughter of a wealthy merchant; the family was of French origin, but had been thoroughly russianized. She was considered beautiful and had a pleasant singing voice. Evidently she was not a particularly gifted actress, for she never rose above minor parts at the Art Theatre and eventually concentrated on a singing career, appearing frequently in popular cabarets. Boleslavsky's marriage to Yefremova did not last.[2] By the end of the coming war, Boleslavsky and Natasha Platonova would both be free to marry again, and she would become Natasha Boleslavsky.

The year 1914 saw the beginning of a new aspect of Boleslavsky's career. Not long after he had opened as Fabrizzio in *The Mistress of the Inn,* he appeared in two new acting roles—not on the stage, however, but on the silent screen. His film acting debut was in a leading role in *Passing Life By* (*Mimo zhizni,* sometimes translated *The Passing Dream*), released on 28 February 1914. His second screen appearance came less than a month later, when he played one of the two featured roles in *Dance of the Vampires* (*Tanets vampira*), first shown on March 22. Both pictures were directed by Yakov Protazanov, one of the more talented of the pre-Revolutionary directors, for the Golden Russia Series at the Thiemann and Reinhardt Studio.[3] Historian of the Russian cinema Jay Leyda describes the several films of this series as an imitation of the popular French genre, "the drama of pathos, where plot-intrigue was replaced by the sentimental sensations of unreal figures clothed in the most exquisite sartorial taste."[4] *Passing Life By* starred the actress Naydenova as Nina, a young girl who is awakening to new experiences and emotions, but who is unable to find real love or genuine meaning in her life. She is caught in a love triangle with an artist named Volin, played by Boleslavsky, and a poet, acted by Vladimir Maksimov, a popular matinee idol.

Contrary to its title, evidently chosen to appeal to the public's taste for sensational subjects, *The Dance of the Vampires* was not a horror movie, but a survey of new trends in dance. It featured Boleslavsky and V. Lasky. Were there any other performers in the film, possibly as anonymous couples on the dance floor? Did the film show popular dances or theatrical performances? Did Boleslavsky (who had studied Greek dancing in the Isadora Duncan style as part of his MAT training and was remarkably agile for a man his size) actually dance in the film? From the surviving brief descriptions, none of these questions can be answered.

In any case, Boleslavsky's appearance in these and later films did not endear him to Stanislavsky, for as Leyda writes: "Stanislavsky's personal feeling about films began as contempt, warmed into antagonism, and never went beyond tolerance, in later mellow years." When he heard that Olga Baklanova and Eugene Vakhtangov had appeared in a film called *The Great Magaraz,* also shown in 1914, Stanislavsky refused to speak to them for six months. Nonetheless, Boleslavsky and several other studio actors, attracted by the twin lures of extra money and the silent cinema's vast audiences, joined what Leyda calls "a constant underground movement" to the film studios "that was too strong to be countered by any measure short of dismissal." Soon, in a relaxation of its rules, the Art Theatre only forbade its players "to take part in any film that does not have serious motives." Most of Boleslavsky's next films were clearly more commercial than artistic works.[5]

During the summer of 1914, Boleslavsky, his wife Maria, and the other studio members retired to a plot of land on the shore of the Black Sea, near Eupatoria, which had been purchased for their use by Stanislavsky. Here, under the strict guidance of Sulerzhitsky they lived in emulation of the peasant *zemstvo.* Each member was responsible for the construction of his own living quarters—built of blocks of stone, with a canvas roof—and each was assigned his communal duty.[6]

The peace of the studio's Eupatorian summer was marred by disquieting news from the outside world. On June 28 the Archduke Ferdinand and his wife were killed in Sarajevo. On July 30, Tsar Nicholas II responded to continuing unrest in Serbia, Russia's ally, by signing an order mobilizing Russia's military forces. The next day the German Kaiser, the Tsar's cousin, telegraphed an ultimatum demanding instant cessation of mobilization. Continuation, the message said, would constitute an act of aggression against the German state. Nicholas, on the advice of his ministers, remained firm; Russia would not demobilize. On August 1, Germany responded to the Tsar's obstinancy by declaring war against Russia. Two days later Germany declared war against France as well. By the time the studio actors returned to Moscow the city was swept with nationalist fervor as the military command launched an offensive into Galicia, formerly part of the Polish kingdom, but in August, 1914, a part of the Hapsburg Empire, Germany's ally.

Mobilization brought to the streets of St. Petersburg and Moscow great parades and processions of soldiers, banners, and weaponry, all moving to martial music. The Tsar ordered the price of vodka to be inflated beyond the reach of common workers and peasants, then banned its sale altogether and closed the drinking halls, in order that Russia's sons might face the coming fight with appropriate sobriety. Some of the MAT's actors had already been called into military service. Others soon volunteered. Boleslavsky did not. This was Russia's war, and none of his affair—except insofar as much of the fighting took place on soil that was historically Polish.

The war did have one immediate effect on Boleslavsky, however. He soon appeared in the title role of a two-reel potboiler called *The Exploits of the Cossack Kuzma Kruchkov (Podvig kazaka Kuz'my Kruchkova)*. Made in a single day by Gardin and rushed into release on 12 October 1914, the film was one of many calculated to boost Russian war-fervor and patriotism. Kruchkov was an actual figure, a Don Cossack who had fought in one of the first engagements of the war. Decorated by Nicholas, his face and heroics were popularized by the press and on posters throughout the nation. Boleslavsky, who must have resembled the hero, portrayed him as a gallant borderland boyar who single-handedly stands off eleven German soldiers. The film's bristling action and Kruchkov's fame combined to make the feature wildly popular.[7] Overnight Boleslavsky was seen by a wider audience than had witnessed his combined performances at the Moscow Art Theatre and the First Studio. The picture's great success did not guarantee Boleslavsky a permanent place in Thiemann and Reinhardt's roster of actors, however. He did not make another film until the fall of 1915, at which time he worked on both sides of the camera—as actor and director.

The outbreak of the World War soon resulted in soaring production costs and reduced personnel for the First Studio. The Studio delayed opening its new productions for the 1914–1915 season until mid-winter, but then it opened two plays in quick succession. The first was Boris Sushkevich's adaptation and staging of Charles Dicken's *The Cricket on the Hearth*. Opening on 24 November 1914, the play was an immediate and resounding success; it "did for the Studio what *The Seagull* had done for the MAT."[8] More than any other play produced by the Studio, *The Cricket on the Hearth* expressed Sulerzhitsky's belief in "the love of mankind.'' Its gentleness, sentimentality, and humor ''radiated the warm hope in man and the victory of goodness over cruelty and greed.''[9] (Boleslavsky is sometimes credited with playing a role in *The Cricket,* and perhaps he did play Caleb, the role created by Michael Chekhov, some time later: an extant photograph of Boleslavsky in an unidentified part shows him in make-up similar to that used by Chekhov in the part.)

The gentle sweetness of *The Cricket on the Hearth* was contrasted sharply by the Studio's next production, which opened on Christmas Day. Directed by Boleslavsky, *The Wanderers* (*Kaliki perekhozhie,* literally, ''the wandering minstrels''), was a new play by Vladimir Volkenstein. Volkenstein had once served as Stanislavsky's secretary and now acted as the Studio's literary manager. He peopled his play with characters who embodied the most mystical, the most superstitious, and the most violent strains of primitive Christianity. *The Wanderers* dealt with ''God-seekers'' in search of peace and salvation at the Heavenly City. Beset by numerous hardships, they eventually slay their leader, a propitiatory sacrifice which was imbued both with primitive religious significance and overtones of archetypal symbolism. The subject evidently interested Boleslavsky. He later recalled: ''The Russian mountains, woods, and river sources are as full of hermits today as they were a thousand years ago.'' These ascetic ''hermits'' settled into small communities in isolated spots.

> They are not monasteries, they are just places where people, who feel ''God's urge,'' go and live in solitude . . . and though they are the result of ''God's urge,'' they do not profess any religion or perform any rituals. . . . These wanderers just move away into the wilderness and remain there by themselves. . . . [10]

Boleslavsky set himself and the actors a two-fold artistic task in *The Wanderers,* that of evoking ''the world of hoary antiquity with crude almost beast-like force, and of revealing the nature of the primeval religious urge.''[11] He was encouraged—in the latter, at least—by Sulerzhitsky, who said:

> It is nothing that they are tired, that they have lost their way, that they are hungry and ragged. To God, to God strain your soul, seek in Him repose when you are exhausted. They follow truth, they are bearers of Christ. Here in the second act they all shine from the consciousness in themselves of a great mission—to carry truth. And the closer you find their capacity of contact with God, the more the audience will understand you.

Markov tells us that Boleslavsky took ''concreteness as the starting point'' in expressing the spirit of *The Wanderers:* ''The tragedy of the thirteenth century . . . was impelled by its subject matter towards a concrete perception of life, even more so than in *The Good Hope.*" Through such means, Markov says, Boleslavsky expressed the monumental, sweeping passions of mankind and the equivocal irony of the play's paradoxical theme: "The insatiable force of love, unconsciously perpetrating evil, with a holy faith in the goodness of the evil perpetrated."[12]

Available critical appraisals suggest that Boleslavsky largely succeeded in realizing the artistic tasks he had set himself. "Ancient, hoary, moss-covered Russia looks at us from the stage," one critic wrote. Another called *The Wanderers* "one of the most painful plays which the Studio has given us." He continues:

> From Norway and Germany—the locales of the previous plays—they have come to our own land, to our own torments. It is no matter that the drama takes place in the beginning of the thirteenth century, that the pilgrims are cowardly and beastly, not very far removed from cave-men, that is only one side of it; on the other hand they are unusually close to us, to our contemporary life.[13]

Beginning on 14 April 1915, Boleslavsky created his last new role as an actor with the Moscow Art Theatre, though he would later act again in plays in the MAT's repertory. The new play was Ilya Surguchev's *Autumn Violins.* This domestic melodrama was an odd choice for its director, Nemirovich-Danchenko; either his generally exquisite literary taste had failed him or he had yielded to the popular mood. Russian victories during the first year of fighting had by now given way to humiliating retreat, and the people of Moscow had sunk into a brooding moroseness. The Art Theatre's public was ready to be amused and diverted by light fare. On seeing *Autumn Violins,* the critic Koiransky felt the production parodied the Art Theatre's methods and found the play "devoid of any literary merit but undoubtedly designed for success with the average audience."[14]

In *Autumn Violins,* Boleslavsky played Baranovsky, a smart young attorney involved in an affair with an older, married woman, acted by Knipper. When her husband (Vishnevsky) begins to suspect them, the woman marries her lover off to her adopted daughter (Zhdanova) in order to allay her husband's suspicions and to rescue her own pride. Koiransky admitted the "dexterity" of Surguchev's "entertaining plot," and continued:

> To keep the play from getting boring the author has provided it with on- and off-stage music . . . dances, a game of forfeits, and cheap lyricism in which the delicate dreaminess of Chekhov's dramas are vulgarized.

Moreover, the play is acted very well. Mme. Knipper in some places moves us to tears, Mr. Vishnevsky is nobly unaffected and gentle, Mme. Zhdanova is young and spontaneous as she should be, and in Mr. Boleslavsky's awkward roughness there is much character—the danger of playing the "first lover" has been successfully avoided.

"The success is indeed great," Koiransky ended. "But, in truth, for the good name of the theatre, it is preferable to produce failures such as a Pushkin drama."[15]

Koiransky's spleen may not have been entirely justified, for the play has been admired by others. His prediction of audience success proved accurate, however. *Autumn Violins* played over a hundred performances. As Slonim notes, the Art Theatre had transformed the work of a minor dramatist who imitates Chekhov into a "spectacular" success.[16]

There is a tempting irony in the juxtaposition of Boleslavsky's first and last new roles with the Moscow Art Theatre. Olga Knipper was the leading lady in both plays, but Belyayev's naïve innocence in *A Month in the Country* has given way to Baranovsky's guilty complicity in sin. Off stage, in his private life, Boleslavsky had also undergone important changes: the enthusiastic sixteen-year-old who presented himself for the judgment of the MAT's directors in 1906 had grown into an established twenty-six-year-old theatre artist who knew firsthand some of the pitfalls of human affairs.

Following the MAT's annual tour in the spring and the Studio's summer retreat to Eupatoria, Boleslavsky returned to Moscow. While continuing his roles on the stage of theatre and studio, he picked up some film work. His next picture was *Tsar Ivan the Terrible* (*Tsar Ivan Vasilievich Grozny*), starring Fyodor Shalyapin in the title role and Pavel Bazilevsky as Boris Godunov. The film, which the famous basso had largely financed, was released on 20 October 1915, for the jubilee of Shalyapin's twenty-fifth year on the stage. Produced by Ivanov-Gai (the very name was "robberish," Shalyapin said later), the picture was a slipshod effort that did not prove popular, despite the great fame of Russia's preeminent basso. The real excitement had unfortunately happened off-camera. Boleslavsky, in the role of Prince Vyazemsky, and Sushkevich as Malyuta, stood on the sidelines and watched as titanic battles raged between opera star and producer.[17]

Soon after, Boleslavsky acted in a film produced by Robert Persky, who had angered the Art Theatre and Tolstoy's widow some years before by releasing an unauthorized film version of *The Living Corpse* a week before the MAT's premiere of Tolstoy's play.[18] Despite Persky's bad reputation at the Art Theatre, his new picture *Mara Kramskaya* (24 November 1915) featured performances by Boleslavsky (as a pianist named Panov), Gzovskaya, Lazarev, Khmara, Geyrot, Rayevskaya, Popov, Kemper, and Count Stakhovich—all from the Art Theatre or its First Studio. The story of a modern woman, the picture failed to win much favor with the public and is notable primarily as the screen debut of Gzovskaya, who went on to become one of the first native actresses to win lasting stardom in the Russian cinema.[19]

Also in 1915—the premiere dates are unknown—Boleslavsky directed his first two pictures, *Three Meetings (Tri Vstrechi)* and *You Still Cannot Love (Ty yeshchë ne umeyesh' lyubit')*. *Three Meetings* was made for "Russ" Studio and photographed by Yakovlev. Based on a poem of the same title by Rozengiema, this four-reeler had a cast of ten, including Gregori Khmara and Alexander Bondarev from the First Studio. The film fared poorly at the box office, though its star, Beatriche Blazhevich, in her screen debut, subsequently made a name in the silent cinema.

You Still Cannot Love did little better. Produced and photographed by Pechkovsky, the somewhat sensational story dealt with a man who struggles to suppress his incestuous feelings for his adopted daughter. Boleslavsky directed the film and played the central role, as well. Kireyevskaya played his stepdaughter Nina as a child, and Kozlyaninova played the grown-up Nina.

Neither of the films Boleslavsky directed in 1915 was a financial success, but that fact in itself does not necessarily suggest that they were of poor quality. Box-office prices had doubled and tripled as a result of a Special Fuel Council's decree requisitioning fuel stocks for the war effort in October. The theatres and cinemas were the first to be affected by the order. Before the winter was out the First Studio's actors were rehearsing in their warmest clothing, and audiences stayed bundled up in their great coats and fur caps during performances. Inflated prices and a badly devalued currency closed a number of cinema theatres and seriously hurt attendance at those remaining open. The public, preferring celluloid thrills to the real horrors of the continuing war, was rapidly developing a taste for films about devils, ascetics, and vampires.

Since the spring of 1915, Boleslavsky had been rehearsing a role in *The Deluge* (sometimes called *The Flood*) by Henning Berger, under Vakhtangov's direction. The play is set in a cellar bar in the American west. There is a torrential downpour and the people trapped in the bar learn that an up-river dam is in danger of imminent collapse. Until now they have fought and schemed, betrayed and accused, but under the threat of group destruction, they come together in the spirit of forgiveness, understanding, and atonement. In the last act, the threat is lifted, and they revert to their former selves, if anything, more vicious than before. Boleslavsky was to portray the shyster O'Neill. For a rehearsal in January 1915, Vakhtangov made the following notes for the play's second act, the act of reconciliation:

> Richard—do his monologue about himself without buffoonery. He is completely inside himself. He is guilt-ridden. Watch the tone. Keep your hands down. "Oh, if I could only cry. . . . It would ease my soul. Alone, I am alone. . . . I am a sensible person, tired of suffering, and around me are such pitiful and empty people. . . ."[20]

The play opened in December 1915, but Boleslavsky was not among the cast. He would play the part of O'Neill only after he had come back from the Great War.

Part II: 1915–1923

Russia, Poland, and Beyond

My dream is to measure the fields, forests, rivers and sea shores with my steps, and my ordeal is that I probably will never be able to stop and say, "This is mine. This is for me. This is the best." Even if I wanted to say it.

—Richard Boleslavsky
Way of the Lancer, p. 257.

6

Years of Decision

For a great many people of Polish descent, the First World War was actually a kind of civil conflict. Boleslavsky explains a situation that was all too common: "My aunt had six boys . . . in 1906 three emigrated, one to Germany, two to Austria—the youngest three remained in Russia. In the war the six served in the different armies. Many families were like that."[1] Each of the major parties to the carnage sooner or later held out to their Polish citizens the tantalizing promise of Polish independence and autonomy in exchange for their loyalty and support in the war effort. Many Polish soldiers mistrusted the word of the Russian Tsar, German Kaiser, or Austro-Hungarian Emperor, but fought under their respective banners just the same, sustained by the hope that the promise of a reborn Polish state might be kept. Only after the Grand Duke Nikolai issued a manifesto guaranteeing freedom for Poland—previously only hinted at by Tsar Nicholas—did Boleslavsky resolve to serve in Russia's army, an army largely paralyzed by the Tsar's indecision, ill-fed, ill-armed, and ill-clothed due to chaotic mismanagement, and demoralized by defeat and desertion. He enlisted in the late summer or early fall of 1915.

Boleslavsky received his training at the Imperial Cavalry School in the bustling port city of Tver (now Kalinin) on the Volga, some one hundred miles to the northwest of Moscow. He claims to have won the highest marks in his class, both for practical proficiency and in theoretical subjects. "For this I was supposed to be made sergeant of the squadron," he writes, "but as a Pole I was given second place. The Russian boy who had the second highest marks was made sergeant."[2] In the late summer of 1916, Boleslavsky, a cornet (the first officer rank in the Imperial Russian Army) was sent to the Border Regiment (probably the Pogranichnaya Stratsa) of the Russian Sixth Cavalry. He was under enemy fire for the first time somewhere along the Galician Front. After some three months' service, he was transferred to the all-Polish first regiment of Krechowiecki Lancers under Moscicki.[3] Wearing the white, amaranthine, and blue uniform of a Polish cavalryman, he served as a lieutenant with other Poles in the south, in an area bounded by the Pruth and Dniester rivers:

> There were two hundred of us in our regiment,— the Polish Lancers—a tiny segment of strangers in the vast body of the Russian army, separated from the main body of Polish infantry legion. During the war, and later during the Revolution, we wandered in and out of the confusion, always a little detached from all of it. Though we fought and were killed, we were in spirit really onlookers.
>
> We were closer to the Poles in the German army than we were to the Russians in ours. And we felt toward the Russians a greater enmity than we did for example toward the Austrians; to the Russians we were never brothers. They looked on us as a conquered people. They did not so much dislike us as disregard us.[4]

In late February or early March, following long months of largely non-consequential skirmishing, Boleslavsky's regiment was taken by train for a long rest near the city of Kharkov in the Ukraine. Here they heard news of the deteriorating situation on Russia's domestic front. Near the end of February—about the time Boleslavsky's regiment left the front—a general strike broke out in Petrograd (St.Petersburg had been renamed) and quickly grew into a full-scale insurrection. On March 8, the police killed and wounded over three hundred people while attempting to disperse the crowds. Within the next three months the Petrograd garrison mutinied and even the Cossacks, traditionally the Tsar's merciless defenders, refused to ride against the mob. Tsar Nicholas, his power and support hopelessly shattered, was placed under house arrest at Tsarskoye Selo. He abdicated in favour of the Grand Duke Mikhail, but the Grand Duke declined the honor. The Duma, which had defied an imperial decree ordering its dissolution, proclaimed itself a provisional government. Leadership soon went to Alexander Kerensky.

These events posed a quandary for Boleslavsky and his regiment. The monarch they had sworn to serve had been deposed; to whom did they owe loyalty? After some indecision, they decided "to stick to our own formation and to work for the resurrection of the Polish state." In a private ceremony, they christened a new standard for the regiment—a white eagle on an amaranthine field—for centuries the emblem of Poland.[5]

Already demoralized, Russia's armies declined into disorder and near chaos. Bolshevik agitators appeared at the front, encouraging desertion when little encouragement was needed. Boleslavsky's regiment sent scouts to the Austrians, the Germans, into Poland, to Moscow, and to Petrograd; they got word back that "Polish legions were forming quickly and were gathering in Galitzia [*sic*] and in Russian Poland."[6] Roused by these reports, the regiment tried without success to skirt the German lines in order to join up with their Polish comrades. Very soon after, Boleslavsky recounts: "We found ourselves at war with the country which we had defended for years. . . . Orders were given to locate 'a band which hides in the forest, travels at night, and which is not an officers' unit. . . . ' "[7] Unable to break through into Galicia, surrounded by a now-hostile Russian army, the regiment decided to disband and disburse:

> Moving out singly or in twos, sneaking through the lines of Reds, mingling with the Communists, we might save ourselves as remnants. We might save those remnants for Poland. . . . Those who could not reach Poland were told to move toward Moscow or Kijow [Kiev] and Odessa and from there to try to find their way. Officers were ordered to go to those towns and serve as points of information and direction. I was ordered to go to Moscow.
> The next place of assembly for the regiment was Warsaw—time, not stated.[8]

Boleslavsky reached Moscow in the late summer of 1917, fearful at first he might be arrested. Soon he convinced himself that chances were slight that Lieutenant Ryszard Srzednicki—he had served under his real name—would be traced to Richard Valentinovich Boleslavsky of the Moscow Art Theatre. He presented himself to the Art Theatre and the Studio: "I was filled with warmth and joy. . . . Even the news about the comrades who were dead could not spoil my inner excitement, because at last I was home. Not Poland, not Russia, not the regiment, not Moscow—the Studio seemed to me really home."[9] His loyalty would remain firm during the approaching Second Revolution, only months away:

> I turned into what I personally always called a "Goddamned civilian." I did not participate in any fight. I did not fire a single shot. I did not take any chances and did not attach myself to any side. All I did was to give hospitality and to distribute money to the people who were smuggling themselves out of the borders of Russia. Those people amounted to about ten or twelve Poles, Lancers from my regiment.[10]

Later, Boleslavsky would admit that while he hated the Revolution, he had loved almost everything he had gone through during the war:

> I went to war influenced by two motives,—by two halves of me. The actor half chose the loveliest uniform, the Polish half chose the traditional hero. It was very childish but I'll never regret it. During the years of war I became a man. I learned camaraderie. I learned compassion. I learned self-reliance. I learned to share sufferings, to despise bluff, to realize that enemies and friends are equally human when taken

separately. I learned that military science in practice does not go beyond the Shakespearean statement: "The Field of Battle," and that the craze of war is a germ like any other germ,—a fever or delirium; that politics had nothing to do with the war, that the only thing the human is always ready for is laughter and the joy of living even in the midst of slaughter and the agony of dying. That everything which happens in war on either side should be understood, forgiven and forgotten as soon as it is possible. Finally, that all war amounts to, after all is said and done, is one colossal "performance" or "show" with a cast of twenty million, and its own "extras," "stars," and "crosses."[11]

The ranks of both the Art Theatre and the First Studio had been reduced by the war. Rationing, shortages of food and fuel, rampant inflation, and general civic disruption threatened the theatre's very existence. In the coming bitter winter, the new Bolshevik government would provide warmth at the Art Theatre, but actor and patron alike would remain bundled up during performances at the Studio and other small theatres. Natasha Boleslavsky, who was seeing Boleslavsky again by now (Yefremova had left him while he was away fighting), remembers that more than once she sat shivering in her fur coat and cap, gnawing on a boiled potato—sometimes also half-frozen, watching a theatre performance.

Immediately upon his return, Boleslavsky began rehearsing his old parts at the MAT and the Studio. Soon he was appearing in his familiar roles. Over the next three seasons, he added some new roles as well, although just when he first played them is uncertain. In Tolstoy's *Tsar Fyodor Ivanovich,* the Art Theatre's premiere production and a continuing favorite of its public, he played at various times three characters: the Courier, Prince Mstislavsky (sometimes acted by Leonidov), and Prince Shakhovskoy (sometimes acted by Znamesky, Bersenev, and Podgorny). And in Gorky's *The Lower Depths* he played first the Tartar and then Satin, a role created by Stanislavsky and previously entrusted only to such outstanding actors as Massalitinov and Podgorny.[12]

Boleslavsky's earlier silent picture, *You Still Cannot Love,* had been re-released (and possibly re-edited) on June 13 (probably just before his return to Moscow), under a new title: *The Family Polenov* (*Sem'ya Polenovykh*). Boleslavsky was still credited as the film's director, though he evidently had nothing to do with its new incarnation. He did resume working in the silent cinema, however, concurrently with rehearsals at the MAT and the Studio. On August 8, a new picture he directed, *Not Reason, But Passion, Rules the World* (*Ne rezum, a strasti, pravyat mirom*) was released. In addition to directing this four-reel drama for "Russ" Studio, he also acted in a film made by

Władysław Starewicz, the gifted Polish director who had been brought by Thiemann from Vilna; and he played the leading role in the picture, *Cottage on the Volga (Domik na Volge)*, an adaptation of Stepnyaka-Kravchinskov's novel, first shown on 2 October 1917.

Yet his real interest was in the activities of the First Studio whose members had been caught up in the revolutionary fervor of the times. Soon after his return he joined a group of Studio actors who met with Stanislavsky to demand a greater measure of autonomy. They wanted more freedom, they said, "to choose our own plays, and produce them in our own way. . . . Why must we always stick to realism?" they demanded. "The theatre with its authority is choking us. They don't recognize modern movements in art. . . . " Boleslavsky joined in the argument:

> In the army, I had been White. Here in the Theatre, in the realm of art, I instantly became Red, the most insubordinate and unruly red of them all. I could not help it. It was in the air. No living being could escape a somersaulting of values in those days. . . . Revolt against authority. Fight for self-determination. . . . Respect remained in form, but in reality only its shadow was present. Against the old troupers who had generously made possible our Studio we now rebelled like so many young fools—or wise men? It was as though a group of consecrated monks rebelled against a conclave of bishops. I took part in the insurrection with gusto. I plunged into the argument, made a speech and won the applause of my friends. Stanislavsky shook his head: "Still fermenting. . . . still fermenting, my boy." He was kind and sad. But he gave in. We demanded artistic freedom and we won.[13]

Efros agrees that a distinct change occurred in the First Studio about this time. "The initial striving to be closer to life and life's concrete truths" gave way to "an urge to rise above life, to ascend to life's very broadest general conditions and to express them in conventional staging." This break with the stage realism which the MAT had achieved was, in Efros's judgment, a necessary moment in the evolution of the Studio: "The idea began to be reflected in the choice of poetic material, in the characteristic use of this material on stage, in the methods used in direction, and, partially, though less visibly, in the acting."[14] The first expression of the Studio's new artistic path was Shakespeare's *Twelfth Night,* already in rehearsal.

As the streets of Moscow grew increasingly dangerous, members of the Studio began living in the attic rooms of their theatre building. Boleslavsky shared a "small cubbyhole" with Michael Chekhov and another actor; Vera Soloviova and Lydia Deykun slept in the next room.[15] When the so-called October Revolution broke into street fighting Boleslavsky and his friends hid out in the Studio, watching through the windows,

venturing outside only when there was no other choice. The girls prepared sparse meals—mostly bread and a watery soup of small bits of
potato, cabbage, and barley. Boleslavsky took turns with some of the
other men standing guard on the roof. The members shared the duties of
running the Studio hospital, which was open to wounded of both sides.
After thirteen days of shooting, the Soviets had control of Petrograd,
Moscow and other important cities; the Civil War, however, would not
be finally over until 1921. Recalling these days, Boleslavsky wrote:

> I did not feel attached to either of the camps. I did not want to belong. I felt a
> stranger to these human beings driven by the inhuman force of their convictions. I
> had no convictions in this struggle. But I was not in one piece. The civil war repelled
> me, but it lured me too. The part of me which was a friend to Russia was tempted to
> take a side. The Pole rejected any participation in Russia's affairs. Between two
> truths, between two lies, I wandered in torment.[16]

He clung to a single conviction. "I'm going to stay here," he vowed.
"I'm going to protect this place and these people." Only the Studio was
worth fighting for: "I knew that I could not, and did not want to, raise a
finger in the street fight, but if some one should try to hurt anything
here, I would fight in a wild fury."[17]

Once in power, the Bolsheviks took immediate steps to bring the
theatre and cinema under state control. In November, the Council of
People's Commissars issued a decree that placed all the theatres of
Russia under the jurisdiction of the Art Department of the Commissar-
iat of Education. In December, Moscow's imperial and academic the-
atres—those with schools—were placed under the control of local
Soviets. The Moscow Art Theatre was henceforth to be administered
by a board of directors composed of five members appointed by the
Education Commissariat and five elected by the theatre collective.
State ownership of the theatres was later signed into law by Lenin (in
August, 1919).

One of the first acts of the newly formed Commissariat of Education
was to issue an order for the expulsion from the theatres of all actors of
anti-Soviet leanings. The Imperial theatres were particularly hard hit.
Many actors were expelled, and a good many, if not all of them, were
immediately arrested by the Cheka.[18] Boleslavsky's exploits with the
Polish Lancers and his generally "white" sentiments were well known
by many of his colleagues. Miraculously, he was not reported.

In *Lances Down*, Boleslavsky recounts that a studio member he
identifies only as "Valka" was named to be the First Studio's political
commissioner. His duty, Valka said, was to watch over the Studio and

"to see that it serves the proletariat and gives the people what they need." Until then, Boleslavsky writes, he and Valka had enjoyed the "warmest relations." Now Valka warned him that his continued presence at the Studio would be tolerated only because he was a "necessary part of the studio," "primarily a specialist" of his craft, and "a person we need at present more than ever." Boleslavsky answered with dangerous candor:

> That's exactly why I hate your outfit. I don't hate you personally, but I do hate your way of thinking. You need me and therefore you make me work for you. You take from my hands whatever you need, but you watch me all the time, and spy on me. The other side held the upper hand because every one had to sell himself for the price of bread and butter. Your side will boss, command and get everybody for the price of fear—fear of losing his life. . . .
> . . . You believe that results justify the means. I don't. I'll stay here and work without thinking for whom I work, only because I worked here before you became a commissioner; for the sake of the work itself. . . . I'll keep on doing the way I did before. You may watch me all you want.[19]

Who was "Valka"? No one by that name was associated with the First Studio. Did Boleslavsky choose the name to mask the identity of a single individual? Or was Valka in fact a composite of two or more people? Boleslavsky describes Valka as being "small and undernourished" and reports that he had twelve teeth removed to avoid military service; he stuttered when he was self-conscious. He played only small parts at the Art Theatre: "He was a poor actor and knew it." The only part he did at all well, in Boleslavsky's estimate, was Sir Andrew Aguecheek in *Twelfth Night*. Boleslavsky offers one final clue: "The only one of us who took an active part in politics, he was a full-fledged member of the Communistic Party."[20] Valentin Smuishlyayev played Aguecheek at the Studio—was he also an active member of the party? Eugene Vakhtangov had been a member of the Social Democrats since his student days and welcomed the coming of the Second Revolution.[21] Was "Valka" a blending of "Valentin" and "Vakhtangov"? There can be no certainty. One thing is sure, however: Boleslavsky had no sympathy for the revolutionary cause and he felt threatened by the new Bolshevik government.

Closed during the street fighting, the First Studio opened its doors again in the last week of November, 1918. It was filled, as were all the theatres in Moscow, with a crowd of Red Guards, sailors, and workers, who stamped their boots to warm their feet in the unheated theatres, talked loudly among themselves when the play bored them, and loudly cheered or booed the performers.[22] The balance of Boleslavsky's productions in Russia were played for such an audience.

In December, the First Studio opened its production of *Twelfth Night,* with Boleslavsky in the role of Sir Toby, his first new role since the war. The direction of this, the Studio's first post-Revolutionary production, has been variously attributed to Stanislavsky, Sushkevich, Kolin, and Boleslavsky—either singly or in combination. The preponderance of evidence suggests that Sushkevich was its principal director, under the close supervision of Stanislavsky. Boleslavsky and Kolin may have served only as Sushkevich's assistants, but there is reason to think that, since returning from the war, Boleslavsky may actually have worked as co-director with his close friend.[23]

Oliver Sayler, an American visitor to Moscow at the time, describes Stanislavsky's reaction, and his own, to a dress rehearsal of the production: Stanislavsky sat "with pencil and paper in hand to note the transgressions of his flock. These implements, though, were soon forgotten and a broad smile of pride mingled with unaffected and unashamed pleasure spread over his face. . . . " Sayler considered this "the heartiest, the most truly Elizabethan performance" of *Twelfth Night* he had ever seen.[24] Marc Slonim characterized the Studio's *Twelfth Night* as "an explosion of gaiety and free spirit."[25] Huntley Carter, an English observer who visited Moscow a little later, noted that the players "frolicked all over the place, even using the cloak-room and lobby as extensions of the stage":

> Sometimes they chased each other in the stalls and circles, sat beside the spectators and saturated them with the odour of grease paint, made trips to the upper part of the building, whence they threw their voices to the stage across the astonished but delighted audience. On one occasion two of the principals, I think Sir Toby and Sir Andrew Ague Cheek [*sic*], went outside the theatre and engaged in an argument that came floating through the open window.[26]

Despite the absence of political content, *Twelfth Night,* which "vacillated between lyrical comedy and a vivid buffonade,"[27] was a great success with the newly "Sovietized" audience. Later, Efros praised Boleslavsky's "remarkable ability for sharp comedy" in the role of the turbulent, roistering Sir Toby,[28] a performance that Soviet historians generally count among his outstanding accomplishments.

Continued fighting between Red and White factions deepened the miserable conditions the World War had brought to Moscow. The economy was chaotic and shortages of food and fuel soon developed into famine proportions. Uncounted numbers died from hunger, cold, and disease. Artists of the theatre were hardly exempt from these terrible hardships. More and more frequently the actors and directors of the Art Theatre and the First Studio worked outside the theatre, most often in quickly thrown-together *khaltury*—literally, "pot-boilers"—performed in exchange for food or fuel or, more reluctantly, for vast sums of devalued currency. Boleslavsky writes that at this time he sold a sketch of himself in the role of Belyayev to the Commissar of Fishery, "an artistic soul who gave me half a million rubles for it." The next day, he adds, "for the half million I bought myself a pair of shoes."[29]

In 1918, Boleslavsky worked on two films, both of which were *agitka,* or short propaganda pieces, approved by the Soviet authorities. He acted in *Love—Hate—Death* (*Lyubov'—nenavist'— smert'*), directed by Perestiani; Zoya Karabanova and Perestiani played the other important roles. Boleslavsky co-directed with Boris Sushkevich a film called *Khleb* (*Bread*) for the Mos-Kino-Committee. Boleslavsky, Vakhtangov, Leonidov, and Olga Baklanova also took roles in the film, and members of the famous Habima Theatre provided the crowd scenes.[30]

Very likely, Boleslavsky directed and acted in his stage adaptation of the Jack London short story, *The Immoral Woman,* with Baklanova in the title role, during the winter of 1918. He also staged *Man of Destiny,* Shaw's one-act play about the young Napoleon, in which he played the role of the young officer.[31] Neither production was ever played at the First Studio. Rather, they were performed in workers' halls and on the stages of available amateur theatres. No reviews of these works are known to survive, but the circumstances of their creation and performance are such that it seems doubtful they were marked by special artistic interest.

Boleslavsky's next production outside the First Studio, however, proved more significant. In May of 1919, at the invitation of Maria Andreyeva, mistress of the playwright Gorky and formerly an actress with the Art Theatre, Boleslavsky and Sushkevich went to St. Petersburg to direct for the recently formed Bolshoi Dramatic Theatre. Organized by the Soviet authorities, the group was headed by Andreyeva and symbolist poet Alexander Blok, and performed in the Mikhailovsky Theatre, formerly an Imperial house.[32]

Boleslavsky directed Sem Benelli's *The Torn Cape,* with designs by Allegri; Sushkevich staged Schiller's *The Robbers.* The company's small group of actors rehearsed both plays concurrently during the summer months. N. F. Monakhov, the Dramatic Theatre's leading actor at the time, recounts that the "feverish work" went on everywhere: "In the theatre, in apartments, on the lawns of the park in Pavlovsk and in the Peterhof parks. Walks taken in groups turned into persistent, stubborn work."[33] Monakhov was frequently present at Boleslavsky's rehearsals and often accompanied the director and actors on long, "instructional" walks. As Monakhov explains:

> These two productions proved that some of our nestlings were already becoming adults. Those group walks had not been in vain. Unbeknownst to us the young people had begun to spread their artistic wings, and already in *The Torn Cape* new young craftsmen had definitely emerged. . . . [34]

Sushkevich's production of *The Robbers* opened on 12 September 1919 and failed to win much approval. It was followed on September 20 with Boleslavsky's staging of *The Torn Cape*. The immediate reception suggested that the production was a great artistic and popular success, but that impression soon gave way to controversy. What Monakhov describes as a "new audience of reactionary socialists" responded angrily to Benelli's play.[35]

N. I. Komarovskaya, formerly an actress with the Art Theatre, played the role of Sylvia, the character in *The Torn Cape* who breaks with the conventional prejudices of an "intellectual elite" to defend the work of a young "poet of the people," acted by the film star, Maksimov. Off-stage, Komarovskaya came to Boleslavsky's defense, as well. In her opinion, the play (which had been selected by Blok) was ideologically sound, and the success of Boleslavsky's production "confirmed the creative position of the theatre's answer to the questions raised by a new audience."[36]

Blok defended *The Torn Cape* for a time, but finally yielded to demands that it be closed. In a letter to Andreyeva, Blok explained his change in heart:

> As for *The Torn Cape,* the more I think about it, about this play, the more it seems to me that it is not right for us, that it is unnecessary, perhaps even harmful to the romantic theatre's entire company. Benelli himself is not a first-rate playwright. Furthermore, Amphiteatrov has mutilated the translation; therefore—I have stopped the performance and finally forced them to listen to what I had to say about the author. There was a strange silence, like after an avalanche, and the brilliantly talented Boleslavsky and the first-rate designer Allegri perhaps increased the danger I sense; I fear that we are in danger of losing them.[37]

Boleslavsky did not return immediately to Moscow, for at Andreyeva's invitation the First Studio opened its 1919–20 season with a tour to Stalingrad. Beginning on September 6, they performed *The Deluge,*

Cricket on the Hearth, and *Twelfth Night,* with Boleslavsky resuming his usual roles of O'Neill and Sir Toby after he was through with *The Torn Cape.* The company played its last performance on October 14 and then, under threat of an impending advance on Leningrad by the White Army in the north, Boleslavsky and the other members of the First Studio hastily returned home to Moscow.

Once there, Boleslavsky resumed work at the Studio on a play he had been developing for some time, *Balladyna* by Juliusz Słowacki, the founder of Polish tragedy. Bolesław Taborski describes the play as "one of the most richly imaginative and poetic plays in the Polish language, and an ever popular classic on the Polish stage."[38] Boleslavsky's production, of course, was performed in Russian translation.

Set in the legendary period of pre-historic Poland, *Balladyna* provided Boleslavsky dramatic material with which to explore primitive peoples and primeval emotions on a grand, epic scale, as Taborski's brief summary of its plot makes clear:

> An ambitious and unscrupulous peasant girl proves herself Macbeth and Lady Macbeth rolled into one: through the murder of her sister, husband, lovers, she attains the crown, but is finally struck by a thunder from heaven, having pronounced a sentence on herself (as the unknown criminal) in an impressive judgment scene.[39]

Boleslavsky had wanted to do *Balladyna* since before the war. By 1915 he had sketched costume designs for some of the characters.[40] Further plans had been deferred when he went into the war, but he had resumed work on Słowacki's play after his return and had shown the production to Stanislavsky in 1919. Stanislavsky had rejected Boleslavsky's concept for the staging, however, and Boleslavsky, evidently unwilling to submit to Stanislavsky's revisions, began working on the production again from the beginning.[41] By the time he returned from Petrograd, he was ready to resume work in earnest.

Boleslavsky began rehearsing the new staging for *Balladyna* on November 4. Stanislavsky, who had talked once of producing the play himself at the Moscow Art Theatre,[42] attended several of the first rehearsals. Normally, Stanislavsky's presence at the Studio would not in itself be remarkable, but it is worth noting here for reasons suggested by Diky:

> *Twelfth Night* was the last production of the Studio in which Stanislavsky took part. He had become an infrequent visitor among us. We didn't praise him. We saddened him more than we cheered him. He could not bring himself to realize that we were developing creatively, that we were acquiring dramatic vigor, that we were collecting

artistic means. . . . The more Moscow loved the Studio, the more indifferent its
founder became towards it, because he saw that we were moving away from him and
were ceasing to be his disciples, ceasing to share common goals in art. We had
become alienated, and meetings became more infrequent. With the passing of years,
Stanislavsky's coldness became apparent to everyone.[43]

Some two months before *Balladyna* opened, Stanislavsky ceased paying
regular visits to Boleslavsky's rehearsals.[44] Was he suffering from one of
the periodic bouts of illness, frequent during this time? Or did he absent
himself because of some personal difference with Boleslavsky? These
questions cannot be answered satisfactorily at present.

Even before *Balladyna* opened to the public, the Soviet press evi-
denced keen interest in it. One journalist wrote:

During these days when the Polish social-chauvinists impertinently brandish their
weapons, when the Polish bourgeoisie aggressive-mindedly prepares to push a frater-
nal nation into an absurd war with The Workers' and Peasants' Russia, here in
Moscow, in the heart of the Soviet Republic, the Studio of the Art Theatre is staging
a tragedy by the Polish poet, Juliusz Słowacki.

This fact is significant—it proves that chauvinism is foreign to us, that we are
prepared to give decisive resistance to the over-confident hirelings of the Entente,
and that at the same time we take from them those values which their true culture
has created.[45]

Another journalist from the same organ reported his response to a
dress rehearsal:

With the staging of *Balladyna* the Studio seems to have taken up the challenge
thrown to it by several ideologists of the new theatre and by all the circumstances of
these present days. *Balladyna* is not a "routine" production, but "the final decisive
struggle" of the Studio for its future. The failure of *Balladyna* would be a deathblow
for the Studio. Its success will convince the members of the Studio that its efforts are
necessary for the modern spectator. It will give them incentive and fire them to new
labor. Judging by the first closed performance, the Studio will have its desired victory. The production creates a great impression and undoubtedly can enrapture an
audience of any social composition. And to completely enrapture the whole audience
in our times is a trick which none of our theatres has successfully accomplished
during the last few years.

Remaining faithful in all respects to the main precepts of its theatrical culture, the
Studio has not, however, merely repeated itself in this production. There will be
enough conversations and reviews about it, but one may even now safely describe
Balladyna as the greatest and most exceptional event in the current theatre season.[46]

Balladyna opened to warm reviews on 16 February 1920, but that
reception soon changed. Shortly after the premiere, Piłsudski led his Polish armies in a fierce campaign against Kiev, and, corresponding with that

event, the same journal voiced its objections concerning errors in the director's judgment and mistakes in interpretation. The critic now noted the unevenness of the actors' performances.[47] *Balladyna* was soon withdrawn from the repertory. (An altered production of *Balladyna* was shown at the First Studio a year or two later, with new staging by Vakhtangov or Sushkevich—possibly both. It, too, failed to win approval.)

The Soviet press was not alone in criticizing Boleslavsky and his production, as Nadezhda Bromley relates in a letter dated 22 February 1920:

> Yesterday at Stanislavsky's apartment, Richard said: "I want to show my work to the whole world." The old man coughed angrily: "That especially stands out in the First Studio—presumptiousness. I'm not going to say a word. You presented *Yorio* and *Balladyna* as you have presented nothing before, but that is still too little. Do you know the secrets of art?"[48]

This conversation took place a short time after *Balladyna's* opening. Had Boleslavsky, inspired by the play's initial success, been bold enough to suggest that the production be moved to the stage of the Art Theatre? Byron's *Cain,* in which Boleslavsky was cast initially as Abel, had originated at the Studio, but Stanislavsky took it over for the MAT.[49] Did Boleslavsky entertain hopes that his production of *Balladyna* might be moved intact to the big stage of the Art Theatre? There can be no firm answer, but Stanislavsky's anger seems to have been directed more at the "presumptiousness" of the Studio's artistic deviation from the established Art Theatre manner than at Boleslavsky's personal ambitions.

The poetic realism of *The Good Hope* had been very much in harmony with the "Chekhovian" naturalness of the Art Theatre, yet in that first Studio production Boleslavsky's sharpening of the actor's expression, his "stripping bare" of the characters, and his use of conventionalized scenery had pointed the way toward the Studio's gradual evolution of increasingly bold theatricality, as even Markov admits.[50] As Efros explains:

> The same characteristics that had advantageously distinguished the first play—a freshness of performance that rejected conventional stamps and hackneyed clichés, its great truth, simplicity, candor, and expressiveness—were also inherent in the Studio's following works, but these characteristics showed through with growing clarity and grew ever more distinct.[51]

Boleslavsky's scenic methods were adopted by Sushkevich in his staging of *The Cricket on the Hearth* and (with Boleslavsky's assistance) *Twelfth Night.* In the area of acting, however, Sushkevich carried the basic approach of "stripping" each character to its essential kernel to a level of expression that was distinctly different, both in mood and degree, from that of *The Good Hope,* achieving almost bravura eccentricity of characterization; in pushing this approach to the point of the grotesque, Sushkevich made his own contribution to the Studio method.[52] Vakhtangov, on the other hand, lagged behind with the naturalism of *The Festival of Peace* and evidently would have compounded his mistakes in *The Deluge* had not Stanislavsky himself intervened to bring the production into harmony with the Studio methods by restaging fully three-quarters of *The Deluge* before it opened. Vakhtangov's reaction: Stanislavsky had violated the tenets of his own system.[53] Only after the revolution did Vakhtangov abandon his pessimistic naturalism and begin to pursue the path of greater theatricality.

By 1919, Boleslavsky had evidently surpassed even Sushkevich in this regard, at least in Monakhov's judgment: Sushkevich's production of *The Robbers* was "academic" in manner—Schiller "smoothed over, combed, solid, respectable"—while Boleslavsky's *Torn Cape* was "seething, noisy, colorful, vivid, impudent, and witty . . . remarkably resolved and unusually joyful."[54]

Boleslavsky's seeking after ever more vigorous and vivid theatricality at the First Studio culminated in *Balladyna,* but not at the expense of internally truthful acting. His approach to the special acting problem posed by the kings, peasants, spirits, and sprites—all of whom speak in poetic rhythms in Słowacki's legendary fairy tale—is suggested by his remarks a year later:

> Thus, since the world has been the world and art has been art, the most abstract creations of the human mind and its most metaphysical concepts have—since the time the need arose to give a visual form to their actions—always been personified and anthropomorphized . . . In the Studio of the Art Theatre, my realism embraced Shakespearean, classical, and romantic themes and, without breaking with the methods of our preparatory work, we have already attempted to go beyond the old style, both thematically and formally.[55]

Boleslavsky's directorial intentions for *Balladyna* can be inferred: he wished to retain the inner realism of the actor's work and to do so through the established methods of Stanislavsky's system; moreover, this inner realism was to apply equally to Słowacki's human characters and his fantastical creatures; at the same time, Boleslavsky sought to go beyond the modes of psychological realism and to discover more theatrical forms of acting and scenery. The substance, mood, and poetic form of Słowacki's mythic tale—a far cry from the realistically drawn characters and the earthbound prose of *The Good Hope* or *The Wanderers*—made it ideally suited to Boleslavsky's purpose.

Boleslavsky himself designed the scenery for *Balladyna*. He devised a basic background of revolving scenic units; one face was covered with burlap adorned with stylized forms done in gold embroidery,[56] and the reverse face was covered with black velvet. By turning the units, the scene could be instantly changed from the primitive splendor of the court to the fathomless void used for the battle scenes. Goplana, the spirit of the lake, made her first appearance peering from behind a stand of reeds; dancing, flickering lights were played upon these to indicate the presence of the lake behind her.[57] In some scenes crude, primitive tables and chairs were used; for subsequent scenes, burlap coverings matching the gold-embroidered background were flung over the furnishings to transform them into tree stumps and forest shapes.[58] The lighting added to the plasticity of Boleslavsky's setting, assisted in the quick transformations of locale, and sculpted the actors' forms so they stood in contradistinction to the backgrounds.[59] Music especially composed by N.N. Rakhmanov underscored the entire performance of mythic human characters and anthropomorphized, fantastical spirits living through a variety of primitive emotions, sharply etched and vividly expressed.

Balladyna was the culmination of Boleslavsky's work at the First Studio. His choice of plays there suggests an interest in what Markov has characterized as "monumentalism." He was drawn to plays dealing with primitive or unsophisticated characters who express themselves in grand, sweeping emotions; in most of his plays at the Studio, the crowd also played an important part. He explored the psychological and dramatic effects of music and sound effects, and rhythmical elements played an ever more important role in his work: *The Good Hope* was suffused with the natural sounds of the sea and a storm, as well as the songs of the sailors and a mournful violin; *The Wanderers* employed the sounds of the forest, ancient religious hymns and chants; by the time of *Balladyna,* music had become an integral part of Boleslavsky's concept of the play.

The poetic realism of *The Good Hope* bore the seeds of a central directorial concern that emerged full-blown in *Balladyna:* Boleslavsky sought to fuse psychological truthfulness in acting with theatricality of scenic expression. This impulse was expressed in his selective simplification of scenic elements, his sharpening of expressive forms of acting and scenery, and his laying bare of the forms themselves. This impulse, inherently experimental and improvisatory in spirit, ultimately led Boleslavsky to assert: "Old, tried forms and methods must never be relied upon. . . . Whether the play is new or is newly revived, a new approach must always be sought for it.''[60]

Most Soviet critics have ascribed the effort to fuse psychological realism with theatricality (as well as the conviction that a new expressive form must be found for each play) not to Boleslavsky, but to Vakhtangov; following their lead, a number of Western observers have concluded that Boleslavsky's work in this direction was the result of Vakhtangov's influence. To accept this conclusion, however, is to ignore the evidence of Vakhtangov's early obsession with naturalism and to forget Boleslavsky's collaboration on *Twelfth Night,* as well as his personal accomplishment in *The Torn Cape* and *Balladyna.* Monakhov, "speaking between ourselves, not for the press," stressed the importance of *The Torn Cape:*

> It is very regrettable and very strange that in the literature about the theatre nothing remains about this play. Very strange, because Aleksander Nikolayevich Blok, for example, was delighted with it. He showed great favor to it; he found its colors very fresh and very bold and thought that in our era in particular they said a great deal.[61]

Balladyna has been similarly ignored in Soviet theatre literature.

Moreover, the evidence of chronology suggests that Boleslavsky influenced Vakhtangov, and not the other way around. Vakhtangov's first signs of dissatisfaction with naturalistic realism came in 1916, following Stanislavsky's "correction" of *The Deluge;* his first significant step toward more theatrical forms of expression was in Ibsen's *Rosmersholm,* which followed *Twelfth Night* at the Studio; Vakhtangov worked closely with Nemirovich-Danchenko on *Rosmersholm,* and Danchenko completed it after Vakhtangov fell ill.[62]

By the time Boleslavsky resumed rehearsals for *Balladyna* in 1919, Vakhtangov's health was seriously deteriorating, and he was engaged in numerous projects of his own.[63] Still, he found time to attend several of Boleslavsky's rehearsals. Stanislavsky noted Vakhtangov's presence at the fourth rehearsal for *Balladyna.*[64] During another rehearsal, Pyshova (who played Goplana) noted with some alarm that Vakhtangov seemed to be taking notes on her work in a scene; she approached him and asked for his comments. In response, Vakhtangov showed her several pages filled with sketches he had made of her and suggested which gestures he believed were in harmony with her role.[65] Later, during final rehearsals, and perhaps performances as well, Vakhtangov brought several of his pupils from the Mansurov (later the Third) Studio for visual lessons in theatrical technique. One of Vakhtangov's pupils, Nikolai

Gorchakov, later recounted that Vakhtangov sat with his pupils "all through the performance and the intervals." Afterwards, "like a general explaining to his subordinates the progress of a battle . . . Vakhtangov propounded the laws of the theatre to us, the reasons for various shortcomings and the ways of overcoming them:"

> It was a real aesthetic pleasure to watch . . . the miraculous changes of backdrops in *Balladine* [*sic*], the perfect harmony between acting and the music, lighting and other elements of the performance. . . .
> We would watch his friends, the wonderful players of the First Studio, with profound respect. . . . Vakhtangov wanted us to make use of all we had seen at the First Studio for our performances at the Mansurov studio.[66]

Vakhtangov's next important production, Anton Chekhov's *The Wedding* (September 1920) at his own studio, was filled with joy and adopted a mode of scenic expression along lines explored earlier by Sushkevich and Boleslavsky, but his first complete repudiation of his earlier naturalism came in his staging of the second variant of *The Miracle of St. Anthony* on 29 January 1921—a year after *Balladyna's* opening. Two months later, Vakhtangov won his first great personal triumph with his theatrical staging of *Eric XIV,* which opened on 29 March 1921, at the First Studio. Efros writes that *Eric* was a continuation along "the same difficult path" Boleslavsky had previously taken in *Balladyna*.[67]

Boleslavsky was not present to witness Vakhtangov's change in direction, for not long after his quarrel with Stanislavsky he left Moscow, never to return. He had one final contact with the First Studio, however. The Studio made its first European tour from June through September 1922, and Boleslavsky was in Berlin when the company played there. As he watched Michael Chekhov's performance in the title role of *Eric XIV,* Boleslavsky kept squeezing Natasha's arm. "Look at that," he whispered. "Brilliant! That's absolutely brilliant!"[68]

Some years later, Monakhov pondered the relationship of Boleslavsky's and Vakhtangov's work in that off-the-record conversation cited earlier:

> Boleslavsky is a brilliant man in the field of art in general, and he is a brilliant director. He has such an imagination, such a vivid and active life. . . .
> It is a pity that just such a talented director as Boleslavsky has left the Russian stage; it is very regrettable because Vakhtangov did a great deal, and he was Vakhtangov's colleague. Vakhtangov was a very interesting man, but I have no idea what Boleslavsky might have done had he accepted the Revolution as Vakhtangov did.[69]

7

Return to Poland

Boleslavsky had a number of persuasive reasons for leaving Russia. His war record put him in jeopardy of arrest and punishment by the Bolshevik government; he staunchly opposed the philosophy and methods of the Bolsheviks; and he deeply resented the loss of artistic freedom he experienced under the Soviet regime. The First Studio—the place he called his "real" home, the only thing he would fight to defend—had passed into the hands of "a force I did not want to yield to" and was "under the control of those whom I hated. Right or wrong, I hated them," because "they had begun to dictate, to control, to inquire, to order."[1]

Boleslavsky recounts how "Valka," a few days after being appointed political watchdog over the Studio, had interrupted a rehearsal being held by Nadezhda Bromley (evidently for *The Daughter of Yorio*) to instruct her in ideological matters as they affected the theatre. There should be "no more human beings" on the stage, Valka explained; the theatre must be guided by "class consciousness, class problems, class beliefs and class aims"; it must present a "declaration of two forces" and not a "conversation between characters." Boleslavsky responded to the implications of Valka's position in a speech heavy with implicit irony and regret:

> You'll have to do it. . . . Forget the human drama. Bring the drama of formulas or the drama of general problems, or splatter around the burlesque and the grotesque, the clownade, the mockery. Don't touch human feelings; they are sore right now. They are burning. Every heart is bursting with them. If you appear on the stage and talk about how you feel, whom you love, what you see in others, you'll sound silly. In comparison to life, you'll be a canary in the midst of a brass band.
> . . . From now on, intimacy or nuances have no place before the kind of audience you'll see here to-morrow [*sic*]. Yesterday their cue was a rifle shot or the corpse of a brother, or a wall pecked with the bullets of a firing squad. Now do you want them to care what Mary, Ann, or Lisa feel or suffer or love? They want to know what throws the masses against masses, what brings a spark into a mob. They want to

justify their own actions of yesterday and to-morrow in a mass. They want to hear the formulated cry of thousands of their own hearts.[2]

Faced by the changes wrought in the First Studio as a result of the October Revolution, Boleslavsky felt "lost and lonely, between two fires. Here I was in the Studio which I had helped to start with the people I loved, where I knew every nail, every piece of furniture, every book, every setting and prop. Now I felt it was no longer part of me. . . ."[3]

Boleslavsky nonetheless remained in Russia for just over two years after 1917, sustained evidently by the hope that the White armies would eventually win the Civil War and restore something of the old order. By the winter of 1919–20, however, the White effort had all but collapsed. By that time, too, the Soviets had taken formal legal and administrative steps to consolidate their control over the theatres and cinema. Boleslavsky had seen *The Torn Cape* censored for ideological reasons, and *Balladyna* come under increasing attack. At the same time, a new factor presented itself: Polish-Russian conflicts had escalated into full-scale war, and free Polish armies were battling Communist forces. Above all else, this may have been the thing that finally persuaded Boleslavsky to act on a plan he had been holding in reserve for some time.

At the time of the so-called First Revolution, which had placed Kerensky's Provisional Government in power, Natasha Platonova had visited the United States to avoid the dangers of the fighting. Returning to Moscow at about the same time Boleslavsky got home from the war, she told him of her trip, talked excitedly about the peace and freedom to be found in America, and urged that they go there together. Travel in the West, they agreed, would be simpler if they were husband and wife; in July of 1918, they were married in a Moscow police precinct station. They devised a plan, but Boleslavsky postponed putting it into action.

Following his quarrel with Stanislavsky, stirred by the news of Polish successes against Red armies, Boleslavsky finally acted, but not without deep regret:

One never knew what Moscow would produce, when it would hurt or when caress. Moscow was a kind stepmother to me, who gave me the best of herself and to whom I, not being her blood son, gave all the enthusiasm of my young years. Because I wasn't her own child I had to know her better than others. Her singing manner of speech was hard for me to master. Her ways I studied as one does those of a dear host who considers you almost a member of the family, who befriends and showers you with gifts. Moscow's gifts to me were generous gifts I could not forget.[4]

Boleslavsky's only surviving written account of his flight from Russia is brief: "I can tell it to you in ten words. I got false papers. I bribed the smuggler. And I was smuggled under the hay for four nights until I reached the border."[5] Natasha Boleslavsky provides a fuller account. Together with Nicholas Kolin and his wife, she and Boleslavsky approached a Soviet official and volunteered to entertain the Red troops at the front with "revolutionary songs" and two short plays they could perform under improvised circumstances. The authorities granted them travel permits. Fearful of rousing suspicion by taking along quantities of luggage, they packed only a few prized possessions: Natasha concealed her best jewelry, sewing some pieces into the linings of the three or four fur coats she wore one on top of the other, hiding others under the coils of her coiffure; Boleslavsky packed a few mementos from the theatre and carried a half-dozen treasured books—including a Russian translation of the complete works of Shakespeare; Kolin took his guitar. They carried nothing else but a few clothes and "costumes" with them aboard the military transport that took them out of Moscow. At a point they judged to be near the Polish lines, they slipped away from their escort.

They had reached the most treacherous point of their journey. A soldier suspicious of their forged travel documents might send them back to Moscow or put them in the local jail—or have them shot. A greedy peasant might accept a bribe to hide them and then cut their throats and search the bodies for hidden valuables; they had heard many such tales back in Moscow. With considerable trepidation, they paid a man to conceal them under the hay on his troika and carry them near Minsk, then in Polish hands, but under periodic siege from a determined Red army. Finally, they stood among some trees, facing a wide snow-covered clearing, beyond which Polish sentinels stood guard. Natasha Boleslavsky vividly recalls their frantic dash:

> The Communists were firing at us from one side, the Poles from the other. We were in the middle. Boleslavsky walked along like a drum major leading a broken band. Kolin and his wife and I crawled on our hands and knees through the snow, afraid we would be shot. Kolin's guitar was on his back, banging up and down. We tried to crawl and carry our few things, but some things we left behind so we could crawl faster. I yelled to Boleslavsky to get down, and pulled at him. He said, "I am a Polish Lancer. A Polish Lancer does not crawl."
>
> I thought he had gone crazy. Then he started to shout to the Polish soldiers not to shoot. I was astonished. I knew he was Polish, but his Russian was perfect, and I never even knew until then that he could speak Polish.[6]

In Minsk they were taken into custody and questioned by Polish officers for several days. Boleslavsky's detailed account of his service with the Polish lancers during the war at last persuaded them that neither he nor his Russian-speaking colleagues were Bolshevik spies. Natasha had come down with a high fever; a doctor was found. She had typhus and was suffering from malnutrition. Natasha concludes: "It was a terrible struggle. It was very difficult to flee—to lose every penny—to lose family and friends—to lose country—to lose everything. It was hard to come to another country, to study the language, to make money, to survive. Thank God we were young then."[7]

They had reached Minsk in late February or early March of 1920. After Natasha was well, they worked where they could, acting the two plays they had rehearsed before leaving Moscow and singing in cabarets, meeting halls, or small provincial theatres. They sometimes received a small salary or donations from the crowd, but most often they played in exchange for food and lodging.

The two plays they performed were *The Harbor,* by Guy de Maupassant, and *The Witch,* a dramatization of a short story by Anton Chekhov, both of which had been done in Moscow in 1916—*The Harbor* at Vakhtangov's Mansurov Studio, and *The Witch* at the First Studio, directed by Gotovtsev and Mchedelov. Very likely Boleslavsky had not acted previously in either play, but Kolin had won great success as the cuckolded husband in *The Witch.*[8] Now he repeated the role, with Boleslavsky playing the mailman who woos the young wife (acted by Natasha). In *The Harbor,* Boleslavsky played the young sailor who visits a prostitute (Natasha) only to discover during the course of the play that she is his sister. The two short plays required a minimum of costumes, properties, or furnishings and were easily adaptable to various playing conditions.

After Minsk, the group stopped briefly in smaller towns and villages along the route to Berlin. By April, they had reached Poznan, some two hundred miles short of Berlin and about the same distance west of Warsaw, which they had bypassed. In Poznan, Boleslavsky was hired to direct at the Teatr Wielkim (Great Theatre), evidently on the strength of his reputation in the Russian theatre. According to Leon Schiller, Boleslavsky was asked to stage Berger's *The Deluge* and Dickens's *Cricket on the Hearth.* Schiller adds: "With these plays Boleslavsky worked to transplant the methods of the First Studio to Poland, among young Polish actors."[9] When *Cricket* opened, or whether in fact Boleslavsky completed that production, is uncertain, but *The Deluge* was presented on 11 May 1920, winning the "great approbation of the critics."[10] This success apparently persuaded Boleslavsky to interrupt his travel toward Germany and to return to Warsaw, the center of Poland's post-World War theatrical activity, and capital of the newly independent Polish Republic. Boleslavsky was no stranger to the Warsaw stage. He had acted here in 1911, in the role of Belyayev in *A Month in the Country*, on the occasion of the Moscow Art Theatre's second European tour. The Polish public had largely boycotted the visiting Russian troupe, but the eminent Polish critic, Kazimierz Ehrenburg, had warmly praised Boleslavsky's performance.[11]

Boleslavsky was also acquainted—though sometimes only slightly—with a number of important figures of the Warsaw theatre, whom he had met while still in Russia. In 1910, he had served as guide and interpreter for Aleksander Zelwerowicz, when the distinguished Polish actor and innovative stage director had visited the Art Theatre. In 1914, Boleslavsky had similarly served the visiting Stanisława Wysocka, perhaps the greatest of all Poland's classical tragediennes.[12] Wysocka had been so impressed by the First Studio that she opened a small theatre modeled after it in her native Kiev. In 1920, both Zelwerowicz and Wysocka were working at Warsaw's Teatr Polski, which was soon to engage Boleslavsky's services.

Boleslavsky's most significant contact with leaders of the modern Polish theatre had come about as a consequence of the War. In 1913, Arnold Szyfman, in an effort to re-establish the national Polish theatre, had moved from his native Kraków to Warsaw and opened the Teatr Polski. When war broke out, Szyfman and a large group of his fellow Polish artists of Austrian citizenship had been interned by the Russians in Moscow. Szyfman soon opened a Polish-language theatre not far from the First Studio. Among his players were Stefan Jaracz, the distinguished character actor who later founded Warsaw's Teatr Ateneum; Josef Wegrzyn, the brilliant romantic actor; and Juliusz Osterwa, then the most famous young actor of the Kraków and Warsaw stages.[13] Boleslavsky had been a frequent visitor to the Polish theatre in Moscow, and a number of the actors there came to see the MAT and the First Studio.

Upon reaching Warsaw in 1920, Boleslavsky first contacted Juliusz Osterwa, co-founder with Liminowski of the Teatr Reduta (Redoubt Theatre). He may have felt that Osterwa owed him a favor, for Boleslavsky had hired the Polish actor for a role in his 1915 silent film, *Three Meetings*.[14] Moreover, of all the Polish directors in Warsaw at the time, Osterwa had most enthusiastically adopted the manner and what he understood of the methods of Stanislavsky and the First Studio. Since its opening in 1918, the Reduta—modeled after the Studio—had become famous for its monastic discipline and its successful emulation of the

Stanislavsky manner. But Boleslavsky was refused a position at Os-terwa's theatre, ostensibly because Osterwa and his partner were not able to afford another director's salary at that time.[15]

Boleslavsky next applied at the Teatr Polski, then the most success-ful and commercially stable of Warsaw's theatres. Leon Schiller, the Polski's literary manager at the time, explains that Arnold Szyfman, its founder and director, "knowing Boleslavsky well from the Moscow days," hired him to direct a single production. Its success or failure would decide Boleslavsky's future at the Polski.[16]

The play was Molière's comédie-ballet, *Le Bourgeois gentilhomme*. Boleslavsky cast the gifted character actor, Stefan Jaracz, in the central role of Jourdain, the common soul who aspires to raise his social status. Madame Jourdain was played by Stanisława Słubicki; their daughter was acted by Gzylewska, and the egalitarian young nobleman who finally wins her hand was played by Wegierko. Grabowski acted the role of the elegantly manipulative Count Dorante.[17]

For his production, Boleslavsky used some of the music composed originally for Molière by Jean-Baptiste Lully, including the overture, the famous minuet, and three short movements of the "Turkish Ceremony." Lully's score was supplemented by compositions by Leon Schiller, who explains:

> This was done because the original interludes, in spite of their undeniable charm, with their forms adapted to the conditions of the courtly theatre, hampered the director's inventiveness, everything being equal. The dynamics of the director's sce-nario required the boldest, mightiest, and most glaring effects, which were not those that could have been produced from Lully's elegantly peaceful music.[18]

Convinced that the production "had to end in a way that was in agreement with the requirements of modern viewers," Boleslavsky re-solved to replace the traditional ending of *Le Bourgeois gentilhomme* (the largely irrelevant "Ballet of the Nations") with a "ballet grotesque" of his own devising.[19] He and Schiller collaborated to write the scenario for a pantomime employing traditional *commedia dell'arte* characters. Special music for this *commedia* pantomime was commissioned from the modernist Polish composer, Karol Szymanowski, generally regarded as Poland's greatest musical genius since Chopin. Szymanowski's music was titled *Mandragora,* a name that has come to embrace the "ballet grotesque" as well. The pantomime, with choreography by Kazimierz Lobojko, was "stylized to some extent in the manner of expressionist primitive art," and Szymanowski "embroidered on this canvas an arche-type of the symphonic grotesque,"[20] producing a score remarkable for its whimsical humor and wit. Natasha Boleslavsky has kept a copy of Szymanowski's music, with brief notes by Boleslavsky indicating cues for key bits of business and dances; the story line evidently combined pantomime, chases, pratfalls, and other bits of comic " *lazzi,* " as well as solo and group dances, to be performed by actors representing the King, the Queen, a Eunuch, a "sham" Eunuch, Harlequin, the Captain, the Doctor, and Columbine.[21]

Boleslavsky employed Wincenty Drabik to design the settings and costumes for the production. Drabik's design for *Le Bourgeois gentilhomme* has been described by Schiller as "a bold step forward:"

> An empty stage was decorated with enormous pavillions draped like a background for portraits or for allegorical images of the 17th century, running with abundant folds from the proscenium opening to the depths of the house as far as the orchestra pit, which was also ornamented in this fashion. Grotesque fragments of the staging for the "Turkish Ceremony" dropped into the audience's view from the colorful parapets or from the stage wings, or else the actors hung from poles linens painted in the fantastic, quasi-expressionistic, or humorous manner necessary for the pantomime.[22]

The production opened on 15 June 1920, and continued for thirty-one performances—an unusually long run at the time in Warsaw, where only one or two weeks of performances were then the rule. Both Boleslavsky's direction and Szymanowski's music were enthusiastically received. Historians and critics have subsequently noted that this was one of the "most notable productions of Molière" ever to grace the Polish stage.[23]

Boleslavsky's success insured his continuance at the Teatr Polski, where he soon made or renewed close friendships with a number of outstanding Polish theatre artists. As Leon Schiller, one of Boleslavsky's most ardent admirers, remarks, both the Polski's younger players and a number of its established stars soon grew fond of Boleslavsky and attended his off-stage discussions of theatrical topics with a "rarely encountered enthusiasm." Boleslavsky spent long hours talking with them about the need for actor training, about the relationship of the director and the actors in a collective theatrical effort, and about the theatre's obligation to serve the "more important cultural problems" of the Polish nation. Such, Schiller says, were the immediate artistic needs as Boleslavsky perceived them. In the longer range, Boleslavsky had even grander dreams. He talked of the need to create in Warsaw a center of theatrical training which would produce a generation of young artists who would branch out into Poland's secondary cities and establish "young, new, independent theatres" and wrest control away from the "businessmen and careerists" who presently monopolized Poland's theatres. Schiller adds: "Boleslavsky's arrival hastened the outbreak of discontent with the poor artistic managers already established on the Polish stage and enkindled dreams of what could be gained only by the collective effort of harmonious groups of actors."[24]

In this regard, Ryszard Ordyński, who had first met Boleslavsky in 1910 in Moscow, writes:

> From the first moment he made himself the darling of the Polish theatre artists. He gave proof of comradeship and modesty, but with an excellent sense, one which was commanding and which carried him to the position of director. . . . With equal enthusiasm he applied himself to both classical and modern plays. . . .
> Boleslavsky's work boded so well over the next few months that we were sure of his eventual marriage to the Polish stage. It turned out otherwise.[25]

Evidently, Polish theatre managers did not share the actors' enthusiasm for Boleslavsky's ideas. But his initial success at the Teatr Polski was sufficient to persuade Szyfman to offer Boleslavsky a contract for the balance of the season.

Immediately after the opening of Molière's comedy, Boleslavsky began rehearsals for Edmond Rostand's affectionate satire on romantic love, *Les Romanesques* (*The Romancers*)—a play perhaps best known to modern American audiences in its musical adaptation, *The Fantastics,* which closely follows Rostand's text. Jaracz and Zieliński played the two fathers whose supposed feud draws their children into an intensely exaggerated romance. Biegański played the ardent young suitor, and Sylvette was acted by M. Kamińska. In addition to directing, Boleslavsky also acted the role of the flamboyant bravado, Staforel. Military matters once again impinged on Boleslavsky's artistic life. By the time *Les Romanesques* opened on 15 July 1920, a Bolshevik offensive was threatening the city of Warsaw. In face of this impending danger, Schiller writes, Rostand's bittersweet comedy seemed empty, false, and trivial. The production was a "fiasco," closing after only thirteen performances.[26]

The Russian advance on Warsaw was a retaliatory response to the Polish occupation of Kiev in May. On July 1, the Soviet general, Tukhachevsky, launched a massive Red offensive against Poland. Minsk, Wilna, and Grodno fell to his armies. On July 23, Tukhachevsky, eager for a definitive victory, ordered a march on Warsaw to be spearheaded by Budenny's vast, seemingly invincible cavalry—the Konarmiya. By mid-August, the Red armies were on the banks of the Vistula River.

Though he did not regret having fought, Boleslavsky's own recent war experiences had persuaded him that: "Every war . . . begins with the highest ideals and it finishes with wolfish instincts aroused and glorified."[27] Still, with Warsaw under imminent threat, Boleslavsky rejoined the Polish cavalry—but this time in the service of Poland rather than the Tsar, and not in a fighting capacity. He was assigned to a communications unit, where his knowledge of filmmaking was exploited to make two propaganda pieces for the Polish government.[28] The films were produced by Sfinx Studios and Orientfilm, but both studios had been temporarily nationalized and brought under the auspices of the Polish War Ministry.

Boleslavsky was one of the very few experienced directors and cameramen working in Warsaw at the time,[29] a fact which evidently made it necessary for him to train some of the members of his camera crew. Equipment was in short supply. Even the successful Sfinx Studio was equipped at the time with only a bare minimum of primitive, outdated cameras.

Boleslavsky produced *Bravery of a Polish Scout (Bohaterstwo polskiego skauta)*, which premiered on 3 November 1920, and *Miracle on the Vistula (Cud nad Wisła)*, first shown on 16 March 1921. *Bravery of a Polish Scout* is remembered primarily as the film debut of the actress Jadwiga Smosarska,[30] but *Miracle on the Vistula*—much of which was made under enemy fire during the Battle of Warsaw and enjoyed wild public enthusiasm upon its release—is of continuing interest, providing as it does an early example of a technique that has come into wider use in more recent times. Much of the footage was shot on location, documenting both the preparations for the battle and the actual fighting. After the battle, Boleslavsky augmented this authentic film footage with reenactments of important events he had missed (and possibly adding fictional elements as well), using some of the actual personages, along with Smosarska and such leading actors from the Teatr Polski as Stefan Jaracz, Jerzy Leszczyński, Leonard Bończa-Stępiński, and Kazimierz Junosza-Stępowski.

In a curious coincidence of history, Lev Kuleshov was recording the events of August 1920 from a Bolshevik point of view. He later recounted how he had mixed "actual war material" with "staged sequences showing the daily life of the front line" during the fighting with the "White Poles." He adds: "Looking back, it seems very much a method of today. . . . Indeed I think that the half-documentary, half-fiction method is one of the most interesting tendencies of contemporary cinema."[31]

Soon after the retreat of the Bolshevik armies, Boleslavsky was permitted to resign from the military and return to his work in the theatre. His next production at the Teatr Polski was *Charity (Milosierdzie)*, a new play Karol Rostworowski, who is widely regarded as the principal heir to Poland's great poetic playwright, Stanisłas Wyspianski. This was the only play by a Polish writer Boleslavsky staged in Warsaw.

Like most of Rostworowski's other plays, *Charity* is deeply concerned with religious and moral questions and is experimental in form. Kazimierz Czachowski considers *Charity* to be an example of the most interesting of the new dramatic forms this remarkable playwright developed: "a *mysterium Mercy,* in which the introduction of the throng as the only actor was handled with rare power and skill."[32]

The play, written in verse, treats the paradoxical theme of man's depravity and his unity with God. Its form blends the allegorical figures of the medieval Polish mystery play with a number of Greek choruses. The characters—such as the Rich Man (Stanisław Stanisławski), the Scholar (Bończa-Stępiński), the Tyrant (Stanisław Bryliński), or Charity (Biegański)—are dramatically less important than the Chorus of the Charitable, the Chorus of Men, the Chorus of Women, the Gang of Thugs, the Chorus of the Wretched, or the Chorus of Criminals who populate scenes set in heaven and hell.

For his production of *Charity,* Boleslavsky again used Wincenty Drabik to design the scenery. Drabik had a natural feeling for the apocalyptic, the stylized, the monumental, and the fantastic.[33] It has been said of him that his "decorative contortions . . . seem a revelation of the Polish soul."[34] Under Boleslavsky's guidance, Drabik reduced the forms inspired by his Krakovian background to the simplest, most expressive stylized elements:

> The decorations for *Charity,* together with all the apparatus of staging, had the gravity and dignity of the mystery play. Drabik expressed his respect for the religious stage and folk art in the architecture designed for the Old-Polish Szopka, in which the action was played on two tiers and in the towering building of the creche, adorned with the most beautiful Krakovian motifs.[35]

Ordyński has described Boleslavsky's production of *Charity* as "remarkable" and "memorable."[36] Schiller considered it the strongest expression he had seen of Boleslavsky's "individuality as a director":

> This production was a revelation of some quite new elements of staging. The originality of the director was exhibited, above all, in the polyphonic rhythmization of the

choruses and in the movement of the extras, as well as in the dynamics of the lighting, all of which were organically connected to the progress of related actions.[37]

An anonymous historian of the Teatr Polski has noted that *Charity's* success depended on "the management of great crowds," and that the production created a "convulsive sensation" in the public.[38] Part of the controversy generated by the production centered about one scene in particular, in which the stage was dominated by a somewhat expressionist rendition of three towering crosses. In Catholic Poland the scenic depiction of Golgotha stirred no little consternation. Boleslavsky was summoned before a government official who challenged the propriety of the production in general and that scene in particular. Boleslavsky stoutly refused to alter the work.[39] The controversy may have contributed to Szyfman's decision to withdraw the production after only twenty performances, though he writes that "such outstanding literary works as *Charity*" were "reluctantly cancelled" in favor of such nationalistic works as De Fler's *The Return,* which had greater appeal for the many military men in the audience.[40]

Boleslavsky's final production on the Teatr Polski's main stage was *Ruy Blas,* Victor Hugo's poetic tragedy set in seventeenth century Spain. Hugo's tangled tale of intrigue, disguise, and deception is regarded by many critics as his finest work for the stage, but the play had little appeal for Boleslavsky. In his view, Hugo's theme—the triumph of the common-born Ruy Blas's lofty sense of honor over the venal plan of vengeance plotted by the supposedly noble Don Salluste—was an excessively "literary idea" with too little relation to genuine human feelings.[41]

Boleslavsky cast some of the Polski's finest actors in the leading roles, including Jerzy Leszczyński in the title role, Marji Przybyłko-Potocka (Szyfman's wife) as the Queen of Spain, and Leonard Bończa-Stępiński as Don Salluste. Again Boleslavsky used Drabik as his designer. For *Ruy Blas's* interior and exterior scenes, Drabik devised a system of flexible, architecturally monumental scenery that was somewhat Craigian in its departure from realistic representationalism.[42] Schiller found Boleslavsky's work on the play dull and uninteresting.[43] Still, its remarkable cast of players and excellent scenery apparently won a reasonably enthusiastic public response, for it opened on 10 February 1921 and continued for twenty-eight performances.

Ruy Blas was the last play Boleslavsky directed on the Polski's main stage, but he directed two other productions for the theatre's small studio adjunct, the Teatr Mały.[44] The first of these was yet another staging of Berger's *The Deluge,* in which he also acted his usual role of

O'Neill. Schiller has characterized this production, which continued for
fifty-seven performances in the small house, as an example of "exquisite
realistic directing."[45] Boleslavsky's other production at the Maly—his
last in Poland—was *Kiki,* a comedy by the French playwright of the
Napoleonic era, Louis Baptiste Picard. *Kiki* ran for forty-nine performances and was similar to *Le Bourgeois gentilhomme* in that it mingled
period music with light, satirical prose thrusts at the newly rich and the
newly risen. But, according to Schiller, Boleslavsky was deeply stung by
the fact that he had been forced to step down from the Polski's main
stage to direct a play which he personally felt was trivial and unworthy.
Nevertheless, Schiller adds, Boleslavsky "displayed as much interest as
was possible for this trifle" and even designed the settings for the production. Schiller, who shared Boleslavsky's disdain for the piece, felt
the production of *Kiki* was only "interesting from the point of view of
form."[46]

    Hiż confirms Boleslavsky's scorn for Picard's comedy: "I was
forced to believe that he had not returned to Poland to direct farce. A
lion lived in him, a lion who was not permitted to roar, or so he expressed it to me. This was our last conversation. A few days later, he
suddenly left Poland—forever."[47]

Despite Boleslavsky's successes at the Teatr Polski, men in positions of
power had apparently grown displeased with him. They took steps
which in turn caused Boleslavsky to grow increasingly dissatisfied with
his theatrical lot in Warsaw. *Kiki* served to bring this conflict into
sharper focus. Schiller explains that Boleslavsky had been forced to
stage the play by a "stronghold of influence," who acted, "according to
some, out of spitefulness." He notes that Boleslavsky was upset by this
disregard of his ambition and talents: "Boleslavsky understood that they
had injured him, that they had put him to the test. We consoled him,
telling him he was not the only one to meet such a fate. . . . We explained that he had us and the theatre."[48]

    What was the specific issue in this dispute, and who, besides Boles-
lavsky, were the parties to it? Neither Schiller nor any other source
presently known supplies a clear answer, but Ordyński offers a tactfully
vague and speculative comment: "Certain people, perhaps not duly ap-
preciating Boleslavsky's great talent, or perhaps desiring that he prove
himself . . . before presenting him with the director's baton, perhaps
finally alarmed him with their increasing authority and discouraged him
from further work."[49]

    In urging reforms for the Polish stage, Boleslavsky had implicitly criticized Szyfman's management of the Teatr Polski, and it is doubtful that Szyfman appreciated such criticism, however indirect. Moreover, Boleslavsky's efforts to introduce a "collective organization" into the Polish theatre amounted to a strong attack on the entrenched star system; while some of the Polski's leading players responded positively to his message, others no doubt opposed this potential erosion of their privileged status. They, too, were a source of opposition.

Evidently Boleslavsky was not consoled by his friends' reassurances, for in May of 1921—not long after the production of *Kiki*—he applied to the municipal authorities in Łódź for the position of manager of the Teatr Miejski (Municipal Theatre) there.[50] Such theatres were supported by the state, but, according to Szydlowski, state support at the time was "meager and paid out irregularly." He explains: "Theatres were leased out to managers or theatre companies who were granted subsidies . . . and held responsible for the commercial success of the theatres." In order to get such a lease, "It was necessary to pull strings and use influence."[51] Possibly the plan for the theatre in Łódź presented by Boleslavsky was considered by the city authorities to be impractical; perhaps he lacked sufficient influence to gain the position; possibly his enemies at the Teatr Polski had interceded to prevent his independence. In any event, Boleslavsky's application was rejected.

At about the same time, Leon Schiller accepted an offer to manage the Municipal Theatre in Lwów, and, he explains, his colleagues from the Polski "planned to go *en masse* with me and help with the organization of a collective theatre." He continues:

> Boleslavsky was an obvious candidate to take one of the leading positions. We had attracted a group of sympathizers, among whom were, besides the youth, a group of choice actors. Like Alcibiades or Coriolanus, however, we had overlooked the town's ingratitude. . . . Boleslavsky gave in to our moment of enthusiasm. Within a few days he worked out with me a plan for our future activity for several years, but again a certain theatrical quarrel angered him so strongly that he irrevocably decided to leave. . . . We gave up the game, and I telegraphed President Chlamtacz that I could not accept the position offered.[52]

Possibly the "certain theatrical quarrel" Schiller alludes to was a matter of internal dissention within the group, but his reference to Alcibiades and Coriolanus strongly suggests that the dispute was rather between the group and the city's administrators. Whatever the source or the specific nature of the argument, it evidently involved principles both Boleslavsky and Schiller valued highly. Schiller's concluding comments suggest that the proposed "collective" organization of the new theatrical venture may have been at issue:

On the day of Boleslavsky's departure, our wine was bitter at the Astoria. We knew that he would never again return and that something had ended in our lives. Ryszard Ordyński still tried a few months later to get his collaboration for the theatres he had organized. But Boleslavsky preferred the poverty he was by then experiencing in Paris to the humiliation he had known in Warsaw.

And thus the Polish stage lost one of its best directors and warriors for the collective cause as the best artistic and organizational form in the theatre.[53]

Ordyński's trip to Paris to see Boleslavsky was but the first of several efforts on his part to coax Boleslavsky into returning to Poland. In 1923, Ordyński spotted Boleslavsky waiting with a group of film extras hoping for work with Famous Players (later Paramount) on Long Island. Again, in 1926 and 1927, while visiting New York, Ordyński pleaded with Boleslavsky. But Boleslavsky's answer was still "no."

The plays Boleslavsky directed at the Teatr Polski cannot be taken as a wholly reliable guide to his directorial interests, for they were chosen by Szyfman, or at least subject to Szyfman's final approval. Boleslavsky cared little for either Hugo's *Ruy Blas* or Picard's *Kiki*. Whether he had a similar lack of enthusiasm for Rostand's *Les Romanesques* is not certain, but little information about its staging has survived in any case. Nor is there much presently known about his production of *The Deluge* at the Teatr Mały; indeed, it is unclear even whether he redirected the play or copied the First Studio's production. Two of his productions at the Teatr Polski, *Le Bourgeois gentilhomme* and *Charity,* although quite different in style and mood, serve to confirm the directorial concerns observed in Boleslavsky's earlier work, and each in its own way marked a further step toward the successful marriage of psychologically truthful acting and an ever greater theatricality of form.

If Leon Schiller's judgment is accepted—and both the success of *Le Bourgeois gentilhomme*'s premiere and the considerable importance subsequently attached to the production by historians of the Polish theatre seem to justify doing so—then Boleslavsky's production of Molière's comedy was masterful. In *Le Bourgeois gentilhomme* he recreated a sense of the play's historical origins in the French court, even as he seemed to comment and pass judgment on Molière's milieu. He achieved this by developing a harmonious formal unity between the acting style and the scenic presentation. Taking the shallowness of M. Jourdain's social pretentions as a comment by Molière—either intentional or not—on the empty grandeur of Louis XIV's court, Boleslavsky opened the play on a virtually empty stage, viewed through a proscenium framed with elaborate curtains hung in baroque splendor. As for the acting style, Schiller notes that Boleslavsky had the actors apply certain aspects of Stanislavsky's system, especially the psychological ones; the comic characters were thus given a human basis, even as they were enlarged into exaggerated, almost grotesque figures.[54] As the plot was unfolded through the enlarged actions of exaggerated and sharply defined characters, realistic illusion gave way to a kind of presentational style, and the scenery grew increasingly bold and grotesque.

As in *Balladyna*, music played an important part. The action was interlaced with Lully's graceful melodies, but these gradually gave way to Schiller's modern compositions and were finally superseded by Szymanowski's unsettling atonalities and modern dissonances; simultaneously, the action of Molière's play yielded to the grotesque ballet-pantomime of *Mandragora*. In this afterpiece, which flowed organically out of *Le Bourgeois gentilhomme*, Molière's characters were transformed—reverting again to the timeless *commedia* figures that had served as the playwright's first inspiration. The tale of Molière's plot was reflected in the actions of these masked mummers, as in a distorting mirror, and told this time through the actor's ancient tools of pantomime, gesture, dance, and tragi-comic pratfall.

Clearly, Boleslavsky had moved beyond illusionism, had dispensed with even a token gesture to the kind of heightened realism that had dominated *The Good Hope;* and if, as the later Soviet critics insist, his theatrical vision for *Balladyna* had been only imperfectly realized, his conception for Molière's comedy—a conception, if anything, more daring and more thoroughly original—succeeded brilliantly. It was a vision of dazzling virtuosity, successfully blending into a unified whole the elements of acting, pantomime, music, dance, and the visual arts.

Similar artistic aims produced strikingly different results in Boleslavsky's staging of *Charity*. Here again music (supplied this time by Schiller) underscored much of the action and again Boleslavsky employed older theatre conventions and dramatic forms to express modern sensibilities. The action was performed in this instance, not by Molière's clowns, but by allegorical figures from the medieval traditions of the Polish mystery play. Likewise the stock *commedia* figures were replaced by choruses inspired by the classical conventions of Greek tragedy. Boleslavsky did not, however, treat these "classical" choruses in a stately, stylized manner. Such an approach would have denied Rostworowski's apocalyptic vision of man's suffering in life, his pain in death, and his struggle for redemption. Boleslavsky transformed the Greek-like choruses into seething mobs of individualized human souls, each of whom struggled after his own goals.

Judging from Schiller's account, Boleslavsky's production of *Charity* was an awesome artistic achievement, one which had an unsettling, even disturbing effect on its audiences:

> *Charity* was more the *succès d'estime* of the director than the author. The work was done as a stylized image of revolution which offended some, though not all. The first turned away from the production, but the second group turned to the "Dantean hell with demigogical enthusiasm." No one could be touched by the sweet-colored chromolithography which reminded them of the images sold in the indulgences booth, or by the decoration of the so-called "divine graves." This was the last act, a mystical finale, but what Boleslavsky created on the stage—today I recall my judgment with great certainty—went beyond the standard of all previous efforts by directors in the area of composition of crowd scenes. This was not the realistic whirlpool in the style of Meiningen or his followers translated into Polish awkwardness, Reinhardt as copied awkwardly and senselessly by his Polish imitators; and these were neither the living marionettes of Tairov nor the human automatons of Meyerhold, whose novelty was then as yet unknown to us. This was Poland's first "composition of naturalistic elements" in the strict sense of the words, elements taken strictly from "life in the raw," unaltered stylistically and thus neither beautified nor deformed. . . . This was a polyphony of ordinary voices, of everyday polyrhythmic gestures, which culminated in the spasms of collective hysteria and terror, the chants of religious ecstasy. This was chaos and nothing other than chaos seen from a flight of creative thought which sought and found order in it.[55]

Leon Schiller later expressed his great debt, and the debt of the Polish theatre, to Boleslavsky. "For people outside the theatre," he writes, Boleslavsky's work in Poland "does not amount to much, for it totals just two shows presented in Poznan and five presented in Warsaw." But for those Polish artists who had worked in collaboration with Boleslavsky and

> formed an intimate, heart-felt friendship with him . . . the result of his activity did not end with a few choice premieres and some unusually interesting, pedagogically valuable rehearsals. Perhaps the firmest trace he left in Polish theatrical life was in the ideas he explained in long and frequent conversations with associates—ideas which we have since been trying to put into effect.

Boleslavsky's ideas, Schiller writes, "pointed the Polish theatre toward the proper road of its development. . . ."[56]

Schiller himself did a great deal to accomplish the goals Boleslavsky had set. Before meeting Boleslavsky, his interest in theatre had been primarily theoretical and literary. But after working with Boleslavsky at the Teatr Polski, he took up stage directing, first at the Teatr Reduta (1921–24), then at his own Teatr im. Bogusławski in Warsaw, where, using principles he had learned from Boleslavsky, he soon became famous as Poland's chief exponent of "poetic realism," or "monumental realism," as his style was sometimes called.

Boleslavsky had dreamed of establishing in Warsaw a theatrical school that would provide trained artists for theatres throughout Poland. Schiller opened such a school, The State Institute of Theatre Art (later, The State Theatre School), just before the Second World War broke out. After the war, he opened a second school in Łódź.

Since his death in 1954, Schiller has been described as "the greatest Polish stage director of the first half of the twentieth century,"[57] and "the greatest stage designer and visionary in the history of the Polish theatre."[58] He personally influenced two generations of Polish directors, and his successors taught a third generation who began working in the 'sixties. Historian Edward Csato notes that Schiller was the teacher of almost all the distinguished directors now working in Poland.[59] As Schiller himself writes, Boleslavsky's departure from Warsaw in 1922 meant a delay in the realization of the dreams Boleslavsky had for the Polish stage, but those dreams were eventually realized by others.[60]

8

Reunion—Separation—Reunion

The dream of Poland—a state of mind, a spiritual ideal, Camelot on the Vistula—had sustained Boleslavsky for much of his life. He had been born Polish at a time when Poland did not exist legally or politically, and had spent his youth longing for its return. His small piece of Polish soil—Dębowa Góra, his family's estate—had been lost, or taken away. Displacement and dislocation followed. A spiritual émigré, he moved from Płock to Bessarabia to Odessa to Moscow. He had fought in the Great War for the sake of his dream of a Polish homeland, and in so doing lost the one place that had come closest to being a home to him— the First Studio. The prodigal son had finally returned to Warsaw, capital of a reborn Polish state, and that experience had tarnished forever— perhaps shattered beyond repair—his sustaining dream of mythic Poland, so long in his mind. He later reflected on his feelings:

> I can't explain it. I must be a freak. I'm immune to patriotism. At the same time I'm sentimental about it in others and in myself in spells. But I can't really say that my dream is to call this stretch of land or another my country and wish it to prosper more than any other land. After all, they are all alike, and they all have to prosper. My dream is in moving over those stretches from hill to hill, from valley to valley, from river to river and to worship them silently while I look at them. Then I begin to wonder again what is beyond the horizon? And this thought becomes my dream until I reach it. My dream is to measure the fields, forests, rivers and sea shores with my steps, and my ordeal is that I probably will never be able to stop and say, "This is mine. This is for me. This is the best." Even if I wanted to say it.[1]

The next few years of his life he spent wandering the capitals of Eastern and Western Europe, until finally he traveled beyond Europe to America, to make his home for a time in New York. His steps during this period cannot be traced with precision, for he moved about a great deal and found relatively few opportunities for theatrical work of any consequence. Still, the highlights, if not the exact chronology, of his travels are known.

Natasha Boleslavsky remembers that she went with her husband directly from Warsaw to Prague, but both Schiller and Ordyński indicate that they visited Boleslavsky in Paris not long after he left Warsaw. Ordyński writes:

> He went beyond the Seine. In Paris the atmosphere inspired him in such a way that his nature responded. He made the acquaintance of a Russian troupe of émigré actors and entered it as an actor, though he could not show his capabilities very well with their repertoire. We visited him there with Schiller. . . . [2]

The émigré troupe Ordyński refers to was most likely a company which had taken up residence at the Théâtre Femina, under the leadership of Maria Kouznetsova, formerly a leading singer with St. Petersburg's Imperial Opera. They specialized in light musical entertainments, comic sketches, and cabaret-style evenings; any roles Boleslavsky may have played with them at this time are not presently known, though his work with them a little later can be documented.

Not long after reaching Paris, however, Boleslavsky made contact (whether by letter or in person is not clear) with a group of his former colleagues from the Moscow Art Theatre, and soon joined them in Prague, Czechoslovakia. By 1 August 1921, he was directing a new production of Shakespeare's *Hamlet* for them and, presumably, rehearsing a number of the roles he had previously acted in Moscow.[3]

Sometimes called the "Kachalov Group" (after Vassily Kachalov, its leading actor) and also known as the Moscow Art Theatre in Prague (where it made its headquarters), the company had existed as a distinct unit since 1919. In July of that year, a large contingent of actors from the MAT—about half the MAT's players—had been performing in Kharkov, in the Ukraine, when an unexpected advance by Denikin's White armies cut off their return to Moscow. Unable to reach home, the group had played various cities in the south of Russia, following a path that led them to the Turkish border. They then traveled through Turkey to Istanbul, thence through several Baltic cities to Vienna and, finally, Prague, where they received an especially warm welcome (Natasha Boleslavsky recalls that when she and her husband joined the company in Prague, they were housed in an ancient castle—damp, drafty, and uncomfortable, but a castle nonetheless, with a lovely garden where they gathered around an open fire in the evenings to drink vodka, joke, and join in singing melancholy, sentimental Russian songs). After establishing themselves in Prague, the company toured Pilsen, Bratislava, Vienna, and Berlin; still later they ventured into Paris and the Scandinavian capitals.

An elaborate brochure published by the group in 1922 featured a photograph-page of its administrators. Sergei Bertonson was Administrative Director. Boleslavsky was named as a director for the company, along with Massalitinov and N. N. Litovtseva. Leonidov and Bersenev were company representatives, and Yakov I. Gremislavsky served as scenic designer.[4]

Their plays were drawn from the Art Theatre's repertoire. With the exception of two of Knut Hamsun's plays (*In the Claws of Life* and *At the Gate of the Kingdom*) and—after Boleslavsky joined them—Shakespeare's *Hamlet,* they showed only works by Russian writers: Anton Chekhov's *The Cherry Orchard, Uncle Vanya,* and *The Three Sisters;* Nemirovich-Danchenko's adaptation of *The Brothers Karamazov;* Gorky's *The Lower Depths;* Surguchev's *Autumn Violins;* Ostrovsky's *Enough Stupidity in Every Wise Man* (also known as *Even a Wise Man Stumbles),* and Turgenev's *Where It's Thin, It Breaks.* Most of these plays contained roles featuring the company's best-known actors: Kachalov and Olga Knipper-Chekhova. Boleslavsky almost certainly took over his former roles (Baranovsky in *Autumn Violins* and Satin in *The Lower Depths),* and a photograph in the company's brochure shows him in a new role—the Player King in *Hamlet.* Other well-known players traveling with the group included Massalitinov, Bersenev, Tarasova, Germanova, Soloviova, and her husband, Andrei Zhilinski.

As a rule, the company followed the Art Theatre's original production for their plays, but Natasha Boleslavsky, who played a number of supernumerary roles in *Hamlet,* remembers that when Boleslavsky's staging or interpretation of Shakespeare's tragedy was at all reminiscent of Craig's 1911 production, Kachalov—who was again in the title role—protested: "No, no, let's have none of that. No Craig, please!"[5] When the Prague production was announced in the *Neue Freie Presse* on 26 October 1921, it was *Hamlet—Prince of Denmark,* with "completely new staging" by Boleslavsky and new scenery by Gremislavsky.[6] The company brochure included a lengthy article titled "Hamlet-Kachalov," by Sergei Makovsky (who apparently was not affiliated with the group), in which he presented a detailed analysis of Craig's Moscow production and concluded:

Thus, the production of *Hamlet* done at Craig's bidding was not successful. The production we see now, outside of Russia, is a very free interpretation of Craig's original idea. The present director of the play, Boleslavsky, and the scenic designer, Gremislavsky, have found their own route to the staging of *Hamlet* . . . . The present director has departed not only from the form of staging, but also from

Craig's entire symbolic treatment, and to a significant degree has approached Shakespeare's realism.[7]

Three of the principal roles in Boleslavsky's *Hamlet* were taken by actors who had earlier played the same parts for Craig: Kachalov as Hamlet, Knipper-Chekhova as Gertrude, and Massalitinov as Claudius, but the other players were new to their parts. Pavlov was Polonius, Ophelia was acted alternately by Tarasova and Kryzhanovskaya, and Bersenev took Laertes (a role Boleslavsky had come to personally despise when he played it for Craig, Natasha Boleslavsky remembers). Kommissarov played Rosenkrantz, Vasilyev was Guildenstern, and Horatio was acted by Sharov.[8]

The setting for *Hamlet* devised by Boleslavsky and Gremislavsky, who had first worked together on *The Good Hope,* was a flexible unit stage, consisting of a system of hanging black velvet draperies (which could be closed, opened, or shifted right or left independently of one another). These were coordinated with an arrangement of platforms and steps of varying sizes and shapes; the platforms were not all rectilinear—some were cubes or rhomboids. Scenic alterations were accomplished through an intricate coordination of lighting with simultaneously moving platforms, curtains, and steps.[9]

The night before *Hamlet* opened in Prague, Knipper-Chekhova started a letter to Stanislavsky, in which she talked about the final preparations for the show: "Today we are playing *Hamlet.* . . . Kachalov performs more interestingly than before, a sort of directness has appeared, he philosophizes less." About her own work, she said, "I am no longer the dead queen that I was—I seem to have come alive, and I now play the 'closet scene' with pleasure. God help us today. . . . We rehearse *Hamlet* from ten in the morning until four or five o'clock, and at night, after the Czech performance is over."

Hamlet opened in Prague on September 18, some six weeks after Boleslavsky had started rehearsals—a short preparation by MAT standards. The next day, Knipper continued the letter she had started:

We played *Hamlet* last night to a full house. Kachalov was handsome and, I would say, more youthful and supple than before. Now he plays superbly the scene with his mother, the scene with the ghost of his father, and "To be or not to be." . . . Both "the king's prayer" and the queen's monologue about the death of Ophelia, which I now speak with love and great emotion, turned out well for us. They say the whole performance produced a very serious, emotional effect. The curtains and the lights, about which we were very apprehensive, went according to command.

She closed with a hasty postscript: "I have written nothing about Gremislavsky's great labor of love—in general both 'slavskys' were on a high level—Richard too."[10]

Hamlet was added to the company's repertoire and first played in Vienna on 27 October and Berlin on 9 February 1922. It roused considerable critical and popular interest in each of those cities. Three of the available reviews of the production remarked the "Russian spirit" of the production and the Chekhovian naturalness of the acting.[11] Makovsky felt that there was still too much of Craig's influence in Kachalov's performance, that his Hamlet was "too ready" for action:

> In Kachalov's Hamlet there is more majesty than helplessness, more raw alienation from the people around him than madness of the heart, more cruelty than kindness. Kachalov's Hamlet is a man isolated not only by what he says, but by the fact that he is scornful to the point of arrogance, the legendary prince—"every inch a prince." In the scene with his mother he behaves like a judge, unerring, unbending, his hands convulsively clenching an enormous Byzantine sword. . . . His threat to the praying Claudius does not sound like a simple excuse for indecisiveness. . . .
>
> Nonetheless, nine years after the first production of *Hamlet* in Moscow, Kachalov now plays incomparably more passionately and more simply. It is as if he has departed from the symbolic tragedy of Gordon Craig and given himself to Shakespeare's poetry. . . . [12]

Regarding the production's scenic effects, a critic in Vienna wrote: "The scene designer has the first word. For the most part by means of the stylized stage [*Stilbühne*], he creates out of curtains very beautiful scenery with intense colors. The sky which peers at the tragedy through columns or apertures is deep green, often violet. . . . "[13] A Berlin critic wrote: "A changing back-cloth with a view on the horizon, the suggestion of columns, pillars, and colonnades, and well-utilized staircases enable them to have changing scenes which are given character by their painter, Gremislavsky."[14] And Ihring, in Berlin's *Der Tag*, wrote:

> Seen in relation to the theatre's development, this production stands—as regards scenery—between Reinhardt and Jessner. In the development of a neutral setting it has already surpassed Reinhardt, for the simplification and organization of space with curtains and staircases is more uniform than with Reinhardt, who emphasized the terrace in the beginning and the graveyard scene in the end. The variations of scenic arrangement—with the alternately narrowing and widening of the stage, with the variety of entrances and exits, with the ease of the architectural distribution of space—avoid stiffness and schematism and here surpass Jessner.[15]

Despite the strong interest in the production, *Hamlet* was shown only five times in Prague, three times in Vienna, and another three times in Berlin.[16] No doubt it would have been performed more often, except that Kachalov did not think he possessed the necessary stamina to do it.[17] Moreover, its life was cut short when, early in 1922, the troupe interrupted its tour to rejoin the main body of the Moscow Art Theatre. Stanislavsky's justification for dropping *Hamlet* and other productions performed by the Kachalov group was that the Art Theatre was preparing to go to America: "Over there they want only Russian authors and to see performances of those works which have established our reputation."[18]

This reunion was the culmination of delicate negotiations that had begun in the first days of the group's separation from Moscow almost three years earlier. Two letters written in the latter stages of these negotiations contain intriguing clues that Boleslavsky may have considered the possibility of returning to Russia. In December 1921, Vassily Kachalov wrote to Nemirovich-Danchenko from Berlin on behalf of the Prague contingent of the MAT. He protested his eagerness to return to Moscow, but confessed, "I feel that I am too soft and unprepared for Moscow." He follows with what seems to be a plea, but his words might be read instead as a set of conditions for his return:

> I alone—or only with Knipper—shall be poor support for you. We have weak, puny shoulders, which can lift little, especially immediately, without training. Only all together as a group shall we help the theatre. I believe that we shall help. Bersenev and Boleslavsky—these are strong shoulders—have a great reserve of strength and they can lift a lot. Doesn't the theatre need our plays, at least in the beginning, in order to set the machine in motion and to give all of you a breathing-space? . . . Be that as it may, the *group* is necessary to the theatre and will help the theatre. I feel this with all my heart. And you must not simply agree to take us into the theatre— you must also make us feel as a group that we are needed, that we are wanted, that Bersenev and Massalitinov and Boleslavsky are not "criminals," but workers who are very much needed in *our* theatre. The group must feel that it is returning home, to *its* theatre [his emphasis].[19]

Knipper, in the letter to Stanislavsky already quoted in connection with *Hamlet,* also wrote:

> Only don't think badly of us, don't think that we are breaking away and don't want to unite. . . . Everything that has happened is fate, and everything will be united again. And I dream that when we are all together, Stanislavsky will wave his wings and create another theatre, which is now needed, and it shall be in Russia.[20]

What did Kachalov, as acknowledged spiritual leader of the Prague Group, and Knipper, its leading actress, have in mind? Did they in fact envision returning to Russia as a body, to be allied with the Moscow Art

Theatre while functioning as an "independent" theatre, with Boleslavsky, Bersenev, and Massalitinov as directors of "our" theatre? Regardless of the hopes of Knipper or Kachalov, or even of Boleslavsky himself, the outcome was quite different. Early in 1922, in anticipation of the Moscow Art Theatre's first American tour, Knipper, Kachalov, and other leading actors of the Prague group agreed to return to the mother company. Another contingent of the vagabond troupe, led by Maria Germanova, decided to return instead to Prague, where they continued to operate as an outpost of Russian theatre at least until 1929. Others— including Boleslavsky—declined either of these options and elected instead to try their fortunes on their own. Whether Stanislavsky ever seriously entertained Kachalov's proposition is unclear. In any event, Boleslavsky could have returned to Russia only at considerable personal risk. As Soloviova put it, "he chose freedom."[21]

Ilya Ehrenburg, who was living in Berlin at the time, writes:

> I do not know how many Russians there were in Berlin in those years; certainly a great many—at every step you could hear Russian spoken. Dozens of Russian restaurants were opened— with balalaikas, and zurnas, with gypsies, pancakes, shashlyks and, naturally, the inevitable heartbreak. There was a little theatre that put on sketches.[22]

Perhaps the theatre he refers to was *Der Blau Vogel* (*The Blue Bird*), where Boleslavsky staged a modest production of *The Cricket on the Hearth*, with a cast drawn from Russian émigré actors and his private students (he taught acting to eke out a meager living). At about the same time he performed in a production of Turgenev's *The House of Gentlefolk* (sometimes called *The Nest of Nobility*) in a German-speaking theatre, and acted "different parts in various German films."[23] Only one film in which he appeared can be identified by title: *Love One Another,* made in Germany by the famous Danish director, Carl Theodor Dreyer. (The film is known in Germany as *Die Gezeichneten,* in Denmark as *Elsker Hvandre,* and in Russia as *Pogrom;* see the Filmography.)

Based on a novel by Aage Madelung, *Love One Another* was a somewhat melodramatic treatment of an extraordinarily complicated plot dealing with a young Jewish girl's suffering during the Russian pogroms of 1905. Boleslavsky played Fedya, her childhood sweetheart, who causes her to be expelled from school. She joins her brother in St. Petersburg but, after a series of complex episodes and subplots, is exiled from the city. Returning to her native village, she is set upon by the grown-up Fedya's "lustful proclivities." A pogrom breaks out and she is

saved from Fedya and a Russian mob by Sasha, her lover. The actors
who played out this story were an international group, from Russia,
Poland, Norway, Denmark, and Germany. A Russian countess with no
acting experience, Polina Piekovska, played the central role of Hanna,
and Torleif Reiss was Sasha."[24] Ebbe Neergaards writes: "Dreyer
found . . . the Russian actors agreeable to work with. They were artistic, but he regrets that he was so occupied with the big equipment, with
the many crowd scenes, that he did not pay enough attention to directing
the actors."[25] In addition to playing the screen villain, Boleslavsky also
served as Dreyer's assistant, most likely helping with the crowd scenes.
As a resident of Odessa during the pogroms there and a man with firsthand knowledge of St. Petersburg, he likely advised Dreyer—a fanatic
for authenticity in settings and other details—on a number of technical
matters, as well.

Boleslavsky left Berlin in the summer or fall of 1921 and returned to
Paris, where he was engaged as an actor and director at Kouznetsova's
Théâtre Femina. Boleslavsky's first documented work at the Femina
was his staging of a mimedrama called *Lâcheté* (*Cowardice*), written by
Leon Bakst, the famous artist most often associated with Diaghilev's
Ballets Russes. Bakst also designed the expressionistic scenery for the
piece, which was set in "the concrete walls of the 'People's House' " in
St. Petersburg after it had become Petrograd. The pantomimic tragedy of
Lâcheté was followed by a short afterpiece of an entirely different
mood, a vaudeville act called "Old Moscow." For this sketch, which
featured the "moujik-bourgeois" and country women dressed in "stiff
skirts that are sky-blue or tri-colored," Bakst designed "two frames,
reaching to the knees of the actors," painted with "a miniature repro-
duction of the orphaned capitol with its forty times forty cupolas, encir-
cled by the crenelated walls of the Kremlin." The effect of this "delightfully exaggerated parody," Bakst's biographer tells us, brought tears to
the eyes of Moscow's émigrés.[26]
    Boleslavsky later incorporated the two pieces by Bakst into a full
evening's entertainment. Songs and other sketches were added, with
additional scenery by Soudekin and Ousounov, and given the collective
title, *Revue Russe*. As staged by Boleslavsky, who also acted as *conférencier*, or moderator, *Revue Russe* played at the Théâtre Femina and
toured Berlin, Madrid, and Nice. In Paris it was seen by Elizabeth
Marbury, a representative of the Shubert theatrical organization.[27] She
contracted to bring the production to the United States, where it opened
at New York's Booth Theatre on 5 October 1922. At last, some two-and-

a-half years after he left Russia (planning to go directly to the United States), Boleslavsky finally reached America.

Revue Russe had been enthusiastically received in Paris. It fared less well with the New York critics. They all compared it with Nikita Balieff's recently-opened *Chauve-Souris* and were all but unanimous in finding *Revue Russe* less entertaining. Both Balieff and Boleslavsky acted as *conférencier* for their respective shows. Balieff introduced almost every number, and his high spirits and fractured English won him a great following; Boleslavsky merely introduced each of *Revue Russe's* two acts. Charles Darnton contrasted the two men. Boleslavsky's remarks, Darton said, were "intensely dramatic instead of humorous"; he is a "gentleman quite unlike that swelling soul of humor on the Century Roof."[28]

A number of critics were favorably impressed by Bakst's *Lâcheté* (retitled *Cowardice*) and wrote admiringly of the tragedy enacted by the young man, his hunchback friend, and his doomed lover, played "in and out and around rows of swaying puppets" which continue rocking indifferently as the youth dies.[29] Still, the reviews were generally lackluster, possibly, as one of the critics suggested, because Americans found the overall tone of *Revue Russe* too thoroughly Russian.[30] Eugenie Leontovich agrees:

> When I met Boleslavsky in Berlin, I became part of the *Revue Russe*, which was very fine in many ways—very tragic and tragi-comic. We were so superior to *Chauve-Souris!* We were very well received in Paris, which is a connoisseur of the arts, especially in those days.
>
> When we finally came to America, nobody in this country at that time was ready to accept an artistic cabaret. The *Chauve-Souris* was the limit that Americans were willing to accept in those days. When we came along, we were absolutely misunderstood . . .

Leontovich also recalls her impressions of her director:

> Boleslavsky was a very knowledgeable man, with marvellous powers of organization. He never did things only because he felt them—only from inspiration. He had a marvellous way of studying things. There was an organization and a responsibility about his work that was not strictly Russian; it was more a Polish trait. He had an aim and he pursued it in carefully organized steps. He benefited from the great artistic heritage of Poland.[31]

The Shubert organization sent *Revue Russe* on the road after only twenty New York performances and closed it in Philadelphia.[32] Some members of the company voluntarily returned to Europe and others, unable to find work, were forced to leave the United States.

Boleslavsky received permission to remain in New York after he showed the authorities a letter from Stanislavsky, inviting him to rejoin the Moscow Art Theatre during its American tour as an actor and an assistant to Stanislavsky. His job, in addition to acting, was to coach the extras (some of whom were hired in New York) for the crowd scenes and to help adjust the scenery and staging of the MAT's repertoire to the various stages they would encounter during the tour.[33]

Boleslavsky was among the large crowd of people who greeted Stanislavsky and his company when their ship docked in New York on 3 January 1923.[34] There was little time for celebration, however, for the Art Theatre's premiere performance in New York was only a week away. Boleslavsky immediately set to work training the extras hired to supplement the crowd scenes in *Tsar Fyodor Ivanovich,* the production which opened the engagement on January 10, at Jolson's 59th Street Theatre. The Art Theatre's success in New York was both instant and phenomenal. The fact that the company played in Russian before a largely English-speaking audience proved no obstacle to their success: "The 'handicap' was no handicap at all, the Art Theatre's art was all the more effective because of its dependence upon acting alone."[35] As Christine Edwards has observed, the New York critics were deeply impressed by three facets of the MAT's playing: "their excellent ensemble; the utter naturalness and lifelike quality of their productions; and the fact that they seemed to be 'living' their roles instead of 'performing' them."[36] Tickets for the Art Theatre's performances were immediately sold out; their New York engagement, scheduled for eight weeks, was extended for four weeks more, after which time they visited Chicago, Boston, and Philadelphia, returning to New York on May 21 for a farewell appearance.

For a great many young American actors, the Art Theatre's performances were a revelation of what could be achieved in the realm of theatre art. They were eager to learn more about the unique methods employed by these Russian visitors, methods that made even the most minor member of the cast seem alive and vital. Beginning on January 18—only ten days after the Art Theatre's New York opening—Boleslavsky delivered a series of several lectures at the Princess Theatre explaining the artistic principles that formed the basis of Stanislavsky's work (later he also gave talks at Bryn Mawr College and at the Provincetown Playhouse). Arranged by Morris Gest, who sponsored the MAT's U.S. engagement, and given with Stanislavsky's approval, these talks stand as the first enunciation of Stanislavsky's ideas publicly presented to an American audience by an artist who had trained and acted at the Art Theatre.

A journalist described the Princess Theatre lectures as "classes in dramatic expression." The writer added: "Now comes word that ten actors and actresses whose names are more or less in electric lights along Broadway have enlisted as a professional class at the Boleslavsky school and will stage, purely by way of diversion, a play from the Russian theatre lore." The reporter's further comments are of interest primarily because they suggest the vague, confused notions most Americans had at the time regarding the Art Theatre's methods:

> They intend taking their time about rehearsals, working out each bit as they think it should be done and not as some American gentleman with the box office deeply rooted in his heart might more or less insist, and, in other words, each more or less directing his own performance. This is the way the Russians up at the Jolson Theatre go about it, with the friendly advice of Stanislavsky to gradually shape the production. Mr. Boleslavsky, of course, will supply that finished Russian touch. Among those who will report for duty, ready to accept anything from a twenty-word speech to a twenty-minute soliloquy as his part, are Winifred Lenihan, Margolo [sic] Gilmore, Jacob Ben Ami, Gilbert Emery, Kathlene MacDonald, Helen Menken [sic], Peggy Wood, Alen [sic] Birmingham, Marine Kirby and Mrs. Edward Carrington.[37]

So far as is presently known, nothing concrete came of Boleslavsky's work with this group, possibly because he was too busy with the MAT's tour. In addition to coaching the crowds, he was soon acting some of his former roles. In February, he appeared as the Tartar in Gorky's *The Lower Depths,* but soon, beginning the week of March 12, he replaced an ailing Stanislavsky as Satin in Gorky's play.[38] That Boleslavsky, rather than Podgorny or Massalitinov (who had also played the part in Moscow) was chosen to take over the role should be taken as Stanislavsky's final compliment to his former pupil.

In picking Boleslavsky to take the role of Satin, Stanislavsky had honored his former pupil. Very soon after, Boleslavsky paid tribute to his former teacher. In an article published in *Theatre Magazine* (March 1923), Boleslavsky described the Art Theatre's leader as "one of the great living geniuses of the theatre," whose efforts had "lifted the actor out of his former position as buffoon, into the sphere of a creative artist" and then made the actor's art a "systematic science."[39]

Though he honored Stanislavsky, Boleslavsky was not content to remain in the great man's shadow; nor did he plan to return to Russia with the Art Theatre when it left America. He had already taken steps to make a place for himself in New York's theatre world.

The ten actors who decided to learn the "Russian manner" from

Boleslavsky after hearing his lectures at the Princess Theatre were not the only Americans who wanted to work with him. Even more deeply impressed by his talks was Miriam Kimball Stockton, who later wrote that the ideas and ideals she heard Boleslavsky enunciate from the stage of the Princess Theatre seemed to her "like the coming of a new religion which could liberate and awaken American culture."[40] In April she sent Boleslavsky a letter asking to meet with him. At that meeting she offered to help found a theatre based upon the ideals he had expressed in his talks. By the end of the meeting, Boleslavsky agreed to work toward this goal, provided only that she, and the American trustees they hoped to recruit, fully understood and accepted his "theory that it would be impossible to impose any foreign ideal upon American soil." She accepted this "theory" as a "fundamental principle" of the theatre they envisioned. As eventually adopted by the new organization, the platform of the new theatre included these basic tenets:

> 1) This theatre must grow here by itself and must get its roots into American soil.
> 2) It must begin slowly, training young Americans for the stage in all its departments.
> 3) It must be recognized and organized as a living social force, recreating itself each generation from the thoughts and material of its own times.[41]

Boleslavsky, Miriam Stockton and her husband, Herbert King Stockton, a lawyer, held several meetings with prospective partners, but without much initial success. The Stocktons continued the effort over the next three months, while Boleslavsky was busy with the Art Theatre. Beginning on April 23, at Philadelphia's Lyric Theatre, he played Prince Shakhovskoi in *Tsar Fyodor,* returning with the MAT to New York on June 2, for the "final" New York appearance. Five days later, on June 7, the Art Theatre sailed for Europe, but Boleslavsky did not go with them. He would see Stanislavsky again the next season, when, by popular demand, the Art Theatre returned to New York.

On 29 June 1923, Boleslavsky, Paul Kennaday, Isabel Levy, Helen Arthur, and Herbert K. Stockton signed a formal declaration establishing The Laboratory Theatre as a business trust.[42] Boleslavsky intended to continue in America the legacy of experiment and innovation he had inherited from Stanislavsky and Nemirovich-Danchenko, but that legacy, as he understood it, would not be served by establishing a kind of Moscow Art Theatre in New York that would emulate its Russian prototype. Such an effort would have contradicted Boleslavsky's understanding of the dynamics of artistic development. As he explained, both his Russian teachers had conducted "laboratories" (Stanislavsky with the group of amateurs known as the Society of Art and Literature, and

Nemirovich-Danchenko with his pupils at the Philharmonic Dramatic School) before coming together to pool their visionary ideas. They had rejected the worn-out formulas employed by the Imperial theatres and through their work at the Moscow Art Theatre had displaced those formulas with new scenic methods.

The process of change and progress did not end there, however. From the ranks of the MAT's younger members had sprung up two "simple theatrical experiment stations with no more than twenty collaborators"—the First and Third Studios. After some ten years, those two laboratories had become "two of the most advanced and lucrative theatres of Moscow." Boleslavsky believed:

> Every laboratory theatre must point the way to the laboratory of the future. A theatre lives no more than a generation. Then it grows old and dies or, if it continues to exist hundreds of years, it comes to have simply a museum value, to become a kind of living archive, a store-house of dead traditions, like the Comédie Française.[43]

—And like the Moscow Art Theatre?

Part III: 1923–1937

America

"... the devil can take me. I have become such an American that I'm amazed. ..."

—Boleslavsky to Ryszard Ordyński

9

Founding the Laboratory Theatre

In Boleslavsky's view, the theatre of the early 'twenties—including the American stage—had already benefited to some extent from the creative infusions of such innovators as Stanislavsky, Nemirovich-Danchenko, Dalcroze, Craig, Jessner, and Reinhardt. Theatres worldwide had adopted the superficial forms of these pioneers' work, had borrowed the external "devices and styles," if not the inner creative vision which inspired them. Despite this international exchange of ideas and experiments, however, Boleslavsky was convinced that the theatre had reached a point of stasis and that the individual theatre artist faced a spiritual crisis:

> Observing the course of the theatre, the new forms, devices and styles that are acclaimed, patented stars, mechanical contrivances, absurd realism, speed of production and triumphant triviality, there are some actors who look tearfully . . . for a solution. They attempt to accomplish something by experiment, but exhausted and unsuccessful, they drop into a chair sobbing: "Everything is over, the Theatre has perished!" Poor Theatre, poor actors, poor designers, poor musicians! They are helpless in their own art. . . . To contemplate, to search, to create—for this there is no place. There are no laboratories of the theatre, there are no tense experiments and achievements, no tedious labor discovering new forms, no fling of the imagination, no joy of attainment. There is no creation, there is only repetition and occasional blind luck, only occasional, as in a card game.[1]

Boleslavsky's personal answer to this crisis was to establish a "laboratory of the theatre," a place dedicated to the solution of creative problems that were not being addressed by the commercial stage. Commercialism, he felt, by its very nature militates against the risks of genuine experiment and innovation. As he later explained to an interviewer, the Broadway producer's eye is always on the box-office; he gambles on productions, knowing that eight out of ten will be financial failures. He spends money lavishly in the hope of success, casts only stars for the big parts, and calls play-doctors to the bedside of the author's child. Yet, all too often, the feeble spark of theatrical life flickers out. "In a sense, of course, every play on Broadway is an experiment, but usually it may be described as a financial experiment rather than a creative one. On Broadway, too, everything is on such a large scale that the trial and error method is too expensive."[2] Still, Boleslavsky did not intend to withdraw entirely from the commercial stage. On the contrary, he felt a two-fold obligation: first, to test and experiment with the forms of theatrical expression; and, then, to "sell" his newly discovered artistic "wares" to commercial producers.[3]

Boleslavsky believed that every theatre artist worthy of the name must necessarily place himself in the avant-garde of his time. But he did not find the alternatives being offered by non-commercial "independent" theatre groups to be efficacious. While he clearly admired individual artists from the independent theatres and respected their basic intentions and aspirations, he questioned the validity of their proposed solutions. He was convinced that most, if not all the independent theatres had misplaced their priorities and that none was dedicated to solving the essential problem of the theatre—the correct training of the actor. In his view, the actor training they offered was a haphazard conglomerate of unrelated disciplines, which did little to further the actor's understanding of the actual processes of acting.

In an address to the Conference on the Drama in American Universities and Little Theatres (November 1925) at the Carnegie Institute of Technology, Boleslavsky made his position clear. He began by apologizing for the "imperfect and rather bad English" at his disposal and confessed:

> I have not the slightest idea of what the words "little theatre" and "little theatre movement" mean. I don't know and I don't care for any "little" or "big" theatre. I do care and I presume it will not be taken for boldness on my part to say that I care for only one sort of theatre: for a good theatre.[4]

And good theatre, he argued, could come about only if the leaders of the independent movement spent less energy erecting expensive new theatre buildings and instead worked to establish centers across the country that would provide sound actor-training and a home for the young actor's growth and development.

> It cannot be called a natural condition when the professional actor has not a chance, has not a proper place to build his creations. But it is still worse that the young professionals in America have no place for development, growth and training: thousands of places for perfect things—no places at all to make mistakes, and only by mistakes the right things are created.[5]

Experimentation with theatrical forms, he felt, should follow two basic lines. On the one hand, he sought "to create new forms which will influence the world."⁶ On the other hand, he hoped to revitalize old forms, grown stale and meaningless from repetition: "There is only one path in art,—the path of search and experience,—personal experience, the experience of one's own sufferings and trials and not that derived from 'superiors.' " In a theatre laboratory "the art of the theatre is eternally reforged. Everything that was good in the old is passed on from one generation to another, not as dead and decayed but as renewed and revivified."⁷

In calling for new "forms," Boleslavsky was not speaking of externally imposed settings, costumes, varieties of lighting, or even novel play structure. In his lexicon, form is an organic, "living" entity which must grow naturally out of the actor's creative interpretation of the life of the play. Form is the external expression of a play's inner meaning, as conceived by the playwright, interpreted by the director, and lived by the actors.⁸ Thus, in calling for the revitalization of established forms and the creation of new ones, Boleslavsky meant forms-of-acting. From these acting forms (given a collective theatrical effort), new and varied forms of scenic expression created especially for each play would result.

Boleslavsky's first priority, consistent with his experience at the First Studio, was to create a laboratory dedicated to training actors in the creative methods of their art. Working collaboratively with such trained actors, he could then conduct experiments in scenic form which, if successful, would advance the development and resuscitation of theatre in America. Boleslavsky did not imagine that he could single-handedly effect such sweeping change. He looked forward to

> a time when every large city will have its own similar organization, dedicated to a dual ideal. First, that the young actor may become a perfect craftsman in the theatre before battering his head against Broadway, the laboratory serving as a post-graduate school for little theatre groups nearby; and secondly, that the results of all these experiments may be available to every group in the theatre, whether professional, semi-professional or amateur.⁹

By the end of June 1923, the theatre envisioned by Boleslavsky had a name, The Laboratory Theatre (or simply, "The Lab," as its members came to call it), and existed as a legal entity. (The name was legally changed to The American Laboratory Theatre, Inc., on 27 March 1925.) In Miriam Stockton, the fledgling enterprise had an enthusiastic, almost fanatic booster and tireless fund raiser. It had a board of directors and, in Boleslavsky, an artistic director, but no real assets. Beyond that, The

Laboratory Theatre was little more than an ambitious plan. In the beginning, the Lab would operate only as a theatre studio and its members would be students. Boleslavsky would train them for two or three years, at which time the most gifted would be selected to become actors in a repertory theatre, which would be opened for regular public performances.

The next steps necessary to put this plan into operation were to publicize the embryonic theatre's aims, to raise money for its costs, and to recruit both staff and students. The first phase of the publicity campaign was an article titled "The Laboratory Theatre." Written by Boleslavsky and published in *Theatre Arts Magazine* (July 1923), the article outlined the new organization's goals. A laboratory of the theatre, Boleslavsky wrote, should embrace "all the workers who take part in a performance: playwrights, directors, actors, designers, musicians, sculptors, architects, costumers, dancers, singers, property men, electricians, carpenters, decorators, tailors, and stage hands." Each of these workers must be "brought up according to the rules and to the laws of collective creation," and be guided by the central rule he had learned from Stanislavsky: "Do not love yourself in your art but love the art in yourself." The laboratory must be ruled by a small board of elected directors, Boleslavsky explained, but the "real master" of the laboratory is the actor, and the elected directors must serve his interests. They must guarantee that "he will be part of the group the entire year and need not worry about his bread and butter." With this assurance the actor "can consecrate his time to education and the perfection of his art; he can be taught singing, dancing, fencing; he can read and can hear lectures." His only responsibility should be to serve his art:

> The actor in such a theatre must never play two parts identically. Because it is "our theatre" he must play Hamlet today, and to-morrow [*sic*] appear as a beggar in a mob scene. And both of those parts must be for him equally objects of creation and to both of them he must give all his force and all his talents.

Mindful that the ultimate success or failure of such a group depended largely on the shared idealism and dedication of each of its members, he wrote in terms reminiscent of the First Studio's monastic zeal:

> The creation of such laboratories of the theatre requires the consecration of its members to the work of the theatre with its disappointments and blunders, its truths and revelations. In such laboratories there is no place for people who wish to make a quick fortune. The groups must be very small. Some of the performances should not even be open to the public. During the first five or six years each laboratory would barely be able to maintain the fifteen or twenty people working in it. But any such laboratory could push forward the theatrical art of the country twenty years. It could

become finally a successful repertory theatre, ready in turn to cede its place to new laboratories, young, fresh, and as enthusiastically searching for newer forms.[10]

Leaving Miriam Stockton and the trustees to deal with the problem of raising the funds necessary to begin the Laboratory's operation, Boleslavsky concentrated on finding prospective students. He had earlier lectured at the Neighborhood Playhouse. Now he approached Alice Lewisohn Crowley, a founder of the group, with a plan to present two one-act plays at the Neighborhood, which had produced no plays the year before. With Crowley's approval, Boleslavsky and Alexander Koiransky, the Moscow theatre critic, retired to Pleasantville, New York, where they spent the summer with sixteen of the Playhouse's actors. Boleslavsky trained the players in the methods of the Moscow Art Theatre, and Koiransky, who was also an artist, taught costume and scene design. They also rehearsed Shaw's *The Shewing-Up of Blanco Posnet* and Yeat's *The Player Queen*.[11]

The two plays opened at the Playhouse's Grand Street Theatre on 16 October 1923. The critics generally praised the Shaw play and all but unanimously found the Yeats play tedious and pretentious. A critic from the *Sun* wrote:

> Richard Boleslavsky is auspiciously introduced to New York theatregoers through the medium of these two plays, which he directed with commendable attention both to the important dramatic moments and the minor matters sometimes lamentably slighted. In both plays the action and speech move together like a dancer and her music, harmoniously and gracefully. From the point of view of production we could find nothing but pleasure in these two fantasies. . . . [12]

Most of the reviewers had similar praise for what Boleslavsky and his young company had achieved in the way of ensemble, colorful group scenes, and sincere acting. Alice Crowley, however, reports that audiences were less enthusiastic and that she personally had come to have grave doubts about the wisdom of using "Russian" methods with young American actors.[13] In any event, as Lab historian Ronald A. Willis has pointed out, Boleslavsky's attempt to assemble a sizeable corps of theatre workers at a single stroke did not bear fruit, for very few of the members of the Pleasantville company were ever associated with the American Laboratory Theatre.[14]

Immediately after opening the one-acts at the Neighborhood Playhouse, Boleslavsky went out of town to direct his first professional New York production with an American cast. The play was Melchoir Lengyel's "heroic comedy," *Sancho Panza*. Produced by Russell Janney,

adapted from the Hungarian original by Sidney Howard, and starring
Otis Skinner in the title role, it opened on November 26 at the Hudson
Theatre to quite favorable notices. After the New York run, Skinner
played it on the road about two years.

Boleslavsky's involvement in a Broadway production at a time
when he was no doubt needed to help organize the Laboratory may have
been justified—or rationalized—as a necessary part of the Lab's publicity campaign. Publicizing its director was a way of publicizing the Lab.
During the next several years, Boleslavsky continued to divide his energies between the Lab and Broadway, and in time this would become a
point of contention between him and Miriam Stockton.

Stockton, in the meantime, had acquired a small apartment located
at 40 East 60th Street, which would serve as the Laboratory Theatre's
first home. It was paid for with money that was largely a personal
donation from the Stocktons and Isabel Levy, one of the Lab's trustees.
They had also hired John Martin (from 1927 until 1962 the dance critic
for *The New York Times*) as Executive Secretary of the Laboratory
Theatre. Miriam Stockton considered the Lab to be officially open on
October 1, but by her description, it was hardly functioning:

> Location—second floor apartment, front parlor and back-room, south side, middle
> [of the] block, between Park & Madison on East 60th St., for which we paid, I think,
> about $125.00 a month. Equipment [in the apartment] consisting October 1st . . . of
> telephone, two chairs, one desk, a secretary . . . no teachers, Mr. Boleslavsky him-
> self absent quite indefinitely with the production of Sancha Panza [sic] in Chicago
> with Otis Skinner, no publicity, except reprint from Boleslavsky's original article in
> "Theatre Arts Magazine," no advertising and only $500.00; pupils enrolled—none;
> definite ideas of what Mr. Boleslavsky wanted—none; instructions for [sic] Mr.
> Boleslavsky—none, except he would come as soon as he could get free. October,
> occasional inquires from occasional individuals, all ages and types, who would hap-
> pen to hear of it, to which we could give no very definite answers. . . . The names
> were taken of several inquirers. About October 15th, Mr. Boleslavsky blew in with
> huge carpet bag and said, "Laboratory Theatre operates." Enquirers were assem-
> bled. Dalcroze, diction, dancing, drawing teachers all sprang up, some voluntary and
> some paid; a table and chairs were bought, lecturers appeared, and a few pupils, all
> of the kind who wished to pay nothing. Everything began to happen in every direc-
> tion, including the beginning of eternal nightmares for Mrs. Levy and myself to sell
> shares and raise money. . . . [15]

The "enquirers" who were taken into the Laboratory Theatre were
not admitted so casually as these remarks might imply. Each was required
to audition for Boleslavsky by performing a prepared piece followed by an
improvisation he suggested. Those who satisfied him that they were serious and had promise were admitted on a six-week trial basis.[16]

In January 1924, the Laboratory Theatre was forced to find a new home. A particularly enthusiastic class in Dalcroze Eurhythmics had jarred loose the plaster from the ceiling of the restaurant on the first floor, below the Lab's quarters. It fell, hitting a waitress in the head. The owners of the building summarily ordered the Lab to vacate the premises. Coming to the rescue, Isabel Levy provided a solution. Her husband had just purchased an abandoned mansion at the corner of 50th Street and Park Avenue. It was scheduled to be demolished that summer, but the Lab was permitted to occupy twelve rooms of the rambling structure until then.[17]

In the meantime, the Moscow Art Theatre had returned to New York, arriving on 9 November 1923. Boleslavsky may have acted with them as before, assuming many of his old roles, but his only documented appearance was in Turgenev's two-act comedy, *The Lady from the Provinces,* beginning on 27 February 1924. Ironically, he played the servant to Count Lyubin—the character acted by Stanislavsky. Probably Boleslavsky took this small role, which he could no doubt perform with relatively little rehearsal, as a sentimental farewell performance with the theatre that had nurtured him for so many years.

The former student had become the teacher of his own studio theatre, but if Stanislavsky took special notice of this enterprise or even visited the Lab during the Art Theatre's return engagement that fact has gone unrecorded. A few months later, on May 11, the Moscow Art Theatre left New York to return to the Soviet Union. No doubt Boleslavsky saw his former colleagues off. He would never again see his great teacher.

Not long after, Stanislavsky's autobiographical *My Life in Art* was published in English. Boleslavsky wrote a short review of the book for *Theatre Arts Magazine's* August issue. The tone of the review was oddly cool and dispassionate—particularly for the usually effusive Boleslavsky: "There is more importance in Stanislavsky's life in art than in the book which he has written about it. . . . " Boleslavsky was disappointed that Stanislavsky's book offered only general comments about acting, rather than specific and practical explanations of the system:

> If you try to find out what Stanislavsky thinks necessary in the theatre, in the art of acting, you will find only hints or generalizations such as those about the feeling of truth, and the actor's belief in his own actions, with which you can neither agree nor disagree. When for instance, he speaks without explanation of the "superconscious through the conscious" it sounds theoretical and may be easily confused with the old-fashioned formula—"be inspired and play."[18]

One positive outcome of the Art Theatre's return visit to New York was that Boleslavsky gained an invaluable ally for his work at the Laboratory. During the MAT's New York stay, Maria Ouspenskaya began teaching at the Lab, interrupting her classes there when the MAT went on to play other American cities, but picking them up again when the company came back to New York for its farewell performances. The Stocktons were enthusiastic about her work, and Boleslavsky wanted her to stay. In the end, the Art Theatre sailed without her, and Ouspenskaya joined the staff of the American Laboratory Theatre.

Born in Tula, Russia, on 16 July 1887, Ouspenskaya was the daughter of a lawyer, who died when she was twelve. Her education after high school was interrupted by work as a governess and tutor. She studied at the Adashev School with Sulerzhitsky before coming to the Moscow Art Theatre in 1909. A charter member of the First Studio, she had worked closely with Boleslavsky on a number of occasions. Of his work at the Studio, she once said, "I do not remember any other director who gave so much of comfort, freedom and who knew how to put the actors into the creative state."

A short, slender woman—often described as "tiny"—with a wizened face that had always made her appear years older than she actually was, she most often played character parts at the MAT and the First Studio. Her personal manner was very intense, and many of the Lab's students were frightened of her; more than once her harsh criticism—delivered in strongly accented, sometimes all but incomprehensible English—reduced them to tears. A few of the students openly despised her, but others were devoted to her—almost all agreed that she was a remarkably gifted and perceptive (if sometimes ruthless) teacher. She had not been long at the Lab before its students reached a silent consensus: Ouspenskaya was deeply, painfully—embarrassingly—in love with Boleslavsky. A few of the boys speculated that perhaps "Madame's" relationship with Boleslavsky sometimes went beyond the purely "spiritual." One of her personal habits was the occasion of furtive smirks and secret laughter among her students: Madame drank. While conducting class, she would often develop a cough or bad throat and call for her "medicine"—bathtub gin (this was the age of Prohibition), kept in a druggist's bottle. The medicine was dispensed by the tablespoon by her current assistant, who stood faithfully at her side, helping with English and tending to her other needs. One such assistant was Marion Crowne, later married to Francis Fergusson. He recalls that sometimes Ouspenskaya's cough was so bad—particularly if class was not going well—that Marion would have to administer repeated doses, sometimes finishing a whole bottle.

Natasha Boleslavsky frankly and openly disliked Ouspenskaya and thought she was vastly overrated as an actress. Still, she reluctantly agreed that Ouspenskaya should stay in the Boleslavsky's apartment until she could get settled and find a place of her own; Ouspenskaya stayed with them some two or three years. Finally, she set fire to her bed one night. She had been drinking and had fallen asleep smoking one of the tiny black cigars she favored. This was all the excuse Natasha needed to have her evicted. Later, after the Boleslavskys bought a farm, a small out-building was remodeled and Ouspenskaya lived there during the summers.[19]

Boleslavsky's farewell appearance with the Moscow Art Theatre was not the last time he ever played on the stage. His final recorded appearance as an actor was in Max Reinhardt's famous spectacle without words, *The Miracle*.

He was not hired by Reinhardt to act in *The Miracle*, however. At first, he worked on the production in quite a different capacity. A playbill for *The Miracle* listed Boleslavsky as "Special Stage Director from the First Studio of the Moscow Art Theatre," but a brief notice in *Theatre Arts* explained that Boleslavsky, whose "direction is expert in the handling of masses, and in the elaboration of detail," assisted Reinhardt "in training the crowds for the New York production of *The Miracle,* and worked alone in welding them into shape for its Cleveland production."[20] Natasha Boleslavsky remembers that he helped hire the American actors for the crowd scenes, coached them, and staged many of the crowd movements, while Reinhardt was busy supervising the overall production, including the transformation of the Century into a massive medieval cathedral by designer Norman Bel Geddes. Given Boleslavsky's efforts in preparing for the 15 January 1924 opening, it is difficult to apportion credit in such comments as Arthur Hornblow's:

> One sits speechless before the astonishing elaboration of detail, the tremendous energy involved, the marvelous handling of the seven hundred supernumeraries, the supreme technical skill, the painstaking, conscientious artistry of the master producer whose genius for creating dynamic scenes and weird mass effects alone made possible a show of such magnitude and beauty.[21]

Following its initial New York run, *The Miracle* went on the road and reopened on Broadway on August 18. By then, Boleslavsky was playing the double role of the Blind Peasant and the Emperor, acted earlier by Rudolph Schildkraut. Alexander Woollcott took a second look at Reinhardt's "wordless mystery" and observed: "It is much as it was.

And where it is not as it was, it is better." Taking note of the new performers in the company, Woollcott wrote: "Bolislawsky [*sic*] emerges from his classroom to give an heroic and finely wrought performance as the Emperor."[22] Another critic commented: "Mr. Bolislawsky has added greatly to the proportions of the ill-fated monarch. . . ."[23] So far as is presently known, this role marked Boleslavsky's last appearance as an actor.

Shirley White, a native of Canada, was accepted into the Laboratory Theatre in early January 1924. Her several letters to her sister provide a rare contemporary insider's view of life in the Lab during its first year of operation. She was greatly impressed that Rosamond Pinchot, who played the nun in *The Miracle,* had become a student at the Lab immediately after the play closed, and she was moved that Boleslavsky, "on account of his faith in his 'children' has just refused to go to Vienna to produce as co-director with Reinhardt."

The members of the Lab's staff and the other students were the "most interesting and enthusiastic workers" she had met in a long time, White continued, "simply the nicest kind of people imaginable, doing their work for the love of it." She writes that "Mr. Webster the architect" watched over work on a miniature stage-set for *Cricket on the Hearth* that was "all to scale and even the smallest item quite perfect." She found diction classes given by "Mr. Clew, an English actor" to be "awfully funny, but perfectly serious underneath." The Lab's physical training was rigorous and left her muscles tired and aching, but she found it "fascinating work: imaginative, creative, and interesting in the extreme." The Lab, she explains, is "emphatically not a school or a theatre as yet," but a studio. "The ten dollars a week they ask can't be called a tuition fee, since we have at least two hours a day of Mr. Boleslavsky," as well as classes in art from Koiransky; work in "tone and voice production" from "Miss Brundidge"; Elsa Findlay's Dalcroze Eurhythmics classes twice a week, and twice-weekly classes in ballet given by "Scott, a pupil of Fokine's." In addition to these regular classes, there were special lectures on the history of fashion. Outside speakers came as well. Playwright Luigi Pirandello spoke to the Lab students on Italian art, and designer Norman Bel Geddes lectured on stage architecture. Eugene Braun, Dhan Gopan Mukerji, Robert Edmond Jones, Rosalind Fuller, Herman Rosse, Roshanara, and Stark Young also talked on their specialities that first year. But Shirley White was most excited about the training she received from Boleslavsky and Ouspenskaya:

The new group had a wonderful hour alone with Boley the other day and he is perfectly justified in saying that whether this training is applied to the theatre or anything else, our lives will be immeasurably the richer because of it. Think of having your powers of concentration sharpened in all five senses, your imagination stimulated so that it is quite under your control and works like a flash, and all of you consciously controlled until it becomes a natural part of you—the control I mean. That's what they're trying to teach us by the process that has proved entirely successful with the Slavic people.

In a subsequent letter, Shirley White described the exercise work intended to develop such capabilities:

First they told me to see a sailboat. Supposedly, I was on the seashore. Then to see a gull swooping down catching fish. And then to look at the moon. You're supposed to be able to concentrate until you really see them with your mind's eye. And when you do you give the actual impression of seeing them to the people watching. It's really true. I've seen all the others doing different exercises, as they're called, and when they're done well you'd swear they were doing the actual thing.

Boleslavsky was dissatisfied with her work on this problem, White continues, and gave her something else to do: "He told me to walk into a room across to where my dog was lying sick on the floor." She imagined her own dog, back in Canada ("It made me awfully homesick."), felt the imagined animal's hot nose, and tried to coax it to take a little water—also imagined. This time Boleslavsky was pleased.

White was impressed with exercises involving the emotions:

What they claim is that you can't impose a characterization on a part, but that to play every emotion in a part you must have experienced that emotion in some form or another, or an approximation of it, or several different forms of it that can be compiled into one. They start you feeling back along the experiences you've had for the different emotions they arouse. And when you find a genuine one, you lock it up in your "Golden Box" as Boley calls it, and bring it out again and again until you are so familiar with it that you can recall it the instant it's needed. But you must never tell your experience to anyone or you've shared your emotion and lost full control of it. It seems awfully funny, but it's quite true, and it's simply amazing the way experiences that you've forgotten come flooding back when you try to remember them. It's all such a new approach to things that to me it's fascinating.

A few weeks later, Shirley White reported to her sister that the Lab was rehearsing three plays. She names *Twelfth Night* and *The Sea-Woman's Cloak* by Amelie Rives Troubetskoy. The other play was likely an adaptation of Dickens' *Cricket on the Hearth*. White also describes a very different kind of exercise:

"Stop" is rather fun, and I'll take a second to explain it. All the group gets in one corner of the room. The command "Hop" means to start running full speed to the opposite corner, followed almost at once by the command "Stop," which means in whatever position you happen to be in—one or both feet on the floor—tense your muscles and not flicker so much as an eyelid. It's marvellous exercise for control. Then comes the command "Fall." You relax and drop flat on the floor by the nearest route. In the middle of the falling comes another command, "Stop," and you hold your position. That's more difficult.

For all her enthusiasm, Shirley White recognized the difficulties Boleslavsky and his fledgling theatre would have to face:

Whether or not creative talents can be found and drawn out of Americans as it was in the . . . Russians is the unanswerable problem Boleslavsky has had the courage to face. . . . On the whole the theatre is comparatively unknown. There's no advertising. People are just beginning to be interested. Really, you feel the size of a minute when you hear the sacrifices people are making down there, students and teachers, for the sake of an ideal. Over half the students are self-supporting and work half the night after their classes are finished. Of course, Boleslavsky, with the Moscow Art Theatre as his background, embodies the ideal, and he is a truly big person and very wonderful to know and to listen to, universally adored by students and teachers.[24]

Even with a minimum of publicity, Boleslavsky's work was beginning to attract attention. In May 1924, Giles Edgerton wrote an article describing the Lab and the aims and ideals embraced by its leader, providing an outsider's view of the goings-on at the Lab. Observing Boleslavsky's class in "dramatic production" he saw a group perform a "sketchy little play" they had worked out entirely on their own from *Cricket on the Hearth*. It was presented in a way that would have "tested the stage presence of quite famous actors": "In a small room with seven or eight rows of chairs, in a space in front of the chairs about twelve feet deep by fifteen feet wide the play was enacted without stage setting or costume, practically without make-up." Edgerton describes the procedure:

At one side of the acting group sat Boleslavsky, crouching down on a little camp-stool apparently regarding the room as quite empty except for his actors, and concentrating upon their work with the intensity of a great surgeon over a serious operation. In turn he watched each face, each gesture, made copious notes, but he never stopped their performance, he never made any suggestions or criticisms while the play was going on.

After it was over, he talked to each in turn, criticized freely and mercilessly, praised rarely and finely, and with each criticism he gave a little dissertation on the beauty of fineness of the art that had been misrepresented. There was no criticism that did not rest on some vigorous philosophy of dramatic production. He never said, "I don't like this," or just "do this differently." His criticism in almost every instance was where he felt the young people were "just acting." His praise was almost invariably for a gesture born of an emotion. He has no interest in, no use for the presenting or expressing of anything that is not the direct result of the actor's feeling about his part. Unless the actor lives his part Boleslavsky does not feel the work worth doing.

As he told one young woman, "you should not *try* to blunder," "you do not seek to be awkward in this part," "you are an awkward, blundering maid-servant; you act like one because you *are* one, not because you are trying to think how such a girl would act." I felt in watching this group that they were aflame with the desire to accomplish something very fine. They were not afraid of mistakes, they were not afraid of criticism. The audience did not exist for them. . . . It seemed to me the most significant kind of dramatic instruction that I have ever seen.[25]

In April, Shirley White wrote her sister:

> I am in an awfully serious mood, and I want you to take this in fully. Out of thirty-four students at the Laboratory Studio, sixteen were selected by the Board of Trustees to be the founding members of the Laboratory Theatre. Blanche and I were two of the sixteen. On April 15, ten days from now, the school term ends. The sixteen will probably go to the country for intensely concentrated work for the summer, with the objective, production in the fall.[26]

The actors chosen for the acting company were not entirely happy with the conditions set for them by the trustees, however. In late June they wrote a letter addressed to Isabel Levy, responding to the trustees' requirements. They refused to pay the ten dollars a week the trustees had asked ("It is financially impossible for many of us."); they refused to sign a binding agreement until there arose "specific legal reasons for doing so, but we maintain that loyalty must be voluntary and cannot be pledged"; but they agreed that their "participation in all branches of production is understood and accepted as an ideal." Moreover, they proposed that the acting group elect a committee, subject to Boleslavsky's approval, that would have "entire charge of all affairs pertaining to school work," and have the right to "plan and organize production as a group"—again with Boleslavsky's approval. The actors, meeting with Boleslavsky (and with his tacit approval of their proposal), had come to believe that the "primary interests" of many of the trustees lay elsewhere and that only those people who were "in living contact with the work in all its phases" were in a position to decide questions affecting the Laboratory's operation.[27]

Isabel Levy died in an accident before she could respond to the actors' letter, but Edith Isaacs, editor of *Theatre Arts* (who had earlier declined to serve on the Lab's board and recommended Levy in her stead), wrote a firm response, questioning the wisdom of the actors' request.[28] The actors were not dissuaded, however. That summer, Boleslavsky and four of the Lab's teachers worked "without a day's vacation, financing themselves the while," to form a working company with the idea of creating a self-supporting repertory theatre through bringing one or more plays to production during the winter of 1924. As Herbert Stockton wrote, "this experiment in independent operation was premature," but at the same time it had become apparent that the experimenters had forged themselves into a "group-organism" that might soon form the core of a self-supporting theatre.[29]

The Stocktons—and most of the other Lab trustees, as well—had been away from New York during the time of the actors' rebellion. When Miriam Stockton returned from Europe at the end of August 1924, she was dismayed by what she described as "a sad situation of disintegration." The Lab's temporary Park Avenue home had by now been torn down. Helen Arthur had resigned as a trustee and Paul Kennaday, another trustee, "had been estranged by Mr. John Martin, the secretary, who would give him no answer to his inquiries as to the conduct of affairs." The theatre's capital had been invested by Martin in *The Sea-Woman's Cloak,* which Boleslavsky and the acting group had been rehearsing over the summer, and Martin held the rights: "He asserted that the trustees were amateurs and that he had instructed [the actors] that they should go on strike and refuse to work for the interests of capital as represented by ourselves and those who had given us money. . . . The whole organization was in a very unpleasant state."[30]

Mrs. Stanley McCormick, a friend of the Stocktons, came to the Lab's financial aid, donating $10,000 to be administered as Miriam Stockton saw fit. A portion of the money was used to rent an apartment on MacDougal Street, off Washington Square in Greenwich Village, despite the fact that Miriam Stockton found the place "extremely scrubby, dirty, uncomfortable, unheated and infested even with rats."[31] Coincidentally, this same apartment had been occupied the previous year by the Provincetown Theatre group, which was just beginning its New York operation.

Earlier, John Martin had told Shirley White emphatically: "I can assure you of one thing—that we'll stay on the East side away from the theatre. And the two places we'll *not* go are to Broadway and among the long-haired Villagers!"[32] Martin might still have disdained the bohemian Village, but evidently he had changed his mind about the desirability of a move to Broadway, for Miriam Stockton reports that by now the Lab's business manager "was negotiating on his own the sale of the immature little production of 'The Sea-Woman's Cloak' to a Broadway manager." Martin and a small faction of actors who supported him were dismissed.

Whatever the trustee's dissatisfaction, no changes were made in the Lab's major personnel: Boleslavsky and Ouspenskaya were issued new contracts.

In the fall of 1924 (whether in September or October is not clear), the Laboratory Theatre resumed work in its new quarters on MacDougal Street. Among the new students accepted that term was a twenty-four year old actor named Lee Strasberg. Together with Harold Clurman and Stella Adler, who would come to the Lab a little later, he would eventually play a major role in spreading ideas learned from Boleslavsky far beyond the boundaries of the Laboratory Theatre.

Strasberg had worked earlier with amateur theatrical groups, but had not become seriously interested in theatre until the previous year when he witnessed a number of performances by the Moscow Art Theatre. For him, these were a revelation of the theatre's potential. In the spring of 1923, he entered the Clair Tree Majors School of the Theatre. After a short time, however, he grew dissatisfied with the training:

> It was routine work—not necessarily bad, but not very invigorating or stimulating. We were looking for another place we could go to. It was a young man whose name I wish I knew—I'd like to thank him—who came one day and said, "I was down yesterday to a place that I think you ought to go to." He was the first one to tell me about the Laboratory Theatre.

Strasberg attended the Lab for only three or four months. Skeptical of the group's potential for sustained future success, he then applied for a job with the Theatre Guild and was appearing in a production there by January 1925. The Lab's intensive program nonetheless made a profound impression on him, Strasberg says. From Ouspenskaya he gained practical experience in the exercises; from Boleslavsky's lectures he acquired "theoretic insight."

> The work that was being done there was, of course, decisive to my own career and has affected everything that I have done, so that Boleslavsky actually represents for me a major post in the history of the American theater in terms of the way in which the ideas of Stanislavsky got into the American stage. Without him I don't know what would have happened.[33]

Natasha Boleslavsky recalls her husband's evaluation of Strasberg as a student: "Lee Strasberg might make a good teacher, but he will never be a good actor." The remark proved at least partly prophetic. The things Strasberg learned during his brief stay at the Lab formed the basis for his own unique understanding—or, as his critics would later insist, his misunderstanding—of Stanislavsky's doctrines. Strasberg's subsequent work at the Group Theatre in the 'thirties and at the Actors Studio in the 'forties would contribute greatly to the triumph in the 'fifties of "the method" as the standard for serious actors in the American theatre.

10

Introducing the System

Boleslavsky's 1923 Princess Theatre lectures were evidently transcribed and revised to serve as the basis for his orientation lectures at the American Laboratory Theatre in its first years. A manuscript of those lectures, though not complete, has survived and provides the basis for summarizing the ideas he presented at the Lab, ideas which inspired Strasberg and Shirley White and a great many of the five hundred other students who attended the Lab during the years of its existence.[1]

Boleslavsky considered art, theatre, and acting to be inherent aspects of human behavior. Art, he said, is "this peculiarity" in man which leads him "to embellish his life" in an effort to "beautify" it. This "eternal striving toward beauty is the seed of the divine in human nature."[2] Likewise, theatre is an urge, rather than than an institution: "That's why the word 'theatre' does not mean a building, with an audience, orchestra seats, a stage and a group of people putting make-up on their faces every night and reciting by heart lines composed by someone else. Not at all! It is a tendency—an innate longing of every living being. . . ."[3] Theatre, in his view, includes games, dancing, parades, pageants, circus-tent shows, and religious mystery plays, as well as the institutionalized theatre of stage, auditorium, and professional actors.[4] Boleslavsky also viewed acting as an inherent and natural part of ordinary life, extending even to lower animals; a cat, for example, pursues a piece of string, knowing full well the string is not a mouse, but "performing" an imaginary chase.[5] Man "acts" and creates "theatre" in real life as an expression of his yearning for perfection, a manifestation of his urge to achieve something more ideal than ordinary existence: "That's why there is a close kinship between the actor and the priest—two professions that used to be years ago but one. Both [have] for their subject—striving toward a better life."[6]

Boleslavsky elaborated the idea that acting is an inherent part of every person's ordinary behavior in an article written in 1927:

The fact that this art is not confined to the limits of the theatre complicates the subject still furthur. Acting is inextricably interwoven into our everyday life. Let anyone follow closely his actions as he goes about his daily tasks and try to separate those moments when he is acting a part from the times when he is really himself. He will soon realize that in the matter alone of those formal smiles of salutation, with which he greets many people he does not actually feel like meeting with a smile, there is a very considerable amount of histrionic material. It almost seems as if the art of acting were born with us.

This notion was a profoundly important aspect of Boleslavsky's thinking, as will be detailed a little later, but the immediate implications can be suggested here: The actor does not have to learn to act—he already knows how; he does it all the time, naturally, spontaneously, and convincingly. The process of acting on stage is not fundamentally different from that which he uses automatically in ordinary life. In a very real sense, then, the actor's training is nothing more than his learning to do consciously—in the unreal world of the stage—what he already knows how to do unconsciously in the real world outside the theatre.

The source of this acting-in-life instinct, Boleslavsky reasons, is idealism:

Even our good manners—which are pure theatre—do not, in the last analysis, come from governesses, tutors, books of etiquette or dancing masters. They come rather from that logical sense of perfection which resides in every normal human being and this longing for perfection may be said to be the true source of that acting power and theatricality which pervades our life. Sometimes this desire to idealize and to avoid things as they really are leads us to absurd lengths, as, for example, when we put ornaments on coffins and feathers and draperies on the hearses going to the cemetery.[7]

He concludes: "If the 'acting' of everyday life is the attempt to perfect reality, within the theatre you get the further attempt to perfect this first perfection."[8]

Central to Boleslavsky's thinking was the belief that all art springs from man's idealism, his urge to beautify life, but in using the term "beautify" with respect to art, Boleslavsky was not arguing for sugercoated trifles in the theatre: "The ideal of 'better life,' " he explained, "is harmony, the substance of our actual daily life—chaos."[9] A play like Gorky's *The Lower Depths,* for example, may depict ugliness, pain, and despair, but Gorky creates a more harmonious and more perfect picture of life in a flop-house; this "illusion" of reality is more perfect—and more perfectly miserable—than the thing itself as it exists in real life.

This "ordering" of the "chaos" of actual life (in which every detail serves the artist's essential artistic statement) is, in Boleslavsky's lexicon, a "beautiful illusion," regardless of the pain and ugliness of the subject. Thus, when Boleslavsky speaks of "perfect" or "better" life he is making a distinction between actualism and illusionism (or theatricality); such a distinction is partly a matter of artistic intent and partly a question of artistic methodology. He had no patience with dialectical or didactic theatre, though he believed the theatre to be "a marvellous teacher" when it deals with its proper subject—"the inner life of the spirit"—rather than propaganda;[10] nor did he approve of writers who follow their "library-imaginations" rather than "truth to life," for they are overly concerned with the "literary side of the play" and fashion artificial and contrived problems:

> As examples of such plays I could take some of the French "romanticists" and so-called "pseudo-classical" plays by Corneille, Racine and even Victor Hugo—plays with long tirades and pompous monologues,—plays abundant in words and showing not the "better life," but ostentatious, bombastic people brought by the author into artificial, pseudo-tragical or comical situations.[11]

Boleslavsky believed that every artist of the theatre—the actor, director, scenic designer, and musician no less than the playwright—must constantly return to actual life, or "nature" as he often called it, to discover or clarify the principles which govern their art: "The laws of nature are immutable and eternal. But nature in its divine opulance expresses them in many different ways." Paradoxically, while nature, or natural law, provides the key to discovering and understanding the laws of the theatre, Boleslavsky vigorously opposed any effort merely to reproduce actual life on stage; the idea of nature as the touchstone of theatrical art is perverted, too, by theatrical movements. In his view, the various "isms" were sheer nonsense:

> It isn't the name which is important. It is an idea which very few people seem to recognize in the theatre, but it is one of tremendous importance to every student in every art to understand before he tries to produce something. This idea or this formula is *useful—beautiful* [his emphasis.] If you put into the piece of art only that which is absolutely necessary for or what can be used for the purpose of action, you have your style. Now it can be expressed by any "ism," starting with *realism* and finishing with *constructivism* [his emphasis]. . . . Well, if it is economical, it will be successful. People will like it but there is no doubt that this is the most difficult achievement in art. To learn to be crisp, of very few means, of very few words and of a single idea at the time, is the big secret of every artist and it is much more difficult

than to drown the stage with the details, foxy lights, hundreds of people, shouting, etc.. . . .

Never mind what it is called, make it good and to the purpose. That is the point. And another thing is that every play is a different play and every play requires a creation on the stage just as much as it requires creation from the author. But we of the theatre are so stale and we like to do everything in just one way. As human beings, we like the way of least resistance. That's why so many people talk about natural acting and real things on the stage. What nonsense! Theatre is theatre and when we go to the theatre we want to see something that is perfected but not something that is reproduced. . . .

How beautiful the acting of Laurette Taylor in "The Furies" is and how subtle, unreal it is. It sounds and looks like a dream, like a vision, and when you look at her, you certainly do forget about all "isms" and that is the only aim.[12]

Ban "nature" from the stage, for the theatre is concerned with imaginary, as opposed to actual life; even so its creative work depends on an accurate perception of actual existance. Every artist of the theatre must return repeatedly to nature and seek to penetrate its laws and "truths": "Because in order to create something that is better one has to know to perfection . . . the actual thing."[13]

The "imaginary life" of the theatre is primarily concerned with "the human spirit in all its simple or complicated manifestations," and in Boleslavsky's view: "A worthwhile play is much more concerned with the inner life of the spirit than with the external happenings of our everyday existence." In his opinion, events are important only insofar as the actor or playwright uses them to reveal human desire or emotion. Indeed, human feeling, or "the desire to attain something," is the entire basis of drama, but it must be "performed" or "enacted" in terms of conflict:

The laws of nature teach us that our entire life is nothing else but a series of struggles for an ideal, for the better things of life.

The dog struggles for a bone. So does a man sometimes, especially if the bone has a piece of steak attached to it.

Yet mostly man struggles for his spiritual ideals.

Every living being, starting from a microbe, is in a constant struggle. As soon as the struggle stops life dies. . . . There can't be a play without a struggle of ideas, passions, feelings, and desires. In life such struggle is expressed by a series of will problems, dictated by our intellect and our spirit and carried out by our physiological apparatus.

I am ambitious—I struggle to satisfy my ambition. I am in love—I struggle to have my love returned. And so forth, down to the smallest problem.[14]

Boleslavsky's belief that drama at its most basic and elemental level is concerned primarily with human desire, which can be understood as a striving to attain some ideal and is translated into a series of conflicts (or "will problems") to be overcome by action, was to play an ever more important part in his thinking. Coupled with his belief that "acting" is an inherent part of actual life, this idea eventually led him to a significant redefinition of Stanislavsky's system.

Boleslavsky believed that the institutional theatre was born when a distinction was drawn between "acting" in life and the "acting out" of an imaginary story. Within the institutional theatre, he believed, four distinct schools of acting had developed, as typified by representative exponents. He quotes Fanny Kemble:

> The art of acting has neither fixed rules, specific principles, indispensable rudiments nor fundamental laws; it has no basis in positive science, as music, painting, sculpture and architecture have. . . .

Coquelin:

> I am convinced that one can only be a great actor on condition of complete self-mastery and ability to express feelings which are not experienced, which may never be experienced.

Talma:

> Acting, like every other art, has a mechanism. No painter, however great his imaginative power, can succeed in pure ignorance of the technicalities of his art; and no actor can make much progress till he has mastered a certain mechanism which is within the scope of patient intelligence.

and, finally, Quintilian:

> The great secret . . . for moving the passions is to be moved ourselves; for the imitation of grief, anger, indignation, will often be ridiculous if our words and countenance alone conform to the emotions, not our heart. . . . Wherefore, when we wish to attain verisimilitude in emotion, let us put ourselves in the place of those who really suffer; and let our speech proceed from the very state of mind which we wish to induce in the judge.[15]

Boleslavsky summarizes:

> I have chosen these contrasting opinions on the art of acting to bring out the four different schools which they represent. Miss Kemble represents the opinion that acting is nothing but inspiration, nothing but flashes of the mere appearance of spontaneity. I might term this the School of Inspiration. To Coquelin's followers,

acting is the "ability to express that which never did happen"—in other words the ability to falsify. This might be called the School of Counterfeiters. To Talma, acting is a mental process, the result of brain work, an exhibition of intelligence and mentality—a very honorable, but none too happy opinion, belonging to the School of the Scholars. Finally, we come to the definition of Quintilian, which begins "for moving the passions is to be moved ourselves." This we may call, with William Archer, "the school of the Emotionalists."[16]

For Boleslavsky, the choice was clear. Recognizing that there have been gifted actors representing each of these schools, he strongly prefers the School of the Emotionalists. He offers reasoned arguments against the methods of the Inspirationalists, the Counterfeiters, and the Scholars, but confronting the more general problem of theatrical effectiveness—the "classic debate between the Emotionalists and the Anti-Emotionalists"—he confesses:

I must admit that I find it more difficult to present any evidence other than my own feelings, based largely on my experience and observation of theatre audiences, to prove as conclusively that the School of Anti-Emotionalism is without meaning. A counterfeit sincerity no matter how cleverly contrived never moves an audience. Pathos which is not genuine never stirs the emotions.[17]

The crux of the Anti-Emotionalists' argument, as Boleslavsky analyzes it, lies in two statements of what is essentially a single premise. On the one hand the Anti-Emotionalists contend that if the actor is truly possessed by heroic emotions he must be incapable of rational acts during this time of emotional stress; conversely, they argue that if an actor demonstrates presence of mind during the time he is ostensibly carried away by a great emotion (by dealing logically with a problem that arises unexpectedly while he is onstage, for example), he cannot then in fact be experiencing the actual throes of the apparent emotion. The resolution of this seeming dilemma, Boleslavsky reasons, can be found implicitly in Joseph Jefferson's well-known statement:

"For my part, I like to have the heart warm and the head cool," which seems to come rather close to the crux of the problem. One might term the followers of this point of view the School of Emotion Makers or creators. It is only comparatively recently, however, that the new psychology and psycho-analysis have made such a thought practical.

Boleslavsky concludes the argument by pointing out that the objective of the Emotionalists is not, as some have concluded, the total and complete fusion of the actor with the role: "It is obvious that no actor, no matter how endowed, can enter absolutely into the character of, let us say,

Lady Macbeth, Othello, or Hamlet. If such a thing could be done, the unfortunate actor would be able to play the part but once and then would be a candidate for the mad-house."[18]

Boleslavsky wonders how the Anti-Emotionalist position ever came into being. The answer, he thinks, has been suggested by "our old friend Talma," who asks: "Is it because truth in all art is what is most difficult to find and seize?" Boleslavsky answers:

> Yes, truth is the most difficult thing in the world to find, but at the same time it is the only thing worth looking for. Like the other arts, the stage is not concerned with what might be called life-truths, but with artistic truth, which is something quite different. Truth in life is positive and materialistic. Life defines truth naturalistically. Truth is simply that which we know to be so. Art, on the other hand has its own laws.

A "stage truth" may override a "conventional truth," Boleslavsky continues, "only . . . when it is entrusted to the hands of a master, who knows how to interpret it. This master is the talented actor."[19] Like Stanislavsky, Boleslavsky believed strongly that the actor is the center of the theatre, its only essential component: the theatre can exist without a director, without a scenic designer, without a playwright—but without the actor, there is no theatre.[20]

Recognition of the actor as the theatre's only essential element, however, did not diminish the importance of the playwright, the designer, or the director in Boleslavsky's scheme of things. Indeed, in his view even stage hands, carpenters, and ushers were vitally important, because theatre by its very nature is a collaborative art, and the success of each artist and worker depends greatly on the work done by every other artist and worker. Recognizing this, Boleslavsky propounded three laws for "collective" creation: every theatre artist and worker, from the star to the lowliest stagehand, must submit to the "single will" of the director; every artist and worker must lend "the maximum of personal participation even in the smallest component part of the collective work"; and every collective creator must be able "to penetrate into the significance and nature of that particular collective work."[21]

Speaking at a time when the importance of the stage director and the role he plays in the theatre was just being recognized in America, Boleslavsky evidently anticipated objections to the "first law" for collective creation:

> One might think that in the theatre . . . the director should be submitted to the single will of the playwright. Yet it is not quite so. The one single will in a creative theatre

belongs to the stage director. The playwright is merely a component part of the production. If he is alive, the director has the right to submit him to his will as far as it concerns the general problem of the production. He may demand of him to make the necessary changes, cuts and alterations. In case the author is not alive, the director has the right, no matter how famous the author's name may be, and how great his classical reputation, to submit to his own will the playwright's literary masterpiece. . . . Only those productions which bear the expression of only one will—that of the stage director—will be complete and successful.

If even the playwright must be submitted to the creative will of the director, Boleslavsky continued, it is "useless to emphasize how completely this submission extends to the other members of the production."[22] The individual actor can depart from the director's conception no more than an individual musician playing in an orchestra can set a tempo for himself that is different from that indicated by the conductor.[23]

The director's fundamental job is to correctly interpret the "spirit and the problems of the author" and to infuse every member of the collective with both his "interpretation of the author's visions" and the "main problem of the play." If the director succeeds in this, "the Theatre has accomplished its task."[24] Lest the director's authority become artistic tyranny, however, Boleslavsky reminds us of his responsibility to the collective: "I once heard a director yelling at the extras: 'Hey— you back there, don't act. You're distracting the attention from the leading characters!' I felt like saying: 'Hey—you there in front, stage your play so that no one is in anybody else's way. Then everything will be O.K!' "[25]

Elaborating the second law of the collective, Boleslavsky explains: "The weakening of any component part weakens the entire body." It follows that: "Everyone in the collective creation, besides lending the maximum of his strength, must have a complete control of his forces and be a real master in his speciality." The artist lacking either skill or commitment to the common cause "has no right to be a member of a collective creation."[26]

The third and final rule of the collective is that every member must be able to "penetrate into the significance and nature of that particular collective work," and, when necessary, to sacrifice "his personal creation for the sake of the general success." Each must be willing to adapt his own talent to the talents of the group and to understand "which of his special qualifications is required for that particular moment."[27] This rule is more than a support for the collective spirit: "One of the most important problems of the actor is the so-called ability to catch the tone of his partner and the mood of the play, which is nothing else but the ability to adapt one's self to the common cause, to find in one's self the necessary color for this particular collective work.''[28]

An interesting corollary of Boleslavsky's understanding of the theatre "collective" was his conception of the role of the scenic designer (and the musical composer as well). Boleslavsky insists that the designer must attend every rehearsal and all meetings concerning a production: "He must be initiated in all the troubles, all the attempts and attainments connected with the work. As much as the artist assists the director and the actors in their work, they should inspire him and help him in all his searches and doubts." Only through such intimacy can there be harmony and unity of purpose:

> It is extremely important, for instance, to an actor playing a scene in his own [character's] home, to be surrounded by furniture and articles responding to his individuality. Do you think it possible to furnish in the same way the rooms of Shylock and of Othello only because it's Venice and more or less the same period? And do you think that the room of Othello as played by Salvini, quick and alert with a tiger-like personality, throwing around the furniture, could be set in the same way as the room of Othello-Mount-Sulley, classically calm and majestic in his tragedy of an outraged lion? . . . Only an artist who works hand in hand with the actors and the other members of the theatrical production, who subordinates his creative power to the requirements and needs of his theatrical colleagues, can be called a theatrical designer.[29]

Boleslavsky offered this as a corrective for the usual commercial practice of the time, in which the designer worked more or less in isolation and delivered his finished scenery to the stage just before opening night. How can an actor perform, Boleslavsky demanded, without knowing what is behind his back? How can he play successfully a scene on a bridge or stairway, rehearsed for weeks "between four old chairs" when "for the first time he has to walk upon a shaky and badly adjusted construction? . . . No one could feel at ease wearing for the first time a new pair of shoes! Yet they want the poor actor to feel at home and to be in a creative mood in perfectly strange and unfamiliar surroundings." And the actor who, at the last moment, is given make-up and costume which contradict his conception of the role "must have the same sensation as a traffic policeman, standing at noon on a busy corner, all dressed up in ballet skirts."[30]

The musical composer, like the designer, must also be an integral part of the collective. Boleslavsky believed that music is the most complicated, abstract, and independent of the arts, and that its great power must be "subordinated to the general problem" of a dramatic production, where it "occupies only a secondary place and is nothing but one of the colors of the whole production, if not merely a background." Accordingly, he believed it is "a great mistake to include in a dramatic production any previously written musical composition which is not specially composed for that particular production," for such music is composed according to musical rather than theatrical laws. The creative theatrical composer, Boleslavsky argues, will experiment with musical effects and discover "music produced not by musical instruments but by means of different sound-devices, depicting various manifestations of life":

> If we . . . listen carefully to the life that surrounds us and . . . lend our spiritual ear to all the sounds produced by life, we shall discover an unexpected amount of them and . . . come to the realization that there are no set instruments to reproduce them. Think of the city noise, the noise coming from a factory, the clamor of an excited crowd. All these sounds in nature are waiting for their Stradivarius and . . . Paganini, but they will be discovered only by the theatre and for the theatre. The theatre of the future, no matter how funny this may seem to a professional musician, will be filled with new instruments and new sound-combinations. It may even create a gamut and a new rhythm—not that of the metronome, but the rhythm of human feelings, heart and soul.[31]

The ultimate aim of such "collective" effort is to meet what Boleslavsky considered the serious moral obligation of the theatre to satisfy the audience's "craving for spiritual food." In his view, the audience is a "gathering of friendly and, as a rule, well disposed people" possessed of a "peculiar childlike quality of trust." A man who would never think of buying a pair of shoes without first trying them on will buy a ticket for "an unknown play almost blindfolded, with complete confidence that his favorite author, actor or producer will not disappoint him." Predisposed to believe in everything that transpires on the stage, the audience "good-naturedly" overlooks hundreds of absurdities, such as: "Moonbeams chasing the leading character all over the stage" or "Lovers shouting tender declarations loudly enough to make all the neighbors come running"; or "Brandished wine cups remaining filled to the brims contrary to all natural laws." All this is willingly overlooked by the public, Boleslavsky said, "if there is only the tiniest bit of truth about the performance. . . . " And when the actor fulfills his obligation to the audience, a "peculiar relationship" of spiritual communion is created:

> The better . . . the actor incarnates his part and "lives it," the more responsive grows the audience and vice-versa,—the more intense and enthusiastic is the public, the more inspired becomes the actor in his performance. A mysterious invisible bond

is created linking the audience with the stage, and as a result we get a truly inspired and creative performance.[32]

Boleslavsky offers a description of such a creative performance that serves to synthesize much of his theoretic understanding:

The theatrical performance is a *collective creation* in *visible, audible* and *rhythmic* images of some *real* manifestations of *imaginary life, places* and *emotions* of the human soul.

. . . It is a *collective* creation because it is the combined work of actors, artists, musicians and other theatrical workers, all of them submitted to the single will of the director.

It's a *visible* image because it is through the medium of our eye that we receive the impression of sets, costumes, make-ups of the actors, etc. It's an *audible* image because our ear receives the impression of all the lines delivered by the actors, as well as the musical tunes played on the stage. It is a *rhythmic* image because the above proceedings are confined to a certain lapse of time, during which the tempo of the action changes from slow to rapid according to the pulsation of the artist-creators, or the musical requirements of the piece.

Through *real* manifestations, because people on the stage use their eyes in order to see, their throat and tongue to talk and their legs and arms to move; the scenery is painted on canvas or cardboard with brushes and paints mixed according to the artist's actual will. In other words, everything that occurs on the stage is *real*.

An *imaginary life* because every artist in his desire to create a bit of "better life" uses his *imagination* to improve reality. Shakespeare's Venice is much better than the real one, and all the drunkards in the world could not beat the "ideal" drunkard Falstaff.

An *imaginary place* because the artist painting the set of a battlefield does not travel to Waterloo to get the actual scene of this place but uses an *imaginary* and more impressive landscape.

Imaginary people because none of the historical characters created by the *imagination* of poets, playwrights and actors has anything to do with their original prototypes. Caesar, Anthony, Cleopatra, as imagined by Shakespeare are certainly different from those who actually existed.

Clear feelings, because only a clear and plain human feeling can be accepted and understood by an audience. As a chord of an instrument would respond only to a pure tone of an identical tuning, so would a human soul respond only to a clear and kindred feeling.

Precise feelings, because every art is knowledge, and knowledge does not accept any haziness or inexactness. A fanciful idea can be accepted only if it has a precise foundation. . . . An artist may design a fantastically long arm, but it must be still an arm with a hand, on which one could lean.

Natural feelings, because the human mind can never invent such variety and abundance of feelings as supplied by nature. The musicians of the whole world will never be able to use all the combinations that they could bring out from the eight fundamental tones known in music. The same holds true regarding the few fundamental human feelings; the greatest genius in the world would not be able to *invent* a new one,—all he can do is to make combinations of those suggested to him by nature.

> *Emotions of the human soul* because the theatre is the art of investing the spiritual emotions of man in a visible form. If a man does not know how to enjoy himself he cannot impersonate joy on the stage, just as an artist . . . cannot design an arm if he has not seen a real one. If, on the other hand, an actor tries to represent joy without actually having experienced it, but just imitating its outer expressions, he would not be an actor but merely a parrot or a photographer.[33]

The actor is distinguished from all other artists by the fact that he is both "artist-creator" and the "material" from which his artistic conception is embodied, combining in a single personality the perception of the artist and the technical skill of the craftsman. The actor must be an artist if he is to conceive his creative task, but a brilliant conception is of little use if he lacks the physical gifts and disciplines needed to embody it; likewise, superlative physical technique is merely decorative and devoid of spiritual content unless it is a formal expression of a truly artistic vision.[34]

Boleslavsky specified eighteen qualities that are important for the actor: "talent; an apt mind; education; knowledge of life; observation; sensitiveness; artistic taste; temperament; voice; good enunciation; expressive face and gestures; well-built body; dexterity; plastique of movements; tenacity in work; imagination; self-control; and good health." Only one is essential: "The first is talent, if one has that, the other seventeen do not matter." Without talent, the actor will never rise to the "class of artist-creators, but always remain among the so-called 'utilities' of the theatre."[35] This is not hyperbole; in Boleslavsky's view, talent is the most crucial, the most elusive, and the least accessible aspect of the actor's nature. All the other qualities may be cultivated, nurtured, or acquired, but Boleslavsky was emphatic: "Art cannot be taught. To possess an art means to possess talent. That is something one has or has not. You can develop it by hard work, but to create a talent is impossible."[36] In another place, he reiterates: "The actor's art can not be taught. He must be born with ability but the technique, through which his talent can find expression—that can and must be taught."[37]

The technique Boleslavsky endorsed was, of course, that first propounded by Stanislavsky as developed at the First Studio, according to which the actor must develop both his "outer" means—the control of his voice, body, and nerves—and his "inner" means—the intellect, the will, and the emotions. Boleslavsky explained the relationship of "outer" means and "inner" means through analogy:

> What is generally referred to as the technique of acting, limited as it usually is to a certain development of the actor's physical resources, is not really technique in the

strict sense of the term. I would call it rather a tuning up of the instrument, just as one might tune up a violin before starting to play. But even the most perfectly tuned violin will not play by itself, without the musician to make it sing. The equipment of the ideal actor, even although he is perfectly tuned up is not complete unless he has what I have already called, for want of a better name, the technique of an "emotion-maker" or creator. . . . [38]

Without "inner" technique the actor is "mechanical" and simply "imitates human emotions without feeling them"; it is "inner" technique that enables the actor to "live his part," making him "sensitive and responsive to his surroundings," enabling him to find "life's truth in all circumstances and situations." Each time he repeats a role he experiences "live, fresh feelings that are each time created anew, but never repeated as something external, learned by heart." He sometimes expresses his emotions "in an entirely different manner, merely following the fundamental lines of his main problem, but without adhering to the once set stage mechanics."

A creative actor lends his ear exclusively to his soul, and does not try to invent new feelings, but merely invests his own in different forms prompted by his imagination. He is never concerned with the external effect of his part but merely in the inner, spiritual side of it. According to Stanislavsky's expression,—"He does not love himself in art, but loves art in himself." He controls his art always and everywhere. He does not look for any artificial excitement furnished by the footlights, the public, the applause, the costume, the sets, a girl friend in a box and so forth—the only thing he needs is to have in front of him a definite problem. [39]

Boleslavsky began his explanation of the actor's inner technique by stressing the importance of "concentration," which was also the topic of his first lesson on acting, published in 1923. He defined concentration as "the quality which permits us to direct all our spiritual and intellectual forces towards one definite object and to continue as long as it pleases us to do so. . . ."[40] The primary object of the actor's concentration should be the "life of the human spirit," or the "life of the inner feelings," his own "soul" and those of the men and women around him.[41] Because the actor's concentration is often partially or totally blocked by muscular or mental tension, he must develop the ability to relax at will all such unnecessary tension; "relaxation" can be mastered through the regular use of certain exercises. Boleslavsky recommended exercises specifically for the relaxation of the muscles, and others intended to ease mental tension. The exercises he suggests to solve "spiritual problems" included work involving such Stanislavskian principles as: sense memory, images, affective memory, imagination, communion, and irradiation (or the ability to transmit moods or even thoughts to a partner by purely mental means, without recourse to speech or gesture.) More generally, Boleslavsky suggested that the actor may solve the "spiritual problems" that create such tension by developing a "boundless faith in his vocation" and through "close communion with the geniuses of humanity who suffered for the triumph of their ideals"; by placing the source of such petty emotions as ambition, egoism, materialism, and irrational anger into perspective and remembering that "most of the things in life are of no consequence"; and finally by developing his "affective memory," through which he can make his spirit "sensitive and flexible."[42]

Affective memory is a phenomenon first described by the French psychologist, Théodule Ribot.[43] Boleslavsky defined it as "the ability of the human organism to retain imperceptibly . . . different psychological shocks and emotions and to live them all over again in case of an identical repetition of the outer physical occurrences of the original event."[44] Boleslavsky considered the subconscious mind a repository of latent emotions and sometimes called it the "Golden casket of feelings." These dormant emotions, he explained, can be stirred by various means; one has only to find the right key: "Sometimes the mere recollection of a feeling enables the actor to live it all over again. . . . But sometimes the mere recollection [is] not sufficient and the actor has to arouse his affective memory by purely physical means." A physical object—such as a letter, a flower, or a dagger, for example—may rouse particular emotions for the actor. In other instances, physical actions—such as a slamming door, a slap, or pouring a glass of wine—may trigger the actor's emotional response. In still other instances, the actor may have to rely on the imaginative recreation of such objects or actions to stir the required emotion.[45]

In this first presentation of the system, Boleslavsky offered memory of emotion as the prime requisite of the actor's work, the starting point of developing a role:

> After having decided what is the feeling necessary for a certain part of his role, the actor tries to find in his affective memory [*sic*] a recollection similar to that particular feeling. He may use all kinds of means in order to bring that feeling to life, starting with the actual lines of the author and finishing with experiments from his own life, recollections from books and finally using his own imagination. Then by a series of gradual exercises and rehearsals he brings himself into a state, enabling him to arouse in the strongest degree the necessary feelings by a mere thought of it and to retain it for the necessary period of time.[46]

This "finding and developing the necessary feelings" is part of the actor's "home-work," a "preparation of the pallette" for his role: "He must not think during this work *how* he is going to reproduce a certain feeling,—his only concern should be to *find it, to sense it with his entire being, to get used to it and to let nature itself find forms for its expression"* [his emphasis].

Having prepared the necessary feelings outside of rehearsals, the actor is ready for the next period of his work and "starts to apply" the emotions "to the lines supplied by the author"; "he never touches the words without being aroused and moved by feelings." The emotions inspire him to "invest them with new forms, prompted not by the rules of elocution but by the great creative mind of the author in complete union with his own creative spirit."[47]

The actor may have difficulty finding the correct emotions from his own experience. ("How do I know what Salome felt holding the head of John the Baptist—I never had a servered head in my hands—") "In such cases," Boleslavsky advised, "one has to use very extensively the 'similar' affective memories and the imagination."

> Here is an example of a complicated feeling which you may find through a series of simple feelings. You have never seen a ghost,—consequently you do not understand how to "live your part" in feeling the reverential fear of Hamlet meeting the ghost of his father.
>
> But have you never experienced a feeling of uneasiness from unknown reasons? Were you never startled at night by a sound from the next room? Don't you remember the feeling you had entering a room where [there] was the corpse of a dead person? Did you never walk at night through a deserted place peering intently through the darkness, being on the look out, listening to the slightest noise in front or in back of you? Were you never startled by the sudden appearance of a person you did not expect to see?[48]

With this example, the surviving text of Boleslavsky's 1923 lectures abruptly ends.

Boleslavsky's emphasis on affective memory as the great secret of the actor's emotional life on stage was compatible with Stanislavsky's early formulations of the system and the ways in which it was applied at the First Studio. Boleslavsky almost certainly discussed at the Laboratory Theatre other elements of the system in talks that have been lost to us. In an article published in 1923, he suggests the importance of another aspect of the system, "dramatic action:"

> Although, in Stanislavsky's technique, much emphasis is placed upon the inner spirit, the emotions, and the soul, he would be the last man to infer that the theatre should be made a laboratory for the exclusive study of inspection [*sic*, introspection]. It is dramatic action that makes the theatre live; his only qualification being that

action, to be real, must be the product of real emotions, otherwise it is merely—acting.[49]

During the course of his work at the Laboratory Theatre over the next few years, "action" would play an increasingly important role in his thinking, culminating in a major shift in emphasis in his teaching.

11

The Lab Opens

In the summer of 1923, shortly after christening the infant Laboratory Theatre, Boleslavsky wrote, but never published an article elaborating the Lab's goals and setting forth its organizational structure. There he wrote: "The Director of the Laboratory Theatre, responsible for its artistic policy, during the first three years will be Richard Boleslavsky; thereafter the director will be elected by the members."[1] Whether he was ever formally "elected" by the members is not clear, but he was to remain the guiding force and principal director of the Lab for all but its last season. Under his leadership the Lab developed a program of actor training unlike any in America up to that time.

In the wake of the troubles between actors and trustees over the summer of 1924, the Lab was eventually reorganized (formally on 29 December 1924) along lines that gave the actors a role in running the theatre. The "Actor-group" was recognized as "the nucleus" of the Lab's "artistic and human structure" and given a voice in making the decisions that would shape their future by serving on various committees, each of which was responsible for a particular phase of the Lab's operation. To avoid the complications and expense of obtaining a theatre license, the Lab was legally designated a "club," a route the Provincetown theatre group had also taken. Randall Burrell, whom Stockton described as "a very charming Harvard boy, who came from Professor Baker," was hired to replace John Martin as business manager. The duties of that position were divided and Elizabeth Bigalow was named executive secretary. Her primary responsibilities would be to administer the Laboratory's school. During the course of the Lab's second year (1924–25), a clearer distinction began to be drawn between the operation of the school and the theatre; actors who enrolled in the school might or might not be considered for membership in the acting company. The school proved to be financially profitable, and there was increasing pressure to admit larger and larger numbers into its ranks. Members of the Lab's acting company, however, were still expected to continue with classes and were exempted from study only when they were needed for rehearsals.

The course of actor training instituted at the American Laboratory Theatre conformed to the pattern Boleslavsky first described in his lectures at the Princess Theatre and later elaborated in *Acting: The First Six Lessons*. For the entirety of its existence, though specific courses and class titles changed from time to time, the Lab offered courses designed to educate and discipline the actor's body, his voice, his intellect, and his "spirit"—or what Boleslavsky called his "outer means of expression," his "inner means of expression," and his cultural awareness.

Courses intended to educate the actor's body included ballet, plastique and mimeodrama, Dalcroze eurhythmics, body rhythm, and fencing. These were taught at various times by La Sylphe, Mikhail Mordkin, Madame Elizaveta Anderson-Ivantzoff, Elsa Findley, Bird S. Larson, Emily Hewlitt, and James Murray. Not all of these teachers were specifically connected with the dramatic stage, but each was a recognized specialist in his own professional field.

Classes for the development and training of the actor's voice included diction, a course called "The Spoken Word," phonetics, and voice production (singing), taught at various times by "Mr. Clew," Margaret Prendergast McLean, Windsor P. Daggett, and Margarete Dessoff. In a later season (1927–28), a special speech course was introduced specifically for members of the acting company and was taught by Professor James Tilly of Columbia University.

In the beginning, the Lab sought to improve the students' intellectual and cultural awareness through special guest lectures. Two visionary scenic designers, Robert Edmond Jones and Norman Bel-Geddes, were regular speakers. Stark Young, the critic and playwright, lectured so frequently that his talks constituted a regular course. Other guest speakers included Helen Arthur, Brian Hooker, Douglas Moore, and Jacques Copeau, the famous French director. On one occasion, George Pierce Baker delivered an informal talk.

Regular courses of an intellectual nature were instituted in 1926–27. John Mason Brown taught theatre history. First Douglas Moore and then Martha Alter taught appreciation of music. Art appreciation—later called "Style and Period"—was taught initially by Alexander Koiransky, then by staff members of the Metropolitan Museum of Art, Huger Elliot and A. Hyatt Mayor. Elizabeth Ward Perkins offered a course called "Observation Through Drawing." A general honors course, which featured readings in intellectual history, was conducted first by Mortimer Adler of Columbia University and later by Clifton Fadiman.[2]

The most distinctive training offered by the American Laboratory Theatre was, of course, that given by Boleslavsky and Maria Ouspenskaya. As Willis remarks: "Boleslavski and Ouspenskaya took personal charge of work on the actor's inner means of expression, and it is this work which formed the core of the Lab's unique training and provides its chief historical significance."[3] In the beginning, apparently, they both taught techniques of acting, but their duties and responsibilities were very soon made separate and more clearly defined. Ouspenskaya was responsible for teaching the basic techniques of acting. Boleslavsky divided his time between teaching and directing. His pedagogical efforts were concentrated in a series of lectures, informal talks, and demonstrations given on a more or less regular basis before the entire assembly of the Lab's students and actors. These talks and demonstrations constituted an on-going course described in the Lab's brochures as "The Art of the Theatre." Boleslavsky was seldom mindful of the time he spent lecturing and talking; often he would spend the whole day and a large part of the night with his students. At other times, when he was busy with an outside production, the Lab members would scarcely see him for a week or two at a stretch.

By all accounts, Ouspenskaya and Boleslavsky formed a potent combination and the work of each complemented that of the other. Lee Strasberg recalls from his study at the Lab:

> Ouspenskaya was a marvellous actress . . . and a wonderful teacher, very precise and very concrete—not theoretic. She gave the actual exercises—simply, clearly, and precisely. And of course, she was a marvellous observer. She could tell who was faking and who was real and was, therefore, very excellent from that point of view.[4]

Donald Keyes provides a somewhat more detailed account of the conduct of her classes:

> To be in one of Madame's classes could be an agonizing emotional experience. Seated in a large circle with Madame a little apart from the group, you were told in rather sharp, staccato tones, "Make for me friendly atmosphere." When this was done—usually in silence—the exercises began. Starting with very simple problems, like concentrating on the construction of one's hand, the exercises grew more complicated until they became little improvised scenes involving partners. Sometimes Madame would outline the steps of the brief story, sometimes the students in a small group or with a single partner would invent. Seldom did Madame praise any attempt.[5]

Despite her diminutive figure, Ouspenskaya could be, and often was, a rigorous, effective, and awesome teacher. Francis Fergusson, who was personally quite fond of her, recalls:

She terrified them in class. She would walk in. (She was very short, you know, very slender—she must have weighed about 95 pounds.) She walked in on her very high heels, carrying a pitcher and a glass. She would sit down and put the pitcher and glass there [on a table] and her monocle in one eye. Then she would have a drink; it looked like water, but it was gin. She would always say, "How 'tis about action." She would give them assignments to improvise some sort of scene that she would invent the situations for. If they didn't do well, she would raise hell with them.[6]

The exercises she guided the students through were intended to develop the basic Stanislavskian elements, including concentration, relaxation, the control of the five senses, the use of images, affective memory, connection (translated as "communion" by Elizabeth Reynolds Hapgood in *An Actor Prepares*), adjustment (which included consideration of the "given circumstances"), and dramatic action. Her frequent use of improvisation—often called "one-minute plays"—emphasized one or another of the elements, while developing the students' imagination and spontaneity.

As the students progressed, classes might well include a combination of exercises, improvisations, and the presentation of short prepared scenes involving first only two and later three or more characters. Ouspenskaya—and often Boleslavsky as well—analyzed and critiqued these scenes, pointing out specific problems and moments the actors had failed to accomplish satisfactorily. She would then suggest specific technical means which the student could employ to improve his work, and the scene would be repeated, incorporating the recommended technique.[7]

As Strasberg remembers, Boleslavsky's lectures complemented Ouspenskaya's class-work:

Boleslavsky did the analytic work. He explained the "why" of the [class] work. I still have the notes I took on his first talk, which was the introductory talk about the work of Stanislavsky and the work of the System. . . . He covered the entire sphere of what may be called the System. I forget how many talks there were, but they covered the theory and the practice, the sense memory work, the emotional memory work. . . . In the early days the important thing was the first outline of the System.[8]

Francis Fergusson recalls Boleslavsky's lectures vividly, for it was the lectures that attracted him to the Lab in 1926. As he remembers, he had just returned to the United States from studying in England:

When I got out of Oxford I decided I wanted to go into the theatre. When I went to New York, I knew very little about the theatre. . . . I wandered around and saw the theatres then existing—the Neighborhood Playhouse and the Theatre Guild. . . .

When I got to the Laboratory Theatre, Boleslavsky was having one of his frequent sessions. He assembled everybody—all the students and all the actors of the theatre—and had them ask questions, and then he would answer. I was very impressed by what he did then. They would stage scenes, and he would criticize them. His English was pretty terrible, but he would act out whatever he wanted to say, and that was good. He would act out almost everything he talked about. . . . I thought he was a marvellously good actor. He was primarily a director, but he could either perform or at least indicate *any* role—even a young lady.[9]

Elizabeth Fenner Gresham joined the Lab in the winter of 1926-27. The forty or so members of her beginning class studied with the other faculty for about a month before they met Boleslavsky. For this first session with him they were told to prepare ten lines of tragedy, and ten lines of "character" acting. At the prospect of "acting for the maestro," she remembers, the whole group was "quaking with awe and stage fright":

We were ushered into the theatre which we were asked to regard as a church, or temple: no smoking, no joking, or loud noise, etc. After we were seated, Boley appeared on the stage which had two wide steps at its front. He greeted us warmly and asked one girl to come up and give us her first selection. She went up, but was shaking so hard she could not begin.

"Look at you," he said gently, "you are terrified, and you must not be."

He looked out at the class. "You are *all* shake [sic] like little leaves." His beautiful voice was full of sympathy. He told the girl to sit on the stage steps and said to us:

"Close your eyes and think of the most calm and beautiful body of water you have ever seen." He waited. "You with the red tie—you are not thinking of calm water . . . " "You who are biting your finger—it will not find you calm water. . . . " And so on, until he was satisfied and we were calm.

"Now my frien'," he said to the girl on the steps, "let us hear your first choice." She delivered her speech from *The Tragedy of Nan* without a hitch. And so it went. After a while he said, "You have all worked hard for me, to try the very difficult. I will try for you. I will be Juliet."

We sat in motionless silence, watching this big man stand center stage, utterly relaxed, with bowed head. You could feel the thoughts—"Juliet? Juliet!—He'll never do it!" Then you could sense a sort of awed expectancy spreading over the group. We began to believe. We believed. And he still hadn't moved. . . .

After fully ten minutes, he lifted his head and spoke. And he was Juliet. When he finished, a sort of moaning sigh came from forty throats and he grinned at us. We loved him.

Gresham adds:

I think we were a difficult class; so many of us were college graduates—not a good time to start turning oneself inside out. We almost literally worshipped him but that was the trouble: we were worshippers, trying feebly to follow his light and worried by our shortcomings. He was enormously patient, but none of us inspired him. . . .

> He counted on Ouspenskaya to limber us up and weed us out and she and her assistants did an heroic job. Many of us were finally able to be "threads going through the eyes of needles" and to "scramble like eggs," without feeling incredibly foolish. And the improvisation classes reached several highs.

She adds: "We were required to watch Boley direct. . . . and it was a terrific experience to see him evoke not just the third, but the fourth and fifth dimensions from the actors. It was like watching a musician play a theremin—pure magic."[10]

In the fall of 1924, at about the time the Lab was moving into the quarters on MacDougal Street, Boleslavsky was asked by Robert Edmond Jones and Stark Young, to take over the staging of Young's play, *The Saint,* starring Leo Carrillo and Helen Freeman, and featuring Ouspenskaya in a supporting role. Harold Clurman, just beginning his career in the theatre, was an extra in the cast, and had attended all the rehearsals: "I did not know anything about direction then, but their work on this production seemed vague and slightly amateurish." After Boleslavsky was called in, Clurman adds: "The change proved instructive, because Boleslavsky was a man of the theatre from top to toe."[11] Years later, Clurman still remembered his impressions of Boleslavsky's work:

> He did a very facile job. In one day he could do more than Robert Edmond Jones or Stark Young could do in a year. . . . Boleslavsky had enormous facility as a director, enormous facility. He could stage a play gracefully in one or two days. He had great, great facility, great constant invention, and a kind of ease. He was almost too facile. He showed his enormous experience as both an actor and . . . director of plays for the First Studio.[12]

Already impressed by Boleslavsky's abilities, Clurman would soon hear his friend Lee Strasberg speak enthusiastically of the Lab's training program. In November of 1926, Clurman would register for Boleslavsky's class in directing at the Laboratory Theatre.

The Saint opened at the Provincetown Playhouse on 12 October 1924. This tale of a young seminarian who abandons his vocation to go in pursuit of a dancer with a traveling tent show was unanimously deplored and dismissed by the critics; Woollcott, for example, found it a "flaccid, inarticulate drama, made listless by a mongrel and amazingly devitalized performance."[13] But Ouspenskaya's performance was singled out for special praise, as were the atmospherics of Jones's set and Boleslavsky's staging of a religious procession, which the *Times'* critic called "magnificent." He added:

There are color and fascination to the strange life of the players. . . . Against
these picturesque backgrounds are set the raw emotions of the leading characters,
and there is much effective balancing between the two. And yet, primarily because play and performance do not quite merge, the effect of the whole is blurred
and uncertain. . . . [14]

In the meantime, Boleslavsky continued rehearsals for two plays at
the Lab Theatre, Shakespeare's *Twelfth Night* and *The Sea-Woman's
Cloak* by Amelie Rives (Princess Troubetskoy), the Virginia-born novelist who married a Russian prince. Rives was at this time a shareholder in
the Lab and a member of its advisory council. [15]

The Lab had been working on both plays since the previous spring,
but *The Sea-Woman's Cloak* received the greatest attention, for it had
been chosen as the theatre's premiere production. Described as an Irish
fantasy, the story is a variation of the Ondine legend, in which a simple
fisherman gains power over Ganore, the sea king's daughter, only to
suffer grief, loneliness and excommunication for the love of her; she
proclaims her love in return only after he has set her free. Together they
go into the sea—she to her home, he to his death. On 7 January 1925,
The Sea-Woman's Cloak was given an informal performance at the Cosmopolitan Club, in the hopes of attracting financial backers. This "dem-
onstration" performance was done on a shoe-string budget. Herbert
Stockton writes that it was well received: "Boleslavsky was exceedingly
clever to have gotten such effects with one or two lights, a little gauze
for the background and varicolored cheap cloth smocks for costumes." [16]

Using the additional money raised at the Cosmopolitan Club the
Lab made final preparations for its first official performance, as described by Blanch Tancock:

For the performance of *Sea-Woman* we transformed our big room into a diminutive
but intensely real theatre. The room was bisected with a curtain. Behind it was the
stage with very simple elements of setting fashioned out of drapes, materials, and
some lights. For the audience some platforms were built up at the other end, on two
levels, and chairs were arranged on these. The little compartments at the back
became dressing rooms, one for the boys and one for the girls. And we all congre-
gated in the main office in complete silence well in advance of performance to play
our parts in the sea-sounds. [17]

This, the Lab's first official public performance, was on 14 April
1925. The following night Amelie Rives visited the Lab. After the performance she and a group of her friends started backstage, but were
stopped by one of the actors and told that "a decision of the Business
Committee" barred such visits. Rives wrote an angry letter to Miriam

Stockton; Stockton responded, but Rives was not appeased. Finally, Boleslavsky wrote the playwright:

> The final aim of everything we do is for the best result of the play and the best atmosphere for the performance of the play. I am accustomed myself, and I teach the actors who are working with me, to pay the deepest honor and respect to the author. It doesn't matter whether that person is William Shakespeare or Amelie Rives, but the author is the man [sic] who starts the life in the theatre and he should be so honored.

Nonetheless, he continues:

> We do not consider it professional to speak with the actors about the play or to correct the actors in all their mistakes on the evening immediately after the play, when the actor is tired and exhausted. It is like teaching a race horse to run after the horse has made her race. If God himself should come after an evening performance to teach the actors, I would say, "My dear God, wait until morning." I consider this regulation as absolutely businesslike—a thing which is necessary in the art because only art which is considered in a businesslike way, is real art. All the rest is *pour s'amuse*.

Evidently one of Rives's friends had written to the actress in the title role, Ganore, suggesting how it might be better played, for Boleslavsky writes:

> The letter is very beautifully written, it is a nice story about Ganore, has few rules about the use of Voice, and it points poetically to the image of Sarah Bernhardt. . . . But after all is said, her letter is the most dangerous and unnecessary sort of literature for the actor while he is working on a part. Why? Because it explains the results, it provides the form, but it does not give the actor the spine—the essence of the part. The actor will have perfectly good understanding in his mind as to what Ganore should be, but he will never learn how he should work and what he should do to achieve what Mrs. Branch has expressed in her letter.

Reacting to Rives's dissatisfaction with the crude and unfinished properties, which had been fabricated from the poorest means, he writes:

> Those things are merely properties, but they play with us on the stage. While they are dead things, through the efforts which we put into building them, they become alive. The knight's chair is made from black plank, but Colum's explaining with your words, Princess, that this chair is a wonderful golden chair taken from the wrecked ship of a mighty king . . . brings this chair to life, and makes it seem not simple black planks, but just what the actor intends it to be. Here is our achievement, and here is our pride. And let me say to you, dear Princess, it is for this illusion that you have written the play, not for a chair which is the art of the cabinet maker, and which every fellow who has $100 can buy.

Please do not consider the Sea Woman as it is played now ready for production. . . . [It] is not ready for production and does not pretend to be yet. We are giving working rehearsals, which is a slow process of maturing and growing. The day will come when we will have the production with a real loom, with real waves and the king's chairs, beautiful walls, and perfected actors, but now it is work, work, work, on an exercise in the art of the theatre, for us. Probably when you brought your friends . . . you had to make a thousand excuses to the effect that we were poor and young. . . . Now if you would say instead of that, that these are rehearsals, you might not be so dissatisfied, and we would not look so poor as we do now in your eyes.[18]

Rives was evidently placated by Boleslavsky's letter, for *The Sea-Woman's Cloak* remained in the Lab's schedule.

In an ironic coincidence, novelist Rachel Crowthers had also attended the Lab's second night performance of *The Sea-Woman's Cloak,* but she had been moved to write, not an indignant letter to Boleslavsky, but a letter of enthusiastic praise to the *New York Times:*

It was my good fortune not long ago to see the students in the Laboratory Theatre, as they call it, and I was so moved and impressed by the work they are doing that I would like to add my work of appreciation for a very wonderful and valuable thing which we have in our midst and which is apt to be overlooked or undiscovered in our overcrowded town.

She considered the play "so very beautiful that it belongs with the best of the Irish plays, and should be known in our town."[19]

Stella Adler also saw one of the *Sea-Woman's* informal, though public performances. As she relates:

I don't recall the date, but I do recall being taken to a very small, ground-floor apartment . . . . There were maybe twenty chairs in the room. And I saw the most beautiful thing I had ever seen on the stage in this small room—some miracle performance. It was directed by Boleslavsky, and in a far corner of the room watching it was Madame Ouspenskaya. . . . [20]

The daughter of Jacob Adler, the famous actor of the Yiddish stage, Stella had acted professionally for some time, but had come to realize that she lacked any firm technique; inspired by what she saw that night in the small walk-in flat, she applied to the Lab and was accepted, apparently in the spring of 1925. She attended classes the fall of that year (the Lab recessed for the summer). A letter from the Lab dated 22 January 1926 notified her that she had been accepted as a "member of the auxiliary group which is being formed on the first of February. . . . "

The letter explained: "You will be given immediate rehearsal work for production, continued training with Madame, and intensive work to counteract personal faults that you may have shown. On the 15th of May, the more permanent decision will be made about you."[21] On April 2, the Lab wrote to Adler again, expressing its sympathy in the death of her father: "He was a most wonderful person whose tradition will always live in the theatre and we are so glad to have for ourselves some of his vitality and genius in you." On May 1, the Lab notified her that she had been elected a member of the acting group of the American Laboratory Theatre.[22]

Highly favorable reactions to the demonstration-rehearsals for *The Sea-Woman's Cloak* persuaded Boleslavsky and the Stocktons that the Lab should seek a new home, one large enough to accommodate its anticipated growth. They began looking about for a suitable location. Finally, they chose the old La Salle School Building at 107 West 58th Street. The contract for the new home was signed on 18 May 1925, with occupancy beginning on July 1. On that date, remodeling began, as Miriam Stockton describes: "Mr. Boleslavsky himself took charge and practically built, with several of the boys . . . the theatre stage and procenium [*sic*] arch. He did everything with his own hands . . . with such inexperienced help as his Group could give him. It was a summer of intense labor for all of us and racking financial strain."[23] An unpublished press release reports that the new quarters contained dressing and work rooms behind the stage which was raised two or three feet. The proscenium itself was about thirty feet wide, the stage area about twenty feet deep. The auditorium was banked, with each level containing one or two rows of seats, accommodating just under one hundred seats. The lighting equipment was selected and installed by Eugene Braun, who had been in charge of lighting *The Miracle*. The front curtain was made by the members of the company and the decorations were planned by the scenic designers (probably Alan Crane and Helen Dresser Peck, who designed the Lab's first two shows) and carried out by the players.[24] In creating the Lab's first real theatre, Boleslavsky clearly had followed the model set ten years earlier by the First Studio.

The American Laboratory Theatre opened its first subscription season in these newly refurbished quarters on 15 October 1925 with *Twelfth Night*. Music especially composed for the production was by Douglas Moore; the playbill credited Alan Crane with the settings and Anna Wille was costume designer. In a few instances only one actor was named for a particular role: George Auerbach played the sea captain, Herbert

Gellendré was Malvolio, and Morton Brown acted Sir Toby. But the other leading parts were played in alteration by more than one actor. Orsino was acted by Oscar Becque, James Daly, and George Macready; Olivia by Adelaide George, Agnes James, Constance McLain, and Shirley White; and Viola/Sebastian by Helen Coburn, Gretchen Comegys, and Blanch Tancock. Boleslavsky continued to use multiple casting for almost every play he produced at the American Lab. Moreover, *Twelfth Night* began rotating with the Lab's other productions as they entered the repertory. This practice of constantly changing casts in rotating repertory made several critics feel uncomfortable, judging from remarks in their reviews.

Boleslavsky reordered the scenes of *Twelfth Night* in a manner similar to that used at the First Studio: the scenes relating to the love theme were placed in the first act; the scenes of revelry usually associated with Sir Toby made up the second act; and the two themes were brought together in the third act. Scenically, however, the Lab production was quite unlike that at the First Studio.

In discussing *Twelfth Night* at the Lab, Boleslavsky explained that both the "long-distant mood" and the "spine" were implicit in the play's full title: *Twelfth Night, or What You Will.* He emphasized the festival spirit of the Twelfth Night of December, "the happiest night in the year, when everyone was supposed to forgive and forget and to bother with nothing but his own enjoyment." He took this approach, at least in part, in an apparent effort to foster in the Lab's actors a sense of naïveté and belief in the play's improbable disguises, mistaken identities, and confusions:

> You must remember [the festive spirit] on the stage and think that everything is all right and true, as you do in carnival times. During Twelfth Night it is all right, and anything may happen. After all, [Shakespeare] says, "What you Will."
>
> You see immediately how your eyes open wide, and you can see that [everything] is possible, and you do not need to pretend at all. And if you can establish this feeling in yourself, you do not need to pretend that you do not recognize Viola and Sebastian, and that Viola does not recognize Sebastian; and you can believe that Olivia would push away the love of a nice young man and . . . fall in love in one second with Viola and, afterwards, in another second . . . not recognize him [sic] . But when you stand on a level with Twelfth Night, when everything is under the wing and guidance of the God of Merrie Olde England, you will say, "Well, that is possible." And many other things are possible too.

The play's title was translated into the "spine" of the production, as he explains:

> After many talks and much discussion we came to the conclusion that the spine of *Twelfth Night* could be expressed in such words as "Playing with life," as you would

play with a toy or a game. Everything in life prompts you to play with it. You do not take it seriously, but you play with it as a child plays with a doll, as a cat plays with balls of paper. You play seriously, but you do play. . . . [25]

The festive spirit and the element of playfulness were also expressed in the scenery for the production. The basic scenic elements were two-dimensional cut-outs in irregular, largely geometric shapes. These were painted in bright, primary colors and, in some instances at least, adorned with cartoon-like renditions of antic figures. These cut-outs were used in conjunction with stairs and various properties, some of which were three-dimensional and some of which were flat. The production opened with the discovery of Orlando—whose "spine" was to "play with love"—sprawling in a three-dimensional bed, listening to music played on a lute by his page. During the duelling scene, Sir Andrew fled up a two-dimensional tree. In another scene, the curtain parted to discover Viola riding horseback before a drop curtain; Malvolio galloped on stage to offer her a ring held on the end of a cane; after a furious chase—with both riders mounted on hobby-horses—Viola "dismounted from the horse and, putting her arm around the horse's neck, making a very pretty picture," accepted the ring.[26] Later, Malvolio carried a candle to descend the steps into a darkened cellar, where he discovered Sir Andrew, Sir Toby, and an inverted Maria disporting amid barrels of wine in the company of the frolicking figures painted on the scenery behind them.

In keeping with the spirit of these proceedings, Boleslavsky played an extended game with the audience by casting an actress to play both Viola and Sebastian. This dual role posed no real problem until the end of the play, when brother and sister must face each other. Blanch Tancock, one of the actresses who played the dual role, explains how this final deception was handled:

> This was worked out by having Viola, who is onstage in the first part of this scene, maneuvered into a position near an exit and with her back to the audience. Offstage, in the opposite wing, a disturbance develops. Sir Toby and Sir Andrew are embroiled with Sebastian and there is much swordplay. The audience's attention is drawn to that side of the stage. Viola slips off, being replaced unobtrusively by a double [who alternated in the role] and reappears from the opposite as the victorious Sebastian.

Tancock adds: "It always surprised me how successfully this deception worked. You could always hear the rustle of surprise and uncertainty when the two figures were there together on the stage"[27]

The reviewers responded favorably to these antics and remarked especially on the bubbling youthfulness, the spontaneity, and energy of the production. Gilbert Gabriel described it as "a performance of zest and fondness and framed by settings of excellent humor." A correspondent for the *Paris Times* was impressed by the "freshness and sincerity that ring true" in the whole performance. "The Laboratory Players inspire us with merriment and gaiety and a little mischievous delight."[28] Brooks Atkinson noted that the production had "released the rebellious spirits of youth in a brawl of drinking and gaming," an approach he found spontaneous and funny in the comic scenes, but one which proved "quite fatal to the romantic beauty of Shakespeare's play." The alteration of the scenes, he believed, did serious damage to "the romantic-beauty, the soft affections, the gentle tenders of love and the heartsickness of 'Twelfth Night'." Still, this flaw was offset by the vigor and energy of the performance: "The scholarly dissector of the Shakespeare cadaver must laugh in spite of himself." The chief quality of the company, he concluded, "seems to be that of a holiday stolen from the grim majestic solemnity of professional Shakespeare producing, and between high spirits and mere practical skill the choice is easy. . . . These crude actors are vastly preferable to barnstormers with sluggish livers."[29] The critical consensus: *Twelfth Night* was flawed, but showed promise of bright future accomplishments for the Laboratory Theatre.

This initial success was followed by an even greater one when *The Sea-Woman's Cloak* reopened on November 4. The cast that night featured Grover Burgess as Colum Dara, the fisherman; Agnes James as Ganore; Blanch Tancock as Widow Dara; George Auerbach as the priest; and Harold Hecht as the fisherman's brother.

The *New York Drama Calendar* dismissed the production as "intelligent" but "too amateurish to satisfy the hardened Broadway patron;" *Billboard,* however, reported that the play was "attracting overflow audiences" and found it an "absorbing drama . . . exquisitely colored with pathos." *Billboard* also had high praise for the actors.[30] Gilbert W. Gabriel pronounced *The Sea-Woman* "utterly entrancing," with its overall "shimmery" texture laced with scenes of "real power and poignancy." He was impressed, too, with Boleslavsky's "stunning" use of "elaborate groupings":

> For the peasant mob of the second act, working upon a stage which gives it about as much freedom as the Lord's Prayer engraved on a pinhead, is packed with vivid pictures, each figure more individual and arresting than the next. The settings, too,

deserve the extra respect of what problems in inches they had to overcome . . . . and are as imaginative and decorative as anything twice their size or their pretension that I have seen in theatre this season.[31]

The critics turned noticeably cool when they saw the Lab's final production of the season: *The Scarlet Letter,* adapted from Hawthorne's novel by Miriam Stockton. To create the play's eight scenes, Stockton lifted dialogue "almost bodily to the stage."[32] The actors were trained in authentic colonial dialect by Windsor Daggett, and four authentic hymns were sung behind the scenes. Settings and costumes were designed after illustrations by F.O.C. Darley for the 1879 edition of Hawthorne's novel and executed by Paul Rover (actually Paul Ouzounoff, formerly the chief scenic artist of the Moscow Art Theatre, who had come to America with Boleslavsky's *Revue Russe*). The opening night cast featured Helen Coburn as Hester Prynne, George Macready as Rev. Dimmesdale, and Grover Burgess as Chillingworth. The play opened on 7 January 1926 to reviews that might well have made Boleslavsky wish he had kept this particular experiment within the confines of the "laboratory," away from public scrutiny.

The critics all but unanimously dismissed the play as being an episodic patchwork, wooden, jerky, and tedious. Richard Watts, Jr., found that some of the groupings added "pictorial value to the production, if not to its dramatic interest": "As is so frequently the case with such organizations, the manner of the production proved of considerable more interest than the play itself."[33] Brooks Atkinson endorsed the Lab's ambitious effort, yet found the acting "sincere" but "amateur" and complained that the players' voices were "harsh," or "raucous and truculent."[34] Gilbert Gabriel, who had so enthusiastically welcomed the Lab's first two productions, agreed that here the Lab's lofty aim was spoiled by amateurishness:

> It is, as the others were, an interesting, aspiringly staged production, acted with that evident love of the task which here must substitute for the graces of professional experience. . . . Groupings and such evidences of an intelligent ensemble training speak strikingly of what the Laboratory Theatre wants most to do, and what it can in part do already.[35]

The critical reception to Boleslavsky's first season at the American Laboratory was encouraging and favorable overall. The reviewers found ample signs of sincerity, sound training, high aspirations, and accomplishment, though not unqualified. Even in the failure of *The Scarlet Letter* they found reason to expect Boleslavsky's work to achieve truly significant results in the future.

The scenic experimentation evident in *Twelfth Night* was equally clear in *The Sea-Woman's Cloak* and *The Scarlet Letter*. Boleslavsky's search for new scenic forms would be strikingly present in most—but not all—of his future Laboratory Theatre productions as well.

Twelfth Night's cartoon playfulness had contrasted sharply with the scenic approach to the other plays in the Lab's first season. The visual treatment used in *Sea-Woman* was a more refined version of the simple scenic enements that had been evolved for the play during the course of a year's rehearsals. For the principal setting, the interior of the fisherman's cottage, Boleslavsky used a background of cloth, which fell in great, swelling folds to suggest the power of the ocean that threatened to sweep Colum to his doom. This cloth background was pierced in places by angular, almost expressionistic doorways to provide entrances. Boleslavsky used the orchestrated voices of off-stage actors to create the sea as an omnipresent character of the play. As Lee Strasberg recalls: "He created the character of the sea . . . the constant undercurrent of the sound of the sea with human voices, which was extraordinarily well done and which I remember as one of the most exciting and impressive theatrical things I've ever encountered."[36] Blanch Tancock, who played the Widow Dara, but participated in the sea-effects when she was off-stage, explains how this was done:

> To create the sea, Boley used his actors in a different way. They became literally the instruments in his vocal orchestra. . . . Using the phonetic symbols as notations and the actors as instruments a carefully orchestrated sound score was developed. . . . Out of these sounds were created the sounds of the sea, the soft wash of water on sand, the crashing of waves on the shore, the angry elements of a brooding storm, the laughter or wailing of the sea-folk.[37]

The climactic moments of the production included a growing body of onstage waves, created by the dance-like movements of actors beneath a lavender cloth stretched across the width of the stage.

The scenic innovations Boleslavsky employed for *The Scarlet Letter,* and their effectiveness, are perhaps most eloquently described by a correspondent for the British publication, *The Stage*. He pitied the "unlettered *nouveau riche*" who wandered into the Lab without having read Hawthorne's novel, but pitied even more "the earnest Hawthornite who misses this stage illustration of the novel." He considered the eight scenes "extremely beautiful and striking," evoking "miraculously in their stiff, studied, pictorial way, the old Boston" of Hawthorne. "And in these same tableaux enough of the stress and mental torment of the novel creeps out to warm their figures into life. It is a bold and almost successful experiment; something new and impressive in the dramatic way; and reaffirms one's confidence that one interesting theatre of the future is here being built up.'' This critic paid considerably more attention than his American counterparts to the director's intentions:

> These tableaux are curiously and ingeniously handled. The forestage is draped in brown, while shifts of scene are indicated by the changing of the decorative back- drops, . . . each suggesting a tapestry woven from . . . Darley's illustrations; and against each of these backdrops the characters are formally posed as nearly as possible in the same position as their tapestry models. Free movement is of course completely sacrificed to this queer, decorative effect, with which, it must be granted, Hawthorne's formal, sombre, unreal dialogue fits well: while between scenes the Puritan milieu and the symbol of the scarlet letter are kept hauntingly in the mind by the singing offstage of ancient hymns and the lowering of a drop curtain with that torturing scarlet ''A''. . . . [38]

The diversity and variety of these scenic forms indicates that the acting forms were equally varied—at least they were if Boleslavsky re- mained true to his belief that scenic forms must be the inevitable and necessary, natural and organic outgrowth of acting forms. The evidence that this ideal was realized is limited, however. The daily reviewers are of little help; in most cases their comments and descriptions of the acting— either individually or collectively—fail to go beyond a generalized state- ment of approval or disapproval. For example, of the acting in *The Sea- Woman's Cloak,* one critic noted that overall it was ''splendid''; that Helen Coburn ''looked attractive enough to lure a lover to the sea''; and that Louis Quince ''gave a sincere and able performance'' as Colum, the fated fisherman.[39] That *The Sea-Woman's Cloak* was indeed marked by psychologically truthful acting—despite the fantastic nature of the subject and the far from realistic scenery—is supported by Lee Strasberg's recol- lection of the production:

> *The Sea-Woman's Cloak* . . . was not directed purely realistically. Boleslavsky was not a purely realistic director in that sense. He was influenced by Vakhtangov's theatricality or fantasy idea. And yet the acting was the kind of acting which im- pressed me and which I later tried to make use of, both in my own work and in my work as a director.[40]

Strasberg's assumption that Boleslavsky's theatricality was a result of Vakhtangov's influence is open to challenge, but Rachel Crowthers, in her letter quoted earlier, supports his judgment regarding the acting in *Sea-Woman:*

There in that tiny theatre downtown—one sees these young people playing old women and men without makeup, and looking old because they have become old through absolute understanding and feeling and the quickening of dramatic imagination to such a flame that they are transported into the little seacoast village of Ireland—actually living the lives of these people in the play—people as remote from these young Americans as anything can be.

In one scene, where they all come on together, the undercurrent of understanding and thinking and feeling, all absolutely part of the central idea, is so much greater and more sincere than one usually finds in the professional theatre that it is amazing. . . . [41]

Emotionally truthful acting evidently underlay the almost architectural severity of *The Scarlet Letter* as well. Brooks Atkinson writes: "So purposeful a performance involves, with unpracticed actors, a certain astringency. The stuff of 'The Scarlet Letter' does not pour out abundantly. Striving after a particular expression, the actors reveal a sort of cerebration that results in action but is not action itself." He goes on to describe the emotional undercurrents and the audience response to several scenes which he found particularly striking: Hester's "defiant tranquility, plays upon human emotions drawn into conflict"; the inquisition in the Governor's Hall "touches several varied chords of feeling, of innocence as against peremptory authority, with the two emotions fused by anguished pleading"; and the scene in which Dimmesdale succumbs to the craft of Chillingworth "likewise sputters with emotion."[42]

12

The System Revised

Boleslavsky's surviving lectures at the Laboratory Theatre for 1925–26 show that, in addition to the difficulties of preparing the theatre's first public season of plays, Boleslavsky was wrestling anew with the thorny problem of emotion in the actor's work. His old solution, which took emotion roused by affective memory as the actor's starting point, had been successful at the First Studio, but had proved to be a cause of confusion and misunderstanding for his American students.

One source of confusion was Boleslavsky's failure to distinguish in his earlier talks at the Lab between the specific technique of affective memory and the broader concept of "memory of emotion," terms that cannot be used interchangeably in any coherent discussion of the actor's work. Boleslavsky began to draw a distinction between the two in his 1925–26 talks and subsequent articles.

The actual mechanism of "affective memory" is relatively simple, but its successful operation depends to a great extent upon the actor's possessing a developed "sense memory," *i.e.* the ability to recall vividly and to a degree re-experience sights, smells, sounds, tastes, or touch sensations. In order to do an affective memory exercise, the actor selects an incident from his own past experience. Forgetting about himself, and making no effort to recall directly the emotions associated with the experience, he recalls instead the sensory stimuli associated with the past event, progressing sequentially through the sensory events. At some point in this process a particular sensory memory will "trigger" the subconsciously remembered emotion associated with the past experience.[1] If the actor is able to identify the sensory "trigger," he has found the "key" to a particular emotion, and the initial arduous and time-consuming process need not be repeated. The "key" is enough: "Through constant repetition and perfection," Boleslavsky explains, it becomes "just like recalling a tune" and can be used without interrupting the flow of the performance.[2]

However, as Boleslavsky now made clear, affective memory is subordinate to the more general concept of "memory of emotion." As a specific technique affective memory has only an indirect bearing on the various means Boleslavsky had previously described for rousing the actor's emotions: by the author's lines; by "the mere recollection of a feeling"; by actual or imagined physical objects or physical actions. These means can be properly understood only in light of Boleslavsky's theory of memory, which he presented in a 1925 lecture.

Boleslavsky believed that memory in the normal individual is primarily a function of the senses (that we "remember" with our eyes, ears, etc.) and that the brain is primarily a repository of sensory stimuli. Through the operation of the senses we are able to remember the lines of a script ("I can see the page. . . . "), the smell of coffee, the feel of velvet, and so on. This he called the "common," or ordinary memory. The normal individual also possesses a motor memory by which his muscles "remember" how to walk or execute a complex dance step. Likewise, every normal individual possesses an emotional memory; however, the empirical evidence for the existence of the emotional memory is less obvious, Boleslavsky suggests, because generally we employ this kind of memory less frequently, and then only on a subconscious level. Nonetheless, he offers proof that "memory of emotion" exists. Every individual sometimes experiences a particular emotion or mood that seems to derive from no logically identifiable source; for no apparent reason, we are simply in a particular mood—we feel exultant, we are depressed, or introspective. Boleslavsky argues that such inexplicable moods, which seemingly arise of themselves without motivation or stimulus, are evidence of the operation of the subconscious mind. The subconscious has responded to a sensory stimulus which it associates with a past emotional experience by "remembering" the emotion connected to that experience (an instance of the *unconscious* use of "affective memory"). The actor can learn to consciously use and control such sensory stimuli, Boleslavsky reasons, by tracing the source of such seemingly inexplicable emotions back to their psychic triggers. If he successfully identifies the Pavlovian source, the actor can then deliberately use that "trigger," either through its literal presence or its imaginative recreation. In the same way that frequent use and exercise of the "common" and "motor" memories will develop the actor's facility for remembering lines and his ability to recall blocking, the actor can develop an increasing facility for remembering emotions. With proper exercise, all three kinds of memory begin to operate on an almost autonomic level; they become almost habitual or automatic with repetition.

Just as the actor comes to remember his lines without conscious effort, or to remember his physical movements without having to stop and think about the operation of the muscles, so may he employ his memory of emotions without deliberate effort or strain. He no longer has to recall the visual image of the page of the script in order to "see" the words— he simply knows them. Likewise, he is able to recall the necessary emotions quickly and easily, without recourse to any conscious use of the psychic trigger—he simply feels.

Because memory is associative, the actor's finished performance constitutes a unique blend of associative memories. The lines prompt physical behavior; a physical movement prompts the actor's next speech; either or both may prompt the accompanying emotion. Picking up a cup, or moving to the window becomes associated in the actor's memory, not only with the lines, but with the accompanying feeling as well. In this way, emotional responses discovered in the course of rehearsal—without reliance on the conscious technique of affective memory—can be learned and memorized as readily as are lines or blocking.[3]

Understood in its broader sense, "memory of emotion" encompasses "affective memory." Clearly, the "psychic triggers" do cause "affective memory" to operate, but "memory of emotion" is not restricted to the conscious technique of affective memory. As a conscious technique, "affective memory" is too narrow and too restricted compared with the complex interactions of the actor's "memory of emotion."

In the surviving 1925–26 lectures, Boleslavsky paid great attention to "dramatic action," an element of the system he had barely touched on in his talks two years before. Again and again he explained at length the value of dramatic action and discussed its relationship to memory of emotion. His tone suggests that by now he was paying more attention to memory of emotion than he personally felt necessary or wise, simply because it was a topic that intrigued his students. Harold Clurman points out that "affective memory" was the element that most excited many of the Lab's actor's, some of whom "to this day . . . have emphasized that almost to the exclusion of the other things."[4]

Clurman's impression is supported by Boleslavsky's opening remarks in one of the lectures:

> It seems to me that I shall have to speak once more—and again try to make myself clear—on a certain part of the method. From what I hear and from a couple of letters that I have received from you, some minds do not seem to catch the point. I

do not think it is the fault of my English, or my words, or of the way I explain. It is probably something much deeper. For me the question is clear, but you do not understand, and I do not blame you, because it cannot be done in four—five—or even six months. You do not, however, understand the way of using the feelings.[5]

In this instance, Boleslavsky sought to explain the proper use of emotions through the use of an improvisation. He called half the students to the stage and suggested an improvisation in which they were passengers on an ocean liner that is sinking. After the actors worked on the improvisation, Boleslavsky offered his critique:

Now, you see, here is the whole thing: what you have done is a pathological case. It is not art. It is a general nervousness. Anyone can do that. Anyone can say to himself, "I am desperate," and then go ahead with physical strength. Where are your souls? I don't see them. I see nerves—I hear screams. Where is the feeling built?

Instead of starting with a generalized emotion, Boleslavsky explains, the actor must build up a logical series of actions. Under the circumstances, the first action is find out whether the boat is actually in danger: "I would go and look myself; then I would have a moment when I would realize that the boat is going down." Such a realization is a kind of "inner" action; it is followed by yet another "inner" action: "In this moment I don't know what to do. This always happens when you are in a trap. . . . Then comes decision." The next action will depend on "who I am"—the individual nature of the actor (or the character). Eventually, Boleslavsky continues, he finds himself a place in line for the lifeboat:

I watch those in front stepping down, one by one. Why don't they move faster? Maybe I can go nearer. Everyone watches, but the hysteria does not start even yet; and it does not start in life until a man has nothing to do with himself—not before. All the rest of the time you can control yourself and . . . go on to the next problem."

He concludes:

This means that you apply your imagination—your memory of feeling. You apply it as part of the whole thing. I don't know if I have made clear to you what I mean, but do you understand the difference between simply plunging into unconscious action and building it up artistically? . . . You see, your imagination gives you the steps to build up your action, but the imagination has a right to exist only when the first line is perfectly prepared and you go from one problem to another.[6]

Was it the complexity of the subject and the students' difficulty in grasping it that necessitated Boleslavsky's returning to the problem of emotion so often? Or was his explanation less than lucid? Apparently both questions must be answered affirmatively. More than once in the 1925 lectures, Boleslavsky begins talking about the use or nature of emotional memory, but ends up explaining the necessity of action. Perhaps he did so in order to suggest priorities, or to demonstrate the interrelationship of the two principles. More likely, his own understanding of that interrelationship was undergoing a transition and had not yet clearly coalesced.

Earlier Boleslavsky had presented emotion or affective memory as the great secret of the actor's work. Now he repeatedly stressed the importance of action: "Life is action," he says at one point. At another, he notes that action is the "function we can build on in our creation of the human soul"—a claim he had earlier made for "affective memory." Again in 1925, he identifies the principle of action as the source of all the exercises employed to train the actor; an understanding of action and its structure, he says now, forms the basis for understanding both the play and every role in it. Action rather than emotion had taken priority in his thinking:

> You know—and there is no use to repeat—that the main thing and the most important thing and the only vital thing on the stage is action. This is a very broad and wide definition, but, after all, if you will analyze you will find that it is exactly as I say. It's action that counts. Even if you don't do a thing on the stage, the words themselves show you that you do something. . . . Through denying the action you establish a new action—which is an action by itself.[7]

Over the next year or so, Boleslavsky reexamined the nature of "acting in life," and from that study deduced the essential "emotion-maker." He was excited enough by this discovery to publish his conclusions in the form of an article, "The Fundamentals of Acting," in the February 1927 issue of *Theatre Arts Monthly*. Near the end of that article (portions of which have already been quoted), Boleslavsky raises the central issue: The ideal actor must have both a well-trained physical instrument and the technique of an "emotion-maker," if he is to follow Joseph Jefferson's advice to "Keep your heart warm and the head cool."

> Can it be done? Most certainly! It is merely necessary to try and think of life as an unbroken sequence of two different kinds of steps, which I would call Problem steps and Action steps. . . . [T]he first step is for the actor to understand what the problem is that confronts him. Then the spark of the will pushes him towards dynamic action. A play has the same structure as life itself, although it may be more condensed, differently expressed and very often abstract. When an actor realizes that the solution of a certain part may consist merely in being able first, to stand on the stage for

perhaps no more than one five-hundredth of a second, cool-headed and firm of purpose, aware of the problem before him; and then in the next one five-hundredth of a second or it may be, five or ten seconds, to precipitate himself intensely into the action which the situation requires, he will have achieved the perfect technique of acting.

Seldom in life do we stop to think how we feel, and almost never do we stop to think what emotion we "should" feel in order to deal with one situation or another; instead we appraise each problem as it arises and take steps to solve it. Most often when we think about emotion, it is emotion in others—we wonder how our actions affect the feelings of someone else. Boleslavsky sees a major advantage in his new emphasis on "dramatic action": it frees the actor from unnecessary preoccupation with his own emotions:

With such fluidity of resource he will never be in the position of being handicapped by the emotion itself or of becoming a nerotic [Sic] from a too constant and too strenuous expenditure of his emotional forces. At the same time he will not have constantly to cheat himself and his audience, working hard at building castles in the air and trying to define what is by its very nature essentially indefinite—thus limiting his art to the production of a series of elaborate tricks.

The great strength of the technique of action, Boleslavsky explains, is that it is natural, logical, and draws on the actor's knowledge of real life:

Such a technique of acting, if completely mastered and diligently practiced, is not so tremendously difficult, because its secret lies so close to nature. It is based on the very essence of that form of acting which we use in our daily life. It is the same realization of a problem with its appropriate sequence in action that is seen in our individual daily dramatic efforts. . . . The younger generation . . . are . . . exceedingly sensitive as to this simple method of connecting problem and action. In my experience with American actors, particularly those of Anglo-Saxon origin, I have found this the only effective way of arousing the emotions and of making their nervous emotion on the stage count for something real and sincere.[8]

Boleslavsky elaborated the technique of the Problem step-Action step in "The Third Lesson" on acting (published in *Theatre Arts* in July, 1931, and incorporated later into *Acting: The First Six Lessons*). As he explains it there, dramatic action is both an analytical tool and a practical technique for the actor. The basic technique of action is a three-step process: "First you want something, it is your artist's will; then you define it in a verb, it is your artist's technique; and then you actually do it, it is your artist's expression."[9]

This formula is elegantly simple, but its consequences are far-reaching. In order to want something, the actor must know first what it is. What does the character really want? What desire, with its implicit motive, lies beneath the words and behavior suggested by the playwright? Once the character's true desire has been discovered, the actor cannot be content merely to pretend to want the same thing; rather, through his will, he must come to truly want it. The second step of the formula compels the actor to define the course of action he intends to take in order to accomplish the character's desire in specific, not general terms. "I want to. . . . " is followed by a concrete active verb. But not just any active verb will do; the actor's choice of action must be logically consistent with the character and the circumstances in which the character finds himself. Moreover, the chosen action must relate to the character's "main" action—the underlying desire he pursues above all others, or the "spine" of the role, as Boleslavsky often called it in his lectures. And finally, the specific action must be in accordance with the actions of the opposing characters in the scene, as well as the "individuality" of the actors in the other parts.[10] The formula of action is completed by the actor's actually "doing," or performing the chosen action. He may employ his physical and emotional means to a greater or lesser extent, but an action is primarily verbal: "You do it through the medium of speech," and it is the choice of action that informs the playwright's words with meaning; intonations and inflections are the "results of action," and not merely arbitrary "juggling with the modulation of voice and artificial pauses"[11]—a claim Boleslavsky had made years earlier for "affective memory."

The technique of action may be applied to an entire role to define the "spine"—or paramount desire—of the character, as well as the individual, or "secondary" actions taken in an effort to accomplish this over-riding desire. The actor's role is like a "long string of beads—beads of action" following "one after another, sometimes overlapping each other but always clear and distinct." The "spine" of the part is the cord upon which the "beads of action" are strung.[12] (Many of Boleslavsky's students call individual units of action "beats," and transcriptions of his Lab lectures have him using the term; possibly he was saying "the first 'bead' of action," but, because of his accent, was misunderstood. Strasberg speculates that Boleslavsky was actually saying "bits.") In a similar way, dramatic action provides the director an analytical tool with which he defines the "spine" of the play (to which the "spine" of each character is related) and designates the individual units of action of the play.[13]

Boleslavsky had not completely abjured the use of affective memory. As his "Second Lesson" on acting (July 1929) reveals, he still considered it a valuable and viable tool that might be used as part of the actor's overall effort to "organize and synchronize the self that is within you, with your part."[14] Boleslavsky cautions, however, that the actor must "be careful not to overdo it." Emotions may be roused by various means, and affective memory is best reserved for those moments the actor cannot achieve otherwise:

> The difficult spots are what you should watch for and work for. Every play is written for one or at most a few "high tension" moments. The audience pays the price of the tickets—not for two whole hours, but for the best ten seconds, the ten seconds when it gets the biggest laugh or thrill. Your whole strength and perfection must be directed toward those seconds.

The actor must not become obsessed with the problem of feeling, however, nor preoccupied with the process of affective memory: "Don't look for 'to be' [affective memory]," Boleslavsky warns, "when you should seek 'to do.'"[15] Properly understood and practiced, dramatic action becomes the actor's "springboard," the technique that enables him to "get the flow of the part" and to "build up an emotion and rise to the unconscious climaxes of real inspired interpretation of a part."[16]

At the beginning of his work in America, one of Boleslavsky's declared intentions was to test the validity of the system for American actors. Implicit in that aim was his willingness to adjust or modify the system to suit the psychological and cultural nature of Americans. Boleslavsky's testing did not lead him to add a single new "element" to the system (though he may well have sought to discover new ones), nor did he delete any of the essential features of Stanislavsky's work. He did invent his own vocabulary to describe some of the elements, but the elements themselves remained constant.

Nonetheless, Boleslavsky made a significant alteration in Stanislavsky's system. At the beginning of his work in New York he urged the actors to take emotion as the starting point of their work and offered "affective memory" as the great secret of "living the role." In 1927, he reversed priorities by announcing his conclusion that—because the process of dramatic action is more organically related to actual life processes, and because it gives the actor conscious control over both his emotions and the technical means of expressing them—dramatic action is, at least for American actors, the most potent and fundamental "emotion-maker."

Boleslavsky's modification of the system anticipated by a number of years a comparable shift of emphasis on Stanislavsky's part. Stanislavsky, as his biographer notes, changed his ideas about the importance of various elements of his system more than once:

> . . . At first he regarded the emotional memory of the actor as of paramount importance and treated it quite independently of the actor's imagination. It was only later that he began to regard the "magic if", that is to say, the actor's imagination, as of much greater importance, and this view, too . . . he subsequently modified, so that by the time his book was already in print [*An Actor Prepares,* 1936] it was the ruling idea and through-action that became the cornerstone of his system.[17]

What Stanislavsky called the "ruling idea," Boleslavsky called the "spine" of the play; Stanislavsky's "through-action" was Boleslavsky's "spine" of the character. If it is true that Stanislavsky did not fully appreciate the value of these ideas until around 1936, then Boleslavsky made the discovery almost a decade before his teacher did.

One consequence of Boleslavsky's gradual shift of emphasis in the system was perhaps inevitable: among his students there sprang up two schools of thought. The majority of Lab-trained actors embraced dramatic action as the fundamental core of the system as Boleslavsky and Ouspenskaya presented it, while a minority endorsed emotional memory as the key to the actor's art. Lee Strasberg would eventually become the leading advocate of the minority view.

13

Dividing Time

The Lab's first public season of 1925–26 had been a crucial one for Boleslavsky. Not only had he produced three plays, but he had also laid the groundwork for a major redefinition of the system. Somehow he had also found time to work on three productions outside the Laboratory Theatre: *The Vagabond King, The Taming of the Shrew,* and *Captain Fury.* The first sowed the seeds of future discord between Boleslavsky and Miriam Stockton; the second won Boleslavsky the most serious critical attention he had yet received as a New York director; and the third closed out of town—foreshadowing events that would lead to Boleslavsky's eventual disillusionment with professional theatre in America.

The Vagabond King was a musical based on Justin Huntley McCarthy's novel and play, *If I were King.* It is the story of François Villon, the beggar-poet who meets King Louis XI. On a whim, Louis names Villon king for a day and, aided by his street followers, Villon saves Paris from the Burgundians—thereby saving his own life as well. Brian Hooker and W. H. Post wrote the book and lyrics, with music by Rudolf Friml. Producer Russell Janney had been pleased with Boleslavsky's work on *Sancho Panza* two years earlier and wanted him for this show as well, but "Boley" was too busy with the Lab. Max Figman, who also played Louis XI, was named to direct instead.

The production did not go smoothly. Janney had trouble raising money for the show, then argued with Actors Equity over the amount of the bond. The musicians walked out of several performances on the road. Janney worried that the crowd scenes, which were vital to the show's climaxes, were not effective. A week or so before the show opened in New York, he persuaded Boleslavsky to come in and "fix up the crowds."[1]

The Vagabond King opened on 21 September 1925 to mixed reviews, but such influential papers as the *Times,* the *Herald-Tribune,* and the *Sun* praised it highly. Equally important to the play's instant success was the effect it had on the public. Almost every critic remarked that the opening night audience cheered and shouted its approval more lustily than in a long while. The major papers agreed that there were two big reasons for the excited reception: Dennis King in the role of Villon, for whom many predicted "instant stardom"; and the handling of the rousing choruses. King, a young actor best known for his Mercutio to Jane Cowl's Juliet, had not been known as a singer, but as Stephen Rathbun wrote, he proved to be "that happiest of combinations, an actor who sings and not a singer who attempts halfheartedly to act. And there was nothing halfhearted about Mr. King's acting. . . . King caught something of the poetic flame of John Barrymore." As for Boleslavsky's crowd scenes, "Mr. King was ably seconded by as lusty and picturesque a chorus of stout lunged thieves and trollops as one could hope to see and hear."[2] As the *Times* put it: "The rabble of Paris would save the day, and it did, for as stirring a third-act climax as can be found between here and Verdun."[3]

The Vagabond King ran in New York for sixty-three weeks and then went on the road. By that time there were already three touring productions in the U.S. and another in Canada, all directed by Boleslavsky.

In Janney's judgment, Boleslavsky's work with the crowds "undoubtedly contributed 50 percent" to the show's initial success, "but he refused to let me put his name on the program as a co-director. He said, 'Some one else has done all the hard work—I just touched it up here and there. I will not take credit from your other director.' "[4] The playbill for the New York opening credited Figman with staging but noted: "Entire Production Under Personal Supervision of Russell Janney and Richard Boleslawsky." Later, after the production moved to the Shubert, Boleslavsky and Figman shared directorial credit. Subsequent playbills for other companies listed Boleslavsky as the sole director.

Later that season—about the time the Lab was producing *The Scarlet Letter*—Boleslavsky began directing another production for Janney, *Captain Fury,* a play written by Cornelia Otis Skinner as a vehicle for her father.[5] Boleslavsky apparently resigned as director while the production (which never reached New York) was still being tested out of town, in February 1926. This evidently did not damage Boleslavsky's relationship with Janney, for they subsequently worked together on two more shows.

The frequency with which Boleslavsky, Janney, and designer James Reynolds worked together suggests—though it does not prove—that Boleslavsky established with them a working relationship compatible with his own ideals of creative effort. They shared a measure of friendship and mutual respect as well.

Boleslavsky and Janney apparently shared a common interest in exploring the role of music in the theatre. Boleslavsky had tested the emotional value of music, using it extensively even in productions of straight dramatic plays and comedies. It was said of Janney:

> He . . . thought to weave a fabric of artistic beauty combining music, romance and drama, into an attractive and compelling form of lasting success. He aimed at a musical play which should offer more than mere clowning, pretty girls, catchy music and touching sentiments. He believed that tense dramatic situations could stir the soul with greater appealing force through a musical play than through a vehicle of the spoken word alone.[6]

These were hardly the goals of the "typical" Broadway producer Boleslavsky so often criticized.

Years later, shortly after Boleslavsky's death, Janney wrote a tribute to him, in which he said: "I . . . probably knew him better than any other theatrical man in the East," and described Boley as "a grand person and a loyal co-worker and friend. . . . The man himself, who could direct others to a dynamic fury, was gentle, modest, retiring—qualities that greatly retarded his 'getting ahead.' "[7]

Boleslavsky's particular gift in handling crowd scenes—so important in *The Vagabond King* 's success—had been singled out for special praise in much of his earlier work, most notably perhaps in *Charity* at the Teatr Polski. Janney tells us that when they worked on *Sancho Panza* he had expected to hire "a lot of 'supers' " to augment the fifteen actors for the street scene in which an angry crowd denounces Sancho, but Boleslavsky said, "No— let me do it with the regular company." So cleverly was the scene staged, Janney relates, that "I used to get great amusement asking my friends who were watching the play to guess how many actors were in the riot scene. They invariably guessed from thirty to fifty." For the New York production of *The Vagabond King,* Boleslavsky had fifty extras (and a full one hundred for the London production later), but that did not simplify his problem. Because of the difficulty of the musical score, Janney had cast excellent singers, "few of whom had ever set foot on stage before." As Janney explains, Boleslavsky's "secret" was to make

> every chorus boy and girl a distinct character. Each one reacted to "cues" according to that character—the coward, the bully, the pious one, the sneak, the skeptic, the braggart, etc. He even studied the speaking voices of the chorus—two tenors shouted

at this point, two baritones at that. He discovered and directed some eighty-seven set cues for crowd reactions in the first act of *Vagabond* alone. And except at several purposeful unison reactions, all these hundred chorus people had an individual reaction. Chorus boys and girls sat up nights developing their "characterizations."[8]

Boleslavsky's final extra-Lab production during the 1925–26 season, *The Taming of the Shrew*, was given only a dozen special matinee performances, beginning 18 December 1925 at the Klaw Theatre. The cast, headed by Rollo Peters as Petruchio and Estelle Winwood as Katherina, was composed mostly of actors who were simultaneously engaged in other Broadway shows. As a "matinee production," *Shrew* was not covered by all the critics, but the available reviews provide more detailed critical comments on Boleslavsky's directorial touch than for any other production he staged in the United States.

Brooks Atkinson provides the most detailed and thoughtful comments on the production. He begins:

When Hortensio's false whiskers came loose in the wooing scene of "The Taming of the Shrew," put on at the Klaw yesterday afternoon, one could not be sure whether it was by accident or design, and whether the explosive laughter from the audience had been sought deliberately thereby or not. One could not be sure because, except for a thin opening scene, the performance had been increasingly louder and broader, with the artlessness of clowning, and also with the incidental stage business that was no more uproarious than delightfully imaginative. For Richard Boleslavsky has staged this lusty farce as vigorously as a year ago M. Gemier produced it in this city. . . . The spirit of this good-humored director['s] . . . art is not cabined, cribbed or confined by the musty traditions of Shakespeariana.

Rather, as Atkinson saw it, Boleslavsky "assumes that Shakespeare sought to amuse the groundlings rather than unleash the rant and oily singsong of the too-professional acting": "The absurdities and grotesque byplays that Mr. Boleslavsky has introduced into 'The Shrew' bring out the full quality of the comedy without defiling Shakespeare's creation." The production had all the refinement of Lucentio's line to Hortensio in their scene with Bianca: "Spit in the hole, man, and tune again!" "Is this refined?" Atkinson asks. "Well, it is not in the idiom of modern books of etiquette. The current 'Shrew' is scarcely more gentlemanly. Without resorting to modern costumes, the director has evoked the spirit of contemporary low comedy."[9]

Atkinson notes the similarities between the holiday spirit that had recently animated Boleslavsky's *Twelfth Night* at the Lab and the high energy of his *Shrew*, as does John Mason Brown, who writes:

In the case of each he had aimed at investing the play with a festival gaiety. In *Twelfth Night* he had been somewhat thwarted in achieving this because of student material. But in *The Taming of the Shrew* his intention ordered almost every moment of the playing, and could be discerned even behind some of the wretched acting of the minor parts. He whipped the old farce into new life by the high spirits and animal gusto of his direction. In particular, the first act swept to a buoyant curtain and achieved the rollicking horseplay Boleslavsky desired.

Brown felt that both Winwood and Peters "fitted well into the director's pattern," but that the production's "chief amusement came from Ernest Cossart's Grumio, exaggerated in costume and in playing to fit glovelike into Boleslavsky's gay scheme."[10]

If *Twelfth Night* and *The Taming of the Shrew* were expressions of the same holiday spirit, they were quite different scenically. As Brown describes: "The permanent setting of four simple arches, suggestive of a loggia in Padua, was designed by Rollo Peters. It gave not only ample illusion of the scenes required, but allowed the play to race to its conclusion without any of the customary and annoying waits."[11] This scenic device was not Boleslavsky's invention, but rather had been conceived by Peters before Boleslavsky was selected as director. As Peters explained to a reporter, friends of his "got Boleslawsky . . . to stage the play, and he felt about the 'Shrew' as I always have, that it is pure, frank farce."[12] The "friends" may have included Jane Cowl, who had played Juliet to Peters's Romeo. She had seen the Lab's *Twelfth Night* and was quoted in a Lab Theatre catalogue (1927–28):

I am keenly interested in the work that Richard Boleslavsky is doing and I have a profound admiration for his ideas and methods. The performance "Twelfth Night" . . . was a joyous experience. I was fascinated by its novelty and the pervading spirit of sincerity with which Mr. Boleslavsky has imbued his young players.[13]

Judging from Atkinson's review, Boleslavsky found the simple setting Peters had devised wholly suited to his directorial needs:

Part of the holiday mood of informal entertainment comes from the scene device. One simple background with four portals and long, low steps serves for all the acts and scenes. To indicate the changes two serfs in costume hang signs reading: "Padua, a Public Place," "Before Hortensio's House," "A Public Road," as the case may be, bow graciously and walk off the stage. Such a device not only sets the key for the performance and keeps the comedy moving swiftly without breaking the illusion, but it also makes vivid the rough-and-ready technique of the comedy as written.

His further remarks suggest that the acting was both convincing and formally consistent with the conventions of vaudevillian burlesque: "Throughout the remainder the clowneries persist, scullions tremble in their boots and fall in a heap, actors chase one another about the stage and trip over the steps, lean against supports that prove inadequate; and the tutor's books for Bianca's instruction are as large as an Alice-in-Wonderland prop. . . . " In agreement with John Mason Brown, Atkinson finds that "as Grumio Mr. Cossart's acting (as well as his part) doubtless fits Mr. Boleslavsky's purpose most closely":

> Mr. Cossart wears a jubilant and jovial countenance, and his eyes are large with naive amazement. His natural tendency toward the obese is enhanced in the present comedy by a Falstaffian costume. His clowneries are well-nigh perfect. His strut, his command of what few subordinates a servant may order and his resentment of Petruchio's temperamental prerogatives are highly amusing. As Petruchio Mr. Peters is not merely the masterful wife-tamer. His conception of the part has form and flow, and effects a high degree of punctuation. At the end of the first act, for instance, he swings Katherina right and left while he is delivering his lines; and with the final "we will be married o' Sunday" flings her violently into her father's arms. If acting has punctuation, this is an exclamation point! And it provides a sententious curtain.[14]

Boleslavsky's treatment of *The Taming of the Shrew* was not universally admired. Alexander Woollcott dismissed it as "a swift-paced, simply mounted and excruciatingly forgettable performance."[15] Perhaps it was in response to such views that Atkinson, in a later piece, considered the broader implications of Boleslavsky's treatment of Shakespeare's play:

> Sticklers for convention complain that Mr. Boleslavsky's direction is nothing more nor less than Russian interpretation of English drama; but such a distinction sounds better than it serves. . . . At any rate, there is no objection to freeing "The Shrew" from the stuffy conventions of Shakespeare playing and making it low comedy for the delight of playgoers. The recent influx of Russian art in our theatre has contributed range to emotions, whether they be of tragedy or comedy. For Russian art in general—literary, musical or plastic—is not restrained by Anglo-Saxon self-consciousness or deliberation; it runs the full gamut with frankness and verve. "The Shrew" comes off well in that interpretation. Accordingly, the reviewer finds himself on the side of breadth and scope.[16]

Boleslavsky had every reason for optimism as he began his second public subscription season (1926–27) at the American Laboratory Theatre. In his first Lab season *The Sea-Woman's Cloak* had been an outstanding success, and *Twelfth Night* had been admired by the critics and proved popular with audiences. On Broadway he had been involved in the financially successful *Vagabond King*, and by directing the Chicago and Pittsburg companies of the musical he augmented the meager salary the Lab was able to pay him.

With his earnings from *The Vagabond King* he and Natasha had bought a second-hand Ford and gone hunting a place they could afford in the country. In Bridgewater, Connecticut, they settled finally on an old farm house with a mill that had been built some one hundred years earlier. It was in a state of near collapse: the roof leaked like a sieve at the first rain; the interior was filled with rubbish; the fireplaces were clogged; the kitchen was a shambles. But it was cheap—and they bought it. On weekends and during the summer they went to the country place, dubbed "The Red Mill," after the operetta, and worked hard to restore it to a livable condition. Boleslavsky loved to work with his hands; he was at his happiest going about in old clothes with hammer or saw, his pipe—an ever-present companion—clenched between his teeth, followed by a host of adopted dogs. German shepherds were his favorites. In time, there were other animals at the farm, too: a couple of cows, a horse, chickens, and a goat (which Natasha hated). Once they found a fawn, wounded and separated from its mother; they nursed the deer back to health and set it free.

Often without warning a carload of boys and girls from the Lab would appear to join in the work. More often, a group of boys would hitchhike out from the city, appearing in the morning and working all day on the house. To cool off, late in the afternoon they would splash in the pond formed by damming up the millstream. Natasha fed them improvised suppers and gave the more threadbare students discarded clothes, begged from "rich people" she had met. Summers at "The Red Mill" were seemingly idyllic and, like Boleslavsky, a bit sentimental.[17]

Of course the new season at the Laboratory Theatre brought its share of problems. In June 1926, the La Salle school building had been torn down, and the Lab again faced the problem of finding another home. Funds for the move and the 1926–27 season were desperately low (as they continued to be for the entirety of the Lab's life). This time the Lab relocated at 145 East 58th Street, formerly occupied by the Terrace Garden, a saloon closed by prohibition. Somehow Miriam Stockton came up with the necessary $9,000 for the yearly rental and an additional $5,000 for repairs and renovation. There were three floors for the school, and a separate one-story building for the theatre, which was remodeled along the lines followed the previous year, but with a stage almost twice the size and an auditorium seating 175 persons.[18]

During the summer of 1926 the Laboratory Theatre launched its subscription ticket campaign and announced its second season of plays: *The Straw Hat, The Trumpet Shall Sound, The Death of Danton,* and *Much Ado About Nothing.*

Boleslavsky wrote Herbert Stockton describing the season, clearly one that excited him. His chief reason for doing *The Straw Hat,* a light comedy by LaBiche, was that it had "more pedagogical value than anything else for the Lab. It is for the sake of the actors' training that we are producing it—the dances, songs, quick dialogue, these things help the actor grow and perfect his technique."

He intended his production of *Much Ado About Nothing* to be "a really beautiful stage definition" of the word "renaissance": "Why not present the festivals, love-affairs, jealousies, controversies, humorous approach of life, constant spirit of adorning life and the fever of seeking and building new aesthetic values for every second and moment of life?—the time when every dress was a work of art" created by artists of the stature of Raphael and Leonardo da Vinci. "Why not create, as *Much Ado* requires, the mood we are given when looking at miniatures of the *Decameron* and the bas reliefs of Cellini?" In his view, *Twelfth Night* is "a gay joke, a carnival, a masque"; it is a "jazz band foxtrot," while *Much Ado* "is a joyful and stylish love serenade. The former is a roar of laughter, the latter a smile of delight." In broader terms, Boleslavsky believed that the theatre which produces one Shakespearean play each season

> must find for each play its own peculiar style and method of production, each as different from the other as *Hamlet* is different from *Much Ado.* But it is meaningless to say that they should be produced in a "modern way." An archaic play can be dressed in modern fashion, and likewise a very modern play can be presented in a once current style long discarded.

Boleslavsky's real excitement, however, was reserved for *The Trumpet Shall Sound,* Thornton Wilder's first produced play, and *The Death of Danton,* by George Buchner. *The Trumpet Shall Sound* was chosen partly as a result of "the general policy" Boleslavsky had set the previous season—"a plan which includes the production of one contemporary American Drama, the best such play suited to our organization and to popular appeal." He wrote admiringly of Wilder's successful novel, *Cabala,* and its "difficult and aristocratic" form. Of Wilder, he said:

> His point of view on life and art is most interesting to me. He doesn't divide them— they are fused together—they are divine in his understanding—he looks for mystery

in realism and realism in mystery. His *Trumpet* is one of those realistic and common-life plays at the first reading, and on the tenth reading it becomes a deep, rich confession of blind human souls, seeking for light and unable to find it—the eternal fairy tale of the Prometheus flame. This is the realism of the nearest future: the lowest and highest elements of the human soul in strange and unsolved relationships—particularly the girl, of whom one may ask, where is she angel? and where is she devil?—a question we cannot answer, no more than we can solve the other human equations likewise propounded. This baffling elusiveness is what we meet now in every step of real life and is what unconsciously keeps us in the search for harmony and truth. The Neo-realism of the *Trumpet* has no limit in time—it isn't the exact moment of any day or month—it could be the realism of the eighteenth or nineteenth century or of nineteen twenty six. . . . It is curious that the original theme of the *Trumpet* can be traced back as far as Plato if I am not mistaken, and probably during the passing of time to come it will be used again.

As for the "general value" of Wilder's play, Boleslavsky explained that

it satisfies our practical domestic requirements, too. It gives us plenty of opportunity for characterization and it gives the actors a chance to look for the sources of inspiration more directly in real life and so transfer them to the realm of art. It will be the Lab's first real opportunity to deal with live, fresh models, instead of the imaginary forms with which it has had to work till now. At the same time the result will not be the mere copying of uninteresting, everyday life.

As much as he admired Wilder's play, Boleslavsky was even more excited by Buchner's *The Death of Danton*. He contrasted it with Romaine Rolland's play on the same subject and found Rolland's work filled with "socialistic tendencies": "It is a protocol—it is not a work of art." He compared Rolland to the "inquisitive mathematician" who examines the Venus de Milo and "solemnly declares that the nose . . . is three and seven eights inches long and her lips . . . seven eights of an inch thick": "Such an issue is too trivial. We wish to see the face of Venus de Milo." And the "face of the revolution" is precisely what Buchner shows us in his *Danton*.

He doesn't give us measurements—he was struck with the greatest creative revolt in the history of humanity, and with his art, with his soul, with his love for the beauty of the eternal cry: "I dare!" he makes us feel as if we were actually living among those people who said about themselves . . . "We will soon be nothing, but our names belong to eternity." Their names belong not only to eternity but to every alive soul who can think, can speak, can profess his creed and deeds freely. . . .

Danton, Boleslavsky felt:

is not a historical play although accurate in historic facts. It is more than that; it is truthful because it is a faithful image of the time which is going on forever, the time between the past and future always—as metamorphosis is unceasing—the time of change—the twilight between day and night when something breaks and a new life is evolved. With this as the theme, it certainly takes young, strong and healthy souls to act the Titans of the drama—and they were Titans. . . .

Boleslavsky explains that for Buchner

Danton is the master of the revolution and Robespierre its servant. . . . Danton lived and died for a revolution that was beautiful and glorious as well as necessary. Robespierre believed only in the cold necessity and the forcing of this into every alive soul; Danton was the Master by the larger vision and more human perspective.

"The form of the play is quite influenced by Shakespeare," Boleslavsky explains, for Buchner "does not adhere to the unity of time, place or action." For him, "the value of the event would be the same" whether the action was consummated in "twenty four hours or twenty four years." Boleslavsky found the structure "strangely modern," with the

flowing, episodic action of a good scenario—a good motion picture director would write a play as this is written. The lines have a staccato, sharp, short quality; every word has its value when taken separately outside of the play, yet it is nevertheless absolutely necessary to and bound up with the action. Some may say it has no story. Has the earthquake a story? The ocean storm? For the scientist, certainly; for us human beings it has a thrill and reminds us of those divine forces which are everywhere and in everything.

Boleslavsky concluded his letter to Stockton by sketching his directorial approach:

Danton will be one of the experimental productions of the Lab. It requires crowd work and synthetic action. We will look for a new form to frame the words of the play, we will look for a new scenery to express its spirit, for a new rhythm to emphasize the beating of the human heart when it first breathes the word "Liberty."
   In *Danton* we also have the difficult problem of creating the atmosphere where the private life of an individual and the public life at large are so closely bound together that the line of demarcation is scarce [*sic*] to be recognized. Fortune made Danton the hero of the people—he wished to be a private man—and lost himself in the opposing demands of what "they" wanted *for* "him" and what "they" wanted *from* "him." When he was acting as an individual for private ends, the deed was recognized as being inimical to the interest of the people. He predicted their destiny for them, told them what they were—but their desire for such exhortations and their demands on him were unceasing and inexhaustible—and when he wanted to find out for himself what he himself was, they killed him in jealousy. This conflict between the crowd and the individual will have to be very strongly portrayed on the stage in

visual and oral form, and in this will be the main experiment in the play's production.[19]

Labiche's *The Straw Hat* as directed by Boleslavsky mingled the components of farce, musical comedy, revue, and zestful harlequinade—served up with a kind of Gallic lightness and gaiety. It was translated and adapted for the Lab by Agnes James and "Paul Tulane" (actually Herbert K. Stockton) in a manner that Americanized, modernized, and musicalized Labiche's airy comedy about the misunderstandings that arise over a lost straw hat on a wedding day. Randall Thompson wrote some twenty tunes for the play. The opening night cast featured performances by Arthur Sircom, Anne Schmidt, Donald Keyes, Richard Skinner, and Shirley White (in a role played alternately by Stella Adler).

The settings and costumes for *The Straw Hat* had what Willis describes as the "comic strip" quality of the production: "One of the settings, for example, was a cartoon-like act curtain with holes for the actors' heads, much like the photographer's device for taking comic photos of grotesque bodies having familiar faces."[20] The basic setting was reminiscent of Rollo Peters's design for *The Taming of the Shrew* insofar as it consisted of three arches across the back and one at each side of the stage, but here the arches were filled by panels painted to represent various locales.

The Straw Hat opened on 14 October 1926 to generally favorable if unenthusiastic notices. Most reviewers found it amusing, but unexceptional light entertainment. One critic was quite impressed by the ingenuity of Lillian Gaertner's scenery and the speed with which the painted panels changed:

> New sets for old appeared suddenly and silently without the touch of visible hands. A millinery shop stood at a breath, and with full equipment, where a bachelor apartment had been a second before. A baroness's reception room turned itself into a bridal chamber. And so things went magically on.
>
> The seeming was as though one scene lingered upon another, even as winter in the lap of spring. We recommend this time-saving mechanism of the stage for extended observation.[21]

Preparations for *The Trumpet Shall Sound* were well underway before *The Straw Hat* opened, as it was Boleslavsky's habit to work on two or even three plays at the same time. By now the Lab's actors had been well trained in his way of working and rehearsals, though still unhurried, accomplished more in a shorter time.

Boleslavsky had known Thornton Wilder for some two years when he selected *Trumpet* from among three or four of Wilder's unproduced plays. In recommending the young writer for a Guggenheim Fellowship, Boleslavsky noted that they had been in "intimate association" at "various" times during that period and "had many discussions . . . concerning the art of the theatre and the writing of plays." Boleslavsky adds that the final version of *Trumpet* fell short of the hopes they shared for it "owing to the fact that Wilder was compelled to accept a salaried position" in Europe "while in the midst of re-writing the last act in conjunction with the rehearsal work" at the Lab. Blanch Tancock remembers that Wilder was a frequent visitor during rehearsals for *The Trumpet Shall Sound,* and adds, "I have always felt that the technique of the bare stage and the imaginary properties which he incorporated in *Our Town* were suggested to him as he watched Boley and Madame at work."[22]

Wilder's first produced play was set in the drawing room of a great mansion on New York's Washington Square in 1871. While the master of the house is away, a tender-hearted serving girl persuades the two other servants to take in an assortment of eccentrics who are down on their luck, including a handsome but heartless sailor, with whom she falls in love. The owner of the house returns unexpectedly and "plays at being God," sitting in judgment upon the erring inmates of his house. He is forgiving, but the servant girl—guilt-ridden and brokenhearted (the sailor has abandoned her)—kills herself.

The Trumpet Shall Sound opened at the Laboratory Theatre on 1 December 1926, with sets designed by James Shute and costumes by Helene Peck. The critics did not share Boleslavsky's enthusiasm for Wilder's drama. The *Times* said the play "furnishes a rather murky evening among the better known symbols," and described it as a rehash of other works "from Ibsen to Sutton Vane," "concocted without any highly piquant sauces." The *Herald-Tribune* described it as a "sophomoric" exercise "besprinkled with a misty symbolism." The *Evening Post* saw the play as "very, very symbolic, and for the most part quite uninteresting" with the exception of "one piece of beautiful writing in the play and one piece of beautiful acting in the rendering of it." The scene was one in which the sailor-sweetheart returns after months of absence, but refuses to marry the girl:

> And then comes the moment of rare loveliness, when Flora takes the crude seaman, to whom she has pinned her delicate love, through the wedding ceremony of her own devising. Standing there before lighted candles, her eyes glowing, her lips tremulous, she marries herself to the jeering sailor, and all the mysterious emotion that there is in any ritual, whether of savage or civilized tribes of the earth, gets into the words she utters.

Of that same moment, the *Time's* critic wrote:

> Last night was chiefly distinguished for one occurrence—a luminous, almost transcendental and vital performance on the part of a comely young woman by the name of Helen Coburn. . . . It was a portrayal as fine and true as it was unexpected. It was not altogether acting, either: Miss Coburn at times was actually living the part and she made credible the somewhat fantastic things she had to do.[23]

Despite the critics' disdain, Wilder's play continued in repertory with *The Straw Hat,* as well as *Twelfth Night,* beginning on December 20, and *The Sea-Woman's Cloak,* on January 3. *The Scarlet Letter* was not revived.

Boleslavsky's next production was not at the Lab, but on Broadway. The play was *Ballyhoo!,* written by Kate Horton, produced by Russell Janney, and designed by James Reynolds. When it opened on 4 January 1927, it was met by all but unanimous displeasure from the critics.

Ballyhoo! is the story of love and morals in a tent vaudeville show, playing a Middle Western fair. Starlight Lil, a champion bronco buster, is a woman of easy virtue until she inadvertently wins the heart of a virginal young man. His brassy mother tells Lil to "make a man of him," but Lil determines instead to shock him into disillusion by offering herself to whichever cowboy cuts the highest card. The young man, hurt and embittered, turns to the arms of an even less virtuous woman. Minna Gombell and Eric Dressler played the leads, and W. H. Post was in a featured role.

The critics rejected *Ballyhoo!* at least partly because of its fairly explicit treatment of this sexual theme. The *Times* noted the "presumptive appeal of the salacious"; the *Wall Street Journal* remarked the "snatches here and there from some of the more daring of the season's sex shebangs." Percy Hammond, on the other hand, believed that the "more callous first-nighters" snickered and made wisecracks in response to the "earnest exhibition" of a "a juvenile, sentimental and unbelievable mess," rather than embarrassment over the play's sexual candor.[24]

The generally brittle Alexander Woollcott was more than usually scathing: " 'Ballyhoo!'. . . . is one of the most arrestingly feeble dramas in the history of America's art life":

> But as a phenomenon of the American stage in one of its more lunatic moments this excruciatingly unimportant premiere was not without its interest. For here was Russell Janney—a great big grown-up manager now, mind you—summoning such men as

Richard Boleslavsky to direct and James Reynolds to adorn a play which in manuscript must have seemed even to the unpracticed eye to be the product of about the same taste, the same imaginative power and the same intellectual attainment, let us say, as produced "My Mother Was a Lady" or any of the sourer ballads of the variety halls of yester-year.

Regarding Boleslavsky in particular, Woollcott wrote:

But when a script of such incredible naiveté and spuriousness is then turned over to a Russian maestro and he brings to its picture of the tent shows in our Middle West all the familiarity and understanding of them which he could acquire through a long life spent in the Russian theatre, you begin to get such layer on layer of unreality that last night's spectators kept pinching themselves to see if they were awake and found, as often as not, that they were not. . . . But then one would also expect a director like Boleslavsky and an artist like young Master Reynolds to decline all association with so childish and trumpery a script. The ways of these people are endlessly amazing. I suppose some one will engage Toscanini to direct "Yes, We Have No Bananas."[25]

Woollcott's remarks inadvertently raise a larger question, for, in one sense, that Boleslavsky worked on Broadway at all is surprising. In his lectures in 1923, he had ridiculed the typical Broadway producer: "glorified janitors," he called them, quoting Hartly Manners. He deplored the "theatre of trade," as typified by the Broadway musical revue, with its lack of coordination between individual artists, its inadequate rehearsal periods, its reliance on the star system and character types, its mindless use of clichés in acting, scenery, and staging.[26] Yet, as he announced in "The Laboratory Theatre," his avowed aim was to help reform such practices and to introduce new scenic forms to the commercial stage as well. A play like *Ballyhoo!* would scarcely seem to offer much opportunity for him to follow that lofty aim.

Why did Boleslavsky take such work? One possibility is that, while his command of English was quite good, it was his third or fourth language; possibly he was not sensitive to nuances and rhythms in the language of scripts like *Ballyhoo!* that jarred native speakers. Or, perhaps he realized the script's flaws but was persuaded to take the play by his friendship for Janney. Then, too, he evidently sometimes worked more out of financial need than artistic interest. Francis Fergusson, who knew Boleslavsky better perhaps than any other member of the Lab Theatre (he worked often as Boleslavsky's assistant and sometimes conducted Lab rehearsals while "Boley" was busy on Broadway), believes that in many cases Boleslavsky felt the shows he agreed to direct on Broadway were "messes," but took them anyway. The reason that Boleslavsky compromised his own artistic standards and directorial aims, Fergusson believes, was simple: "He needed the dough. He was very lousily paid at the Laboratory Theatre, as everyone was."[27] This opinion is supported by Harold Clurman, who felt that in agreeing to "doctor" Stark Young's *The Saint,* Boleslavsky "knew very well that the play was not very sturdy and there was no way of his making a success of it. The idea that you can get a good director—a fine director—into a poor script and save it is just nonsense. All he can do is make it a more presentable show."[28]

In the meantime, at the Lab Boleslavsky had been rehearsing *The Death of Danton,* for which he himself was designing the scenery. In his letter to Stockton, cited earlier, he had said "the scenery will consist mainly of lighting and the use of certain principles of stage groupings."[29] Willis reports: "One tentative plan called for a unit setting, bathed in red and dominated by a huge guillotine directly up center."[30]

Early in January 1927—evidently shortly after the *Ballyhoo!* fiasco—Boleslavsky was faced with a dilemma: Janney wanted him to go to London to direct *The Vagabond King* there, but if he accepted the offer, he would have to sail on February 11. Boleslavsky did not feel he could do justice to *Danton* in the time remaining, nor could he produce *Much Ado About Nothing* satisfactorily if rehearsals were suspended until his return in late April. Boleslavsky had displayed more passionate interest in *Danton* than in any play since *Hamlet* in Prague. Should he go ahead with the Buchner play and give up the trip to London and the chance to win an almost certain success with *Vagabond King?* Or should he remain true to the principles he so vigorously espoused in his lofty talks with the Lab students, turn his back on the easy commercial success, and produce *Danton* for the sake of his vision as an artist of the theatre?

On 22 January 1927 various newspapers reported that *The Death of Danton* would not be included in the Lab's season of plays. Two days later, the press announced that the Laboratory Theatre would instead produce Clemence Dane's *Granite,* a success in London during the summer of 1926 with Sybil Thorndike and Lewis Casson. The Lab production would mark the American premiere of the play. Eighteen days after *Granite* was announced in the press, it opened at the Laboratory Theatre. That same night, 11 February 1927, Boleslavsky sailed for London.

Blanch Tancock, who played Judith, the role created by Sybil Thorndike, recalls that "*Granite* was the most hurriedly prepared of all our plays." Boleslavsky's decision to go to England was "abrupt" and it advanced the deadline for a new production sharply. *Granite* was one of the plays under consideration. It presented no great problems [in terms of production] . . . and had a small cast. It was put into rehearsal at once and was rehearsed intensively for just over a fortnight, I think. This time there was no double casting and the onus for preparation in depth became the actor's responsibility. The cast were all experienced actors, used to playing together, and alert to Boley's direction.[31]

Francis Fergusson believes there was considerable cynicism and calculation behind Boleslavsky's choice of plays to replace *Danton*. Moreover, in its staging he deliberately employed the kind of "stage tricks" he felt would please the critics. Fergusson remembers:

Granite he did frankly to make money. The Lab was badly in need of dough, as always. And he simply looked around and found this play. He didn't like it. He knew exactly how to stage it: he was able to use the natural tensions in the acting company and to use [actors'] "yens." He did it beautifully: the atmosphere was so thick you could cut it with a knife . . . He spent very little money on it . . . But he did it with complete cynicism.[32]

Tancock remembers that the night of *Granite's* opening

was also the night when Boley sailed for England. It was a very emotional night all around. Most of the first line critics had been in the house. Those of us who had been in the play were keyed high. Others who had only watched were depressed. One and all we rushed down to the docks to see Boley off. We tried to give him a gay, happy, confident send-off. But when he was gone and we turned away, depression descended and we went sadly back to home and to bed.[33]

Evidently Boleslavsky understood New York's critics better than they understood him. Clemence Dane's tale of repressed passion, double murder, and demonic powers won for the Lab its most enthusiastic reception ever. Nathan Zatkin praised the production's "rugged sincerity" and wrote: "Richard Boleslavsky effected a masterpiece of direction, using every device known to drama, every subtle touch possible to extract from the play the last vestige of power."[34] Atkinson felt that in *Granite* "the American Laboratory players now give the best molded performance of their interesting career." Boleslavsky, he said, had "separated" the "several differently colored threads" woven through the pattern of the drama "with uncommon skill."[35] R. Dana Skinner had high praise for Boleslavsky's staging of the play's ending: "This is the most clearcut example of creative direction I have ever seen."[36] Percy Hammond urged a commercial producer to transfer the play to Broadway where it might serve as an example for the "unenlightened." The production, he said, might be profitably studied by Woods, Belasco,

Erlanger, Ames, or McBride: "There is a strange door, for instance, in 'Granite,' which, whether closed, opening or ajar, provides more drama than many of the noisier expedients prevailing in Broadway."[37]

Tickets for *Granite* sold out at once; several days passed before Boleslavsky learned that the Laboratory Theatre had its first popular hit. By the time the news reached him, the Lab had already received offers to move *Granite* to the Shubert Theatre, the Greenwich Village Theatre, or the Mayfair Theatre. The Lab sent news to Boleslavsky, even as they deliberated the options. Pressed by the producers for a decision, the Lab council voted unanimously to accept the offer to move *Granite* to the Mayfair, a small Broadway house on 44th Street with a stage almost exactly the size of the Lab's. They reasoned that they had to turn down the larger houses because Boleslavsky was not in New York to re-stage the play.[38]

On 25 February 1927 Boleslavsky sent a cable:

OPPOSE BROADWAY PRESENTATION STOP IF MOVED ALREADY MAKE BEST—RICHARD

A return cable was dispatched:

COUNCIL UNANIMOUSLY APPROVED MAYFAIR PROJECT LIMITED EN-GAGEMENT REPERTORY CONTINUE FIFTY EIGHTH STREET TOO LATE CHANGE CONTRACT PLEASE CABLE ENCOURAGEMENT.

On 26 February Boleslavsky answered:

MAKE BEST GO AHEAD[39]

Granite opened at the Mayfair on February 28, and continued playing to sell-out business for seven weeks, at which time it returned to the Lab for a final week of performances before the summer break. The commercial producers financed the move, allotted money for salaries, and paid the Lab fifty percent of all production profits. Every night Herbert Gellendré, after being "killed" as Jordan in *Granite,* took the first available taxi and dashed across town to get in make-up for his appearance as Dexter in *The Trumpet Shall Sound.* Blanch Tancock felt cut off from the Laboratory Theatre:

I think I felt quite soon that it was a mistake, but I may be flattering myself with hindsight. Anyway, I do think it was a mistake. In the first place, it broke the unity of the group in a run and took them out of regular performances of other plays. What was worse, all the values that had been built into us were in some way diminished by this surrender to quick success tactics. And on the very lowest plane, surely it would have been sounder to attract audiences to our own theatre which had a strong atmosphere and personality, to encourage their patronage, rather than lift a momentarily successful production into a completely impersonal theatre where it had no connection whatsoever with the rest of our plays. There may have been financial considerations, of which I know nothing, that made it a wise decision, but by any other standard, I am sure it was bad. Anyway, for the rest of that season I was almost completely out of touch.[40]

Boleslavsky felt cut off, too—and was irascible. He wrote from London complaining that the advertising for *Granite* mentioned neither the Lab's name or his. He met with a London producer who asked him if he had anything to do with the play:

I'm very seldom mad. I was after this question. But I could not help it. That is why I send nasty cable. I'm sorry. . . . Cable me please how *Granite* is doing on Broadway. And ask them to play strong and vigorous every night—I have very little news from you—and it upsets me. I'm sure after *Granite* news—you all have forgotten me. . . .

Clemence Dane, pleased with the success of her play, met with him and offered a new work: "It is no good. We shan't count on it in the next season." In his absence George Auerbach (who had acted in every Lab production except *Granite*) was rehearsing *Big Lake,* a new play by Lynn Riggs; there was talk of opening it as the Lab's final production of the season: "If *Big Lake* gets Madame's OK I have nothing against its opening. . . . as an experimental production—without my participating in it . . . " Stella Adler had been absent from the Lab working on a professional production; she had returned a few weeks earlier and now there were Lab members and trustees who were pushing to have her replace Blanch Tancock (who had received both highly favorable and quite negative reviews) in *Granite:* "Don't change cast in *Granite*. If we have something that is good—believe me it takes plenty to improve it— wait until I come back. . . . " In closing, Boleslavsky reiterated: "Write me more. I'm lonely without Lab. Ask everybody to write me," and ended with: "Do not undertake a *thing* without notifying me first. God bless you all. . . . "[41]

Elizabeth Bigelow wrote Boleslavsky on March 11. Among other things, she enthusiastically praised the progress of *Big Lake* under George Auerbach's direction. Four days later Boleslavsky cabled his instructions: they should close *The Straw Hat* and concentrate entirely on *Big Lake* and open it without him as an "experimental production."[42]

Big Lake opened on 8 April 1927, staged by Auerbach under Ous-penskaya's guidance, and featured Helen Coburn, Frank Burk, Stella Adler, and Grover Burgess in important roles. The critics found this drama of false accusation, murder, and suicide in a rural setting to be a "promising" evening—promising playwright, promising director, and promising actors.

That same month, on April 19, Boleslavsky's London production of *The Vagabond King* opened at the Winter Garden Theatre, featuring Derek Oldham as François Villon, Norah Blaney as Huguette, and H. A. Saintsbury as Louis XI. Russell Janney describes the play's reception: "The audience remained in the theatre cheering for half an hour after our opening performance. Boleslawski was shouted for and recalled again and again."[43] *The Play Pictorial* summarized the critics:

For the most part it makes a bustling, spirited show, full of rich colour in a succession of lavish scenes that happily avoid the merely garish. . . .

—*Daily Telegraph*

Picturesqueness of staging, melody, a strong story, lilting music—all these contribute to a production that promises to be a big success.

—*Daily Mail*

The Vagabond King puts the last dab of whitewash on the character of François Villon—and does it to the strains of tuneful music. The result is quite irresistible. This is no vagabond king; it is a kingly vagabond. . . .

—*The Times*

The Vagabond King is one of the best of the musical plays seen in London for years. The first act in the tavern, which is a riot of colour and movement, is a magnificent piece of production. *The Vagabond King* should break all records at the Winter Garden.

—*Daily News*

The Vagabond King proved last night a triumph. It is the most romantic musical play staged in London for years. It has colour, movement, beauty. The chorus singing roused the audience to tremendous enthusiasm. "The Song of the Vagabonds" could stand up against a dozen similarities. It was sung by a crowd of cutthroats with a fury that forced from the audience a thunder of cheering. They acted it. They shouted it. They "bit" it in their intensity. Their well-chosen voices blended in perfect balance.

—*Daily Express*[44]

Boleslavsky sailed for New York on 23 April 1927. *The Vagabond King* continued at the Winter Garden for 480 performances.

Miriam Stockton wrote Boleslavsky a letter, which she evidently never sent, in the early summer—probably in July 1927. It read in part:

My Dear Mr. B—

It is impossible and ridiculous to attempt to build up a noble young theatre without a director. This theatre has been created for you—do you want it, do you wish to do by it as should be done —or do you not—? We need to know.

I do not think you know how to estimate the quality of friendship which many American people have put back of you—and which you accepted—such generous financing as you have had for five years is almost unknown in the world. . . . You signed a letter for Mrs. McCormick last spring which was virtually a contract with her and with Herbert and me—and you have since then broken it in spirit and in letter. You have involved yourself and put the money, the lives and honor of your many friends at the mercy of a Broadway producer whom you know to [be] tyrannical and utterly without respect of anyone but himself. Since the *Straw Hat* went into rehearsal—15 months [ago]—you have made five Broadway productions, spent three months building up your fame, and three months in England. Meanwhile look at the scanty half-prepared work you have given to the Lab, which has the potentialities of really great and important opportunity—to say nothing of matters of honor.

It is wicked in my opinion for me to involve other people's money, my husband's and my own name . . . and the lives of everyone in the Lab behind a man who puts us all at the mercy of Mr. Janney . . . in order that he may make money himself. This seems to me a betrayal of trust and honor and I cannot share in such ways . . . which have been to my mind dishonest and sly—[45]

At the end of the 1926–27 season the Terrace Garden building was torn down to make room for the Roxy movie theatre. During the summer and early fall of 1927, the Lab moved from the former saloon to a former brewery, located at 218–224 East 54th Street. Stockton raised money for the most expensive renovation yet, one which provided the Lab its most comfortable and spacious quarters. The Lab would remain here until it closed in 1930.

14

Season of Change

Miriam Stockton had reason to question the degree of Boleslavsky's personal and emotional investment in the Laboratory Theatre's future. The depth of her own commitment was such that earlier, at a time when the Lab was particularly hard pressed for funds, she had considered mortgaging her house to keep its doors open. The Lab's chronic financial problems would grow so intense during the coming season that she would finally take this step. Understandably she was deeply disturbed by Boleslavsky's ever more frequent—and ever more lengthy—absences from the theatre she had fought so hard to create for him.

The problem ran deeper than she suspected. Boleslavsky was discouraged. More and more often he was beset by what he called his "Polish gloom." He worried about money. The New York run of *The Vagabond King* was about to close, cutting off one source of income. True, he would earn something from the London production, but his total income in 1927 from his most commercially successful show was only $1,250; his income from the Lab for the same period, $2,600.[1]

Immediately upon his return from London he set about trying to get work to supplement his meager earnings from the Lab. He sent letters to his friend Basil Sydney about a possible Broadway production involving Sydney and his wife, Mary Ellis (she had wed Sidney at "The Red Mill"), and they eventually agreed to do Bruno Frank's *The Twelve Thousand*, with Boleslavsky directing. Boleslavsky also wrote to Russell Janney: they would do a musical adaptation of *The Squaw Man*, to be retitled *The White Eagle*. He wrote to Rollo Peters, but nothing came of it. He agreed to direct *A Midsummer Night's Dream*, for a modest salary, as a benefit for the Actors Equity Home. Later in the season, The Snarks, a women's amateur theatre club, wrote the Lab asking whether one of their advanced students might direct for them Austin Strong's pantomime, *Popo;* Boleslavsky took the job himself and agreed to accept the usual $500 fee the club paid its directors. He had not forgotten completely about the Laboratory Theatre; at his request Francis Fergusson was reworking the translation of *The Death of Danton* for the Lab's coming season.[2]

Just two or three weeks after his return from London, while these plans were taking shape, Boleslavsky investigated another avenue of possible work, one which might take him beyond Broadway. Early in May he met with Robert Edgar Long, a "Counsel in Public Relations," who was visiting New York from his home base in St. Petersburg, Florida. Whether Long approached Boleslavsky or Boleslavsky instigated the meeting is not clear. In any case, Long wrote him on 14 May 1927, "after thinking over this whole business of securing for you 'a place in the sun' in the motion picture field." For only $100 (of Boleslavsky's money), Long promised to get an article with pictures featured in the next issue of "a publication here in town called 'The National Review,'" which publishes the careers of men who have become prominent in the world of the theatre" and reaches "the desks of the higher officials and their secretaries" in the film industry. Boleslavsky thought the proposition over for three days and wrote back that he had just paid his debts and finds himself "as poor as I was before." "Without being greedy," he continued, "I must tell you frankly that the sum of $100 means so much to me that I really cannot spend it now—I just can't, that's all." He expressed his liking for Long personally and added: "I hope that our business relations, though they start humbly, will some time bring a nice crop."[3] Incredibly, Boleslavsky had the Lab's regular secretary type his response to Long; no doubt word of this exchange reached Miriam Stockton soon after.

Boleslavsky's mood at the beginning of the summer is perhaps most vividly reflected in a long letter he wrote to Gordon Craig. Boleslavsky had been greatly excited the previous season by one of Craig's books—probably *The Theatre Advancing* (1921); finally he had Elizabeth Bigelow inquire of Craig whether he would consider coming to the United States and lecturing at the Lab during an American visit. Craig wrote a warm and encouraging response, but said he could not come to America just then. On June 9, Boleslavsky wrote Craig a reply. In response to Craig's offer to write about Boleslavsky's work at the Lab, Boleslavsky answered that the Lab was not yet worthy of such serious artistic attention: as yet, he writes, "we are doing nothing but, as I call it, 'smelling the theatre.' " Boleslavsky explains that he recently directed "a musical comedy" in London that "isn't of special value," but that his earnings from it will finance "a few months" of serious work "trying to find worthy things in the theatre." Of his own career, Boleslavsky says that he is not writing, nor is he designing very much:

All I am doing is trying to educate the young people as much as it is possible in every element of the theatre . . . When the actors will learn as much as they can about the science of the theatre and the handling of instruments of the theatre, those instruments being themselves, we will produce one, two or three plays as we want and not as we must. At present we are producing the plays as we must do them, for the sake of squeezing a certain amount of money necessary for their expenses and convincing the people who give us the rest of the money that we are doing something. I do know that this is the only way that we can succeed here in this country . . . We don't do yet what we want and what we dream to do sometime. All these four years of our existence, I am trying to kill what you call "imitation of an actor," and believe me, as Herod, I am unmerciful and kill them when they are still babies.

Actors, Boleslavsky adds, are the "same all over the world": "They love effect, and they miss plenty of beautiful things which are right close to them in nature, and they work hard to do the things which were done a thousand times in a thousand past years. Well, I am one of them." His only virtue, he writes, is that every day he reminds himself of the lessons learned from Stanislavsky, Craig and "a few others—almost nobody." And what will happen to the young actors he is training? They will either do "what human beings do in the theatre or they will disappear in the Great White Way" called Broadway, where they will win "glory" or find "oblivion"—which, he adds, are one and the same thing.[4]

A Midsummer Night's Dream was scheduled for only a single performance as a gala extravaganza for the benefit of the Actor's Fund. It was played in a natural outdoors setting at the Forest Lawn Tennis Stadium, which seated some fourteen thousand people. Because of unseasonably cool weather and rain, it was delayed a week and then presented on 26 June 1927. The performance began with a Prologue delivered by Tyrone Power. This was followed by a thirty-five instrument chamber orchestra playing Mendelssohn's Overture. The cast included a hundred member ballet corps choreographed by Alexin Kosloff of the Metropolitan Opera and another hundred persons singing in choruses directed by Leo Braun. Boleslavsky had wanted Douglas Moore to write special music for the production, but Moore declined, saying there was not enough time.[5] The setting was an oblong white platform with four white columns, placed on the lawn of the tennis stadium, which was also used by the actors; the costumes were brightly colored to contrast with this background.

A critic from the *Herald-Tribune* praised the "intelligence and imagination" of Boleslavsky's direction, particularly his use of the "vast and undecorated stage he had to deal with." The reviewer was impressed also that the actors' lines were delivered with the "sensitive appreciation of both their metrical and literary values," when generally "lines must be bellowed forth to be heard at all" in such open-air performances.[6]

A few additional performances were scheduled in August on Broadway, but plans to extend the life of the production were soon cancelled, most likely because Reinhardt's celebrated production of the same play was announced for the coming season.[7]

Immediately after *A Midsummer Night's Dream* the pace of planning for the Laboratory Theatre's 1927–28 season accelerated—and heated up. On July 23, Boleslavsky wrote to Miriam Stockton, apologizing for his "rudeness on Friday night" and assuring her he had not intended to hurt her. He assured her, too, that everything she had done on the Lab's behalf was "recognized and valued highly": "I think you act just like a silly little girl when you say that I don't want you in the Lab and so on— I won't even answer that. . . . " He then outlined the problems relating to the Lab's operation that most deeply concerned him, starting with the "policy towards productions and purchase of plays":

> . . . More and more I catch myself trying to work on proposed plays (and even on selecting them) with the reason "this play is the cheapest to produce" dominating my mind. I do understand the necessity of economy—and I am not one who asks uncontrolled and unlimited means for creating a theatrical performance—but entering a new section of the Lab's road to stability we should remember that after all it is abnormal in the theatre to pay for everything but for the most organic and vital element of theatrical organism—this element being productions and plays. . . . I'm handicapped with material (actors). I'm handicapped as a matter of fact with everything—For God's sake don't understand it as a complaint—God knows I would like to work for nothing and do everything for nothing—but even God Almighty could not do it. . . .

Regarding the financial policy of the school, Boleslavsky argued that there should be more money for scholarships—not less, as Stockton proposed. One reason for the Lab's existence, he said, should be to provide training for the truly worthy student actor who cannot afford tuition. On the other hand, he felt that many students were getting too much for their money and that tuition rates should possibly be raised: "I would not hesitate to give anything extra for talented ones—but why spend precious money for dumbbells?"

Next he raised what he evidently felt was a crucial issue, one that penetrated to the core of many of the Lab's problems: the conflict between the "human and professional" in the Lab's operation. He had raised the question with Craig, and begins his response with a quote from one of Craig's letters:

> One is raised from the seeds of revolt
> Kept flourishing by Discipline
>   but Discipline
>   the hardest drilling known
> I see no discipline in theatre
>   I see appalling Vanity.

These words hit me over the brain and I saw in them the reasons of many of our troubles—they concern myself just as well as the last pupil.

. . . To get the best results for the whole institution, I'm afraid [that for our] $9,000 budget we are a little bit too *human* in our relations to our comrades and fellows—human to the point where we stop being wise—human in sympathy and hatred. We love and hate personalities a little bit too much for the even and productive function[ing] of a whole body. It goes everywhere—Miss Larson is invited [to join the faculty] because Ann Schmidt loves her—

Patsy [Walter Duggan] is thrown out because Madame [Ouspenskaya] hates him.

Morton [Brown] is proposed [for a] position he does not fit because Boleslavsky loves him.

Mary Steichen is proposed to the group because she is so charming—everybody loves her.

Pupils don't go to [Elsa] Findley's lessons because they hate her.

We don't produce *Danton* because we hate it—.

We suspect [Blanch] Tancock hates [Stella] Adler and Boleslavsky [hates Frances] Wilson.

We all love the Lab to such a degree that if it were a child we would give him nothing but candy—and wonder where the indigestion comes from—it all makes me sick.

Theatre is a *machine*—it should be emotional in results but not in means—it produces emotions but does not work by emotions. . . . What is human? To give pain but create a loyal character, or to give pleasantry and create indifferent creatures? What is human is strict business, where production and creation are our aims. I get a tremendous amount of love from the Lab—but I'm absent for eleven weeks and three-quarters of my words are forgotten by everybody. . . .

. . . I am the weakest on this point perhaps because I was in such a forge [at the MAT] that there was not a night when I did not weep and consider myself the worst kind—it was too hard—I know how hard it is—and try as much as it is possible to spare the others [such suffering]. . . .

As I said before, I'm lecturing myself primarily but I need everybody to understand my point of view and to help me start this new policy of relations among us in the new building. Kindness and understanding should be normal and fundamental, but not [when] they come before the needs and necessities of the institution.

He closed by apologizing for "this crazy and 'wordy' letter . . . it is difficult for me to write."[8]

The Lab's problems escalated. They had to vacate their East 58th Street location soon, but the brewery on East 54th Street would not be ready for occupancy until November—after the expenditure of over $30,000 for the lease and renovation.[9] Miriam Stockton was now functioning as the Lab's Administrative Director, in which capacity she fully intended to enforce Boleslavsky's new policy of businesslike, unemotional operation. She and Boleslavsky agreed that classes should begin at the old address but the season's plays would not open until the move to the new address had been accomplished. The John Price Jones Corporation was hired to devise a scheme for a long-range fund-raising program. At their suggestion, the operation of the Lab's school, which had always been more profitable than the theatre itself, was separated further from the running of the acting company and renamed the Theatre Arts Institute.[10]

The new season would begin in November with Shakespeare's *Much Ado About Nothing,* which Boleslavsky had worked on the previous year but postponed when he went to London. This would be followed by the first in a projected trilogy of Knut Hamsun plays, *At the Gate of the Kingdom.* Next would be Arthur Schnitzler's pantomime, *The Bridal Veil,* directed by Elizaveta Anderson-Ivantzoff. Boleslavsky would finish the season with two plays by French authors: Jules Romaines's *Dr. Knock* and Jean-Jacques Bernard's *Martine.*

In keeping with the Lab's new policy of professionalism, the acting company was reduced; only the most gifted and popular actors were invited back. Beginning this season, only one actor would be assigned to each role. Moreover, the regular company was augmented by older, more experienced players from the professional stage; Joaquin Souther was hired for $50 a week plus, at his request, tuition-free training at the Lab's school. Boleslavsky thought Souther was talented but that his work bore the stamp of the "Broadway style"; he wanted the actor's maturity and experience, but would let him go if he did not absorb the Lab's methods.[11] Other professionals were considered. In one or two cases, entering students were brought into the acting company for small roles ahead of the "auxiliary group" that had worked its way through the Lab's training program; Elizabeth Bigelow was quite concerned by this breach of the Lab's stress on "training before stepping foot on the stage."[12]

Some unexpected changes in the Lab's acting company occurred as well. Early in September 1927, Stella Adler resigned; Boleslavsky urged her to stay. She explained her desperate financial situation: "You will say, Stella why didn't you tell us before. I can only say I didn't intend leaving you. My position at home is such that were there no other theatre engagements obtainable I should have to secure other steady employment." Boleslavsky answered: "I understand your problem only too well. So completely so that I cannot find it in my heart to urge the decision upon you although I would like to." Still, he offered her $30 a week, apologizing that he could not offer more.[13]

On October 6, Boleslavsky wrote George Auerbach—previously a mainstay of the company—demanding his resignation. Auerbach, Boleslavsky wrote, had been insubordinate and lazy:

> Please do not come to me and do not try to talk to me. I don't want to yell at you as I should and I can't talk kindly and calmly with you anymore. I am ashamed before everybody. Katherine Squire and Elizabeth Tyler, kids, do a thousand times better than you do. I am ashamed before Souther who thinks I am a silly fool to suffer your indignant attitude. This letter is final and decisive.[14]

Until now, Auerbach had been one of Boleslavsky's personal favorites.

Later in the season, in December, Grover Burgess, one of the company's most popular actors with critics and public alike, sent a nonchalant note to Elizabeth Bigelow: "My 'game' leg has forced me to return from New York to my country 'villa' for medical attention. . . . Circumstances may force me to join the Neighborhood . . . again as soon as I can meander about." Boleslavsky was out of town with *The White Eagle* at the time. When he heard about Burgess' note he sent the following cable:

> TRY TO PERSUADE GROVER HE CANNOT LEAVE NOW IT IS COWARDLY AND INHUMAN STOP SENT HIM WIRE STOP WILL BE BACK SUNDAY NIGHT MAYBE SUNDAY MORNING THERE IS NO UNDERSTUDY FOR HIM REGARDS—RICHARD[15]

Burgess did not return.

Boleslavsky started rehearsals for the Lab's season in September. On October 12, he advised the Stocktons of the days he would have to spend rehearsing *The White Eagle* for Russell Janney, including some periods out of town, during which his assistants would continue the work at the Lab. The Stocktons had evidently gained confidence in Boleslavsky's dedication to the Lab during the course of many letters and conversations over the summer and early fall. Nonetheless, on October 18, Herbert Stockton asked Boleslavsky to sign a one-year contract with the Lab, backdated to September 10.[16]

On November 18 the American Laboratory Theatre opened its

1927–28 season with *Much Ado About Nothing,* with Blanch Tancock as Beatrice, George Macready as Benedick, Francis Burk as Claudio, Martha Johnson as Hero, and—in one of the few instances of doubling this season—Thomas Hayes and Louis V. Quince alternating as Dogberry. Douglas Moore wrote special music for the production; settings were credited to the Laboratory Theatre Workshop "and were inspired by the Fifteenth Century illuminated manuscripts of 'Roman de la Rose.' " Paul Rover painted them.

The critics divided about equally on the merits of the production, but it raised a storm of controversy within the Lab. As several of the critics pointed out, the stylized acting against mannered scenery was hopelessly marred by terrible diction and mangled line readings that made the dialogue all but unintelligible. Constance McLean, the Lab's speech teacher at the time, wrote an angry letter to Boleslavsky in which she attacked the actors for spurning the speech training she had offered them repeatedly: "I cannot say enough in praise of the acting, the staging, the setting, the coloring and the costuming. I cannot say enough in denunciation of the absolutely unintelligent reading of the lines." She reports that "one whole division of students in the new group simply rebelled last Thursday" because such poor speech was being permitted on the Lab's stage.[17]

On November 29, Miriam Stockton wrote Boleslavsky of the "many and genuine" praises for the sets and costumes for *Much Ado,* for Douglas Moore's music, and for the building and theatre. However,

> There were comments from all sides that the play itself was only half produced, the esprit and quality of the play was blanketed and muffled by lack of intelligent inner-understanding on the part of the actors and atrocious and illiterate diction. There were many unfavorable comments from the inside of the Theatre and from the entourage of friends upon your being absent and occupied with the engrossing Janney production of *The White Eagle* [at a time when] a great deal of capital and backing rests upon your powers.

Many people believed, she added, that the chances were equally good for "distinguished achievement" or "shameful fiasco" at the Lab. "It is certainly necessary that none of us delude ourselves as to the critical affairs of the next two or three months or I may even say weeks."[18] Shortly after that, the Lab reopened its success from the previous season, *Granite,* and withdrew *Much Ado.* Assistant directors Francis Fergusson and Shirley White rehearsed the play for a few weeks and it was placed back in the schedule, incorporating the changes they had made.[19]

In December, Boleslavsky came back to New York briefly for the final rehearsals of Hamsun's *At The Gate of the Kingdom* and then went back out of town to continue the final preparations for *The White Eagle*. On December 8, Miriam Stockton wrote him: "As you know, our institution cannot last much longer upon a diet of faith, hope and charity . . . even prayer is not very fattening."[20] That night, the Lab opened its second play of the season. Paul Rover designed the settings, and costumes were by Rose Bogandoff; Grover Burgess, Florence House, Joaquin Souther, Herbert Gellendré, and Katherine Squire played important roles.

Again critics were divided, but mildly favorable toward the play by the Nobel Prize winning Hamsun. The reviewer from the *Times* noted that the "setting, while of a school which permitted coats, hats, and pictures to be painted on it, was atmospheric and colorful." The play, he pointed out, was Ibsenesque, but an "interesting and provocative drama," and it benefited from "one excellent and one good performance," given by Florence House and Grover Burgess respectively. "In the lesser parts one might sometimes have wished for a better cast than was recruited among Mr. Boleslavsky's amateur-professionals," but all in all, *At the Gate of the Kingdom* "was a most creditable undertaking." Joaquin Souther, whose presence Boleslavsky had hoped would create a more professional level of performance, was not singled out for special mention.[21] The first three performances were sold out to members of New York's Norwegian community, but after that attendance fell.

On December 15, Miriam Stockton wrote yet another letter to Boleslavsky, explaining her own personal feeling about *At the Gate of the Kingdom:* "I love the play and feel it very poignant and real and eternal. . . . I think, considering it went before the world with so few rehearsals and under such abnormal conditions of production, that it was a marvel it was delivered so smoothly." She returned to her central concern: "We understand, Bolie, your problems and the desirability from several points of view that you should do outside work," but "last year was very bad for the theatre," and the Lab's productions since *The Trumpet Shall Sound* were impoverished by your successive distractions:"

When you are not divided in mind and spirit then you are most reasonable, mellow and inspiring to everyone who works with you, but when you are driven mad with conflicting pressures and over-fatigued, you are sometimes so unapproachable and irritable that it seems as if the work and adjustments with everyone do not go smoothly. You have a thoughtful, earnest fine group of assistant Regisseurs, fairly intelligent. Is it not possible to give them more of your confidence before and during a production and get the benefit yourself of their constructive reactions upon the total conception before money is spent?

In the future, she concludes, "I feel that before money is released for any of these coming plays, the assistant Regisseurs and Francis [Fergusson] should have a voice as to whether they are reasonably convinced of a good result. . . . "[22]

On December 26, *The White Eagle*—the reason for Boleslavsky's extended absences from the Lab and cause of much of the Stockton's consternation—opened at the Casino Theatre in New York. Rudolf Friml, composer of *The Vagabond King,* wrote the music; the book and lyrics were by Brian Hooker and W. H. Post. James Reynolds designed the settings and Busby Berkeley was the choreographer.

A minority of the critics pronounced the show a hit, along the lines of *The Vagabond King,* but the *Times* reflected the general opinion: The operetta derived from Edwin Milton Royle's play "combined the best and worst features of an effort to get the most out of poor old Puccini, Gilbert & Sullivan and the conventional Broadway musical show. There was a little bit of everything and too much of some things. The result was a sort of musical cafeteria where one might take one's choice." Some of the songs were good, the *Times* said, the stage-settings were "marvelously effective," the choreography "bizarre and original," but the tale of the Englishman (acted by Alan Prior) who finds love in the Old West with an Indian Girl (Marion Keeler) was not well adapted and seriously needed "cutting": "The construction is enept, the action drags deplorably and every act suffers from a misplaced musical climax which does not match the dramatic climax."[23] *The White Eagle* closed after forty-eight performances.

Earlier, on 8 October 1927, Boleslavsky had been involved in an automobile accident, in which he was injured, though not seriously; still, he was evidently held liable for damages. On 14 January 1928, he wrote to Janney: "I don't like to bother you with my own private affairs. You have so much on your mind but I am in a pretty bad hole by now. As you see from the enclosed bill, the next move will be a lawsuit against me." He asked Janney to pay him what he was due from *The White Eagle,* "and for that I would call the deal of *The White Eagle* off and through. If you will consider that since Toronto, I received only $25.00, maybe that would not sound so bad to you." Janney evidently did not come through, or if he did, it was not soon enough, for on January 20, Boleslavsky sent a "strictly private" letter to Clarence Luce, Jr., asking for a loan of $500 "for one year, with reasonable interest. . . . You understand that I must be in pretty bad shape to be writing you this

letter. If you are not in a position to do it, just forget about it. . . . ''[24]
After this time, Boleslavsky never worked with Russell Janney again.

Shortly after this, Boleslavsky was rehearsing *Popo* for the Snarks and directing *The Twelve Thousand,* starring his friends Basil Sydney and Mary Ellis. He did not complete either production. He worked about half the number of rehearsals he had agreed on with the amateur group, then offered the services of one of the Lab's teachers to do the final work. The Snarks were not satisfied with the replacement. Sometime later, they paid Boleslavsky half the $500 director's fee. *The Twelve Thousand* opened at the Garrick Theatre on 13 March 1928 to unenthusiastic notices. *Billboard* noted: "Richard Boleslavsky, it is said, started the direction of *Twelve Thousand.* Basil Sydney finished it, however." Summing up the production, *Billboard* wrote: "Without knowing anything about Bruno Frank, one would size up *Twelve Thousand* as the work of a college freshman, pretentious without amounting to much."[25]

Why had Boleslavsky left the two shows? Evidently he quit them for some two or three weeks' work staging the ensemble scenes for Florenz Ziegfeld's production of a musical *Three Musketeers,* starring his friend Dennis King. Ziegfeld's play opened at the Lyric Theatre on March 13—the same night that *The Twelve Thousand* opened at the Garrick. Boleslavsky's work on the extravagant production did not win any particular notice from the reviewers.

Boleslavsky may have broken with Janney, but his friendship for James Reynolds continued. He asked Reynolds to design the setting for the Laboratory Theatre's production of a pantomime, *The Bridal Veil,* staged by choreographer Elizaveta Anderson-Ivantzoff, who was on the Lab's teaching staff. When Ivantzoff saw the sketches she rejected them, because, in her mind, they were static and did not "move." Boleslavsky interceded on Reynold's behalf and went to extraordinary lengths to persuade her to change her mind. Francis Fergusson remembers that Boley at one point got on his knees on the stage and pleaded with Ivantzoff. Next he tried the "high and mighty" line. "He tried every emotional trick—none of it worked." The volume of the argument escalated and the actors, hearing the noise, gathered to watch the spectacle. "If you accept his design the production will be worth $1.50," Boleslavsky argued, "but if you throw it out, it'll be worth thirty-five cents." Ivantzoff answered that she did not care what it was worth, she would not accept it. Finally, Fergusson finishes, "Boley took a vote and the vote was on his side and not hers; she departed in great anger, but that settled that." Anderson-Ivantzoff used the designs, and Reynolds stayed on at the Lab to teach a three-month course in stage design.

The Bridal Veil opened at the Laboratory Theatre on 26 January 1928. A number of critics frankly admitted that pantomime was not to their taste. Those few who appreciated the form were generally pleased with the production, and several wrote admiringly of the "excellent settings." The Lab had a modest success.

The critics divided more sharply—and much more heatedly—over the Lab's next show, Boleslavsky's production of *Dr. Knock,* which opened on February 23. Almost all the reviewers liked Romains's satirical tale of a quack doctor who mesmerizes an entire town; and they approved Harley Granville Barker's translation. At issue was Boleslavsky's directorial approach. Almost without exception, the reviewers compared Boleslavsky's treatment unfavorably with what they had heard or read of Louis Jouvet's production in Paris, which had been running successfully for three years. Jouvet had played the farce more or less realistically; Boleslavsky transformed it into a light, bizarre grotesque, played in what Brooks Atkinson described as "lampoon scenery with murderous knives and saws. . . . and putty noses, clown pants and furious moustachios." Atkinson pondered the director's role at some length:

> We have all heard and said a good deal these past years about the importance of stage direction. Mr. Boleslavsky has the ideal qualities of generalship; he commands his productions absolutely, as a good director may. The styles of acting, the costuming and the scene designing bear the stamp of his individuality. And his love of spirited acting, his readiness for comic antics unrestrained, his contempt for rigid and airless forms of producing, lead to the spontaneity we all relish in native drama.
>
> In "Dr. Knock," however, he has subordinated an "intellectual farce" to a formula of burlesque parsiflage. Translating wit into low comedy renders it heavy and dull.[26]

Percy Hammond wrote along similar lines:

> Mr. Boleslavsky, being a student and an explorer, has changed the original decor of the play. In Paris, one is told, it was done with sane scenery; but in Fifty-fourth Street the dress and settings are futuristic, reminding you of the brilliant hysteria of the *Chauve-Souris.* The change, I suspect, is ill advised.[27]

The most virulent attack came from John Anderson, the only New York critic who had actually seen Jouvet's production. He notes that he had worked to have the play performed in New York only to see it "virtually ruined by arty clap-trap" and "almost wrecked by a stylized production in the gimcrack and meaningless monkeyshines of clownish foolery":

> Instead of realistic characters, through which Romains, and certainly Jouvet meant, presumably, to convey some warmer touch of feeling, he has turned out his cast in absurd costumes, reducing it all to farce, and often burlesque. The actors are directed to the same ruinous errect [sic] so that the delight of finding one of my favorite plays done at last in [sic] the chagrin of finding it, at the same time, done in.[28]

To be sure, the production had its defenders. The critic from the *Sun* thought it was "rollicking good fun . . . very modern in conception, in scenery and in characterization. . . . Yet it is not mere clowning, for it contains wisdom and truth to nature."[29] Barclay V. McCarty, writing in *Billboard*, went even further; he thought the production was "played excellently" and showed "unique, original directing that produces effective tho [sic] at times startling results. Richard Boleslavsky attains his best work of the season by interpreting a piece prone toward heaviness in a light, bizarre manner."[30]

Boleslavsky often claimed that he had little regard for the opinions of critics; now, however, he was angered enough to write a lengthy letter addressed to John Anderson, the apparent leader of the pro-Jouvet faction. But Boleslavsky did not defend his production of *Dr. Knock* so much as his rights as a director. His central point was that had he merely copied Jouvet's production he would be guilty of artistic plagiarism. He went on:

> Why did we have to produce "Doctor Knock" exactly as it was produced in Paris? Even if their production was a thousand times better than ours—what is the reason for it? Should we be the importers of foreign goods and nothing else? Would you be satisfied with the best kind of reproduction and do you seriously think that the reproduction of a Paris success would be right and adjustable to New York theatrical conditions? This is for me, personally a tremendously important subject. The rights of production do exist in Germany and Russia. They do not exist elsewhere in the theatrical world, with the exception, if I am not mistaken, in Denmark. Nobody ever heard about it in New York. . . .
>
> I don't know when the day will come in New York when the rights of the producer will be respected as they are respected in Germany and Russia but those days will come. . . . Dear Mr. Anderson, this is the reason why I haven't done the production of "Dr. Knock" as it was done in Paris.[31]

A few months earlier, at a fund-raising dinner for the Lab, Boleslavsky had expressed the opinion that there had been nothing new in the world theatre since the World War; America, he said, was still "consuming the theatre food which was prepared in Europe before the war," but when that material had been used up, "the renaissance will spring forth from America" and he wanted to be ready for it.[32] Now, in writing to Anderson, he reiterated that theme: "We want to talk to you about things like realistic acting and realistic producing, which is gone from the theatre" and will not return for "many years." Periods of realism, Boleslavsky continued, always precede "periods of romanticism." "The theatre of Belasco and his pupils has done its good"; American theatre stands poised "between the past realism and romanticism and imaginary realism. . . . The new generation is coming and is believing more in symbols than in actual things." To produce *Dr. Knock* realistically would "sound false" in their ears—it is "a farce," "a cartoon," "a funny picture—a burlesque. One has to be naive enough to take it as it is and not to look at it as it would be a Bible. . . . " Boleslavsky concludes:

> Another colleague of yours finishes his criticism that I have produced on the stage the kidneys and microbes which do not exist anywhere on land or sea. Does he want me to put real human kidneys into a jar of alcohol and put them on the table in front of the audience? God Almighty, how far this absurd hunt for realism in the theatre goes! . . . But let us agree on what we are talking about. The first thing will be that there is no such thing in the theatre as realistic characters. The realistic character is something that is contradictory to the idea of the theatre itself. It's impossible. It is hopeless.
>
> . . . The trouble is that here in America, we don't want to give the young generation of designers a chance to fulfill their dreams and visions on the stage and to the young generation of actors a chance to find their ways to unite their work with the new movement. When Reinhardt comes, we all rave about it but I can show you thousands of Reinhardt's methods spread all over the American theatre, mostly in the vaudeville, and nobody raves about them.[33]

Boleslavsky never sent that letter; Herbert Stockton persuaded him that it might do serious damage to the Lab's public relations during its crucial fund-raising program. John Mason Brown, who was teaching at the Lab, may have taken up the issue in Boleslavsky's stead, in a review signed only J.M.B.:

> It is critical bad manners to compare things that are not comparable, not to mention the fact that it is idle. In this instance there is no need to say who has accomplished this task better. But there seems to be a great, a lusty-shouting need to defend M. Romains and Mr. Boleslavsky, from the impertinent animadversions of Divers and Sundry. . . .
> The American Laboratory actors, with their grotesque make-up and their exagger-

ated gestures, rendered perfectly plausible, by a simple phenomenon of overempha-
sis, a character and a situation which would be incredible and silly if rendered
realistically. Judging on the sole allowable basis of the English script, we recommend
Mr. Boleslavsky unconditionally for his interpretation of what is expressively called
in French a "charge," that is to say, an intentional overloading of character, situation, etc. with comic material.[34]

Boleslavsky demonstrated the kind of realism he could endorse in
his next production, the Lab's final offering of the 1927–28 season. The
play was Bernard's *Martine*. Bernard's story is a simple one, simply
told: a French peasant girl falls in love with a young man visiting next
door, but he fails to notice her and she cannot speak of her feelings; he
leaves, and she marries another young man, whom she does not love,
and settles down for a barren, joyless life. As ultimately produced at the
Lab, *Martine* was realistic in both acting and scenery, but this was
realism of a very special kind and had little in common with the naturalistic detail of Belasco.

Martine also provides the only clear example at the Lab that Boleslavsky put into practice one of his cardinal beliefs: the final scenic form
of a production, in order to be an organic, unified whole, must result
from the collaborative work of director, designer, and actors.

The designer for *Martine* was Robert Edmond Jones. Jones and
Boleslavsky had first worked together some four yerars earlier, when
Boleslavsky took over the final rehearsals of Stark Young's *The Saint* at
the Provincetown Playhouse. Since then, Jones had been a frequent
guest at the Laboratory Theatre, lecturing on various subjects. Clearly,
he and Boleslavsky shared many of the same ideals. Ruth Nelson, who
played the title role in *Martine,* recalls vividly the working relationship
that developed between the two men and the actors during rehearsals:

It was Boleslavsky's belief that the designer should be implicitly a part of every
moment, and Jones was there every day. I don't know who I loved more; they were
simply wonderful. . . . There was such an intimacy in rehearsals between the director and the designer and the actors. Jones came to me and said, "What do you think
Martine should wear?" I suggested, and he brought me everything I suggested, but
absolutely more perfect than I had dreamed of. He went to the Salvation Army and
such places where you get second-hand clothing and went through barrels. . . . He
didn't have things made, he found real things himself. For one scene I wanted her to
wear a coat that hung on a hook by the kitchen door, and everybody used it—the
women could use it, the men could use it—it was just something you put on when-
ever you went out. And he brought me such a coat and a stocking cap. Everything I
asked for—he brought, with such love. That was all part of the relationship. Everyone worked with everyone else so lovingly.

She remembers, too, the principal setting Jones devised, which featured a blossoming apple tree, denuded of blossoms and most of its leaves in later scenes:

> [The settings] were magic, because they were real. Austere is a good word—simplified. He could put one tree there and when he lit it a certain way, the whole world opened up to you. There was a farmhouse and it had a real bureau, and it looked like a farmhouse—but there was just one object instead of several. It was done with such simplicity that it was extraordinary. The lighting was out of this world, which of course Jones did. And what he did to this tree with his lighting was something that will never be recaptured.

Nelson had not always been so favorably disposed to the Lab's methods. She had enrolled in the Lab's school at the beginning of the year but had dropped out because she found the overall tone of Ouspenskaya's sessons on Stanislavskian techniques—which Nelson, a veteran of the Group Theatre, considers lessons in "the Method"—too negative and too critical. Boleslavsky persuaded her to return, because he wanted her for the title role in Bernard's play, but she approached the first rehearsals with a measure of skepticism and caution. Her fears soon melted away, for unlike Ouspenskaya, Boleslavsky "was most gentle and loving with the actors during rehearsals":

> When it began I went to him and said, "I am most happy to play this role. I have only one favor to ask. Please don't suggest my using 'the Method.' Just tell me what you want, Mr. Boleslavsky." I had such confidence. His eyes twinkled. He nodded solemnly and agreed as how he would not bring up the Method. And he never did. Except that little by little—.
> I had a scene where I was sewing. Fairly soon in rehearsals I brought a piece of something to sew, a needle and thread. This went on a few days. Then one day Boleslavsky said, "You know, Ruth, the audience can't see that needle, and it makes it too small for you to use that needle. You must use the needle in your imagination and *give* it to them, and then they'll understand the needle."
> "Ahhhh, of course!" [she thought].
> That's the way he gave me the Method. It was always like that. Little by little he taught me as much about the Method as anyone in my whole life did. But it was always out of the action—out of something [specific], so that I understood it completely.[35]

Martine opened on 4 April 1928. The critics were unimpressed with the play; overall, its tone was too delicate, too muted, too elusive, they felt, to be very interesting. A number of the reviewers were quite impressed, however, with the intelligent artistry of Robert Edmond Jones's settings, Boleslavsky's direction, and Ruth Nelson's acting. Leonard Hall found Nelson's performance:

one of the best . . . I have ever seen turned in by an apprentice Duse. Boleslavsky has evidently directed her expertly, and between the two of them her Martine is almost airtight. It is an interesting role for a fledgling actress, with its rapid changes from gawky girl to suffering young woman to peasant wife already beginning to ossify mentally and physically, and Miss Nelson seems to have a grip on it every minute. She comprehends it; she feels it, and she plays it. . . . [36]

Robert Littell also praised the "genuine feeling" and absence of theatricality in Nelson's "expressions of joy, longing, despair and resignation" in this "gentle tragedy done in silverpoint"; the production was remarkable, he wrote, primarily because of her "sincere, finely shaded and living acting" and for the "delicately beautiful sets" of Robert Edmond Jones.[37] But an anonymous critic from the *Graphic* wrote most perceptively of Boleslavsky's achievement in this production. Nelson's performance, he began, might easily be called great:

Her bewildered, tortured, uncomplaining Martine became, not a girl in a play, not even a girl in real life only, but a pitiless picture of all of us. The character had a touch of the universal. The author and the actress joined malicious hands to hurt us. The play and the actress cannot be forgotten. . . .
   The sets, the tempo—everything is attuned to the simplicity of the central character. . . . The direction and the acting are a delight to the intellectual theatregoer.[38]

No other reviewer expressed so clear an understanding of Boleslavsky's artistic aim.

Boleslavsky ended the Lab's 1927–28 season on a much more hopeful note than he had begun it, despite the fact that the season itself had not been a particular success: *Much Ado About Nothing* was a hastily prepared failure, an embarrassment artistically; *At the Gate of the Kingdom, The Bridal Veil* and *Martine* were modest successes, but did little to enhance the Lab's prestige or financial stability; *Dr. Knock* had generated interest through controversy. Still, Boleslavsky's apparent break with Russell Janney had alleviated the Stockton's fears and presumably signalled Boleslavsky's intention to devote more of his energies to the Laboratory Theatre. Most importantly, during this season Boleslavsky had found two important new allies for his work at the Lab—John Mason Brown and Robert Edmond Jones.

   In April 1928, Boleslavsky was asked: "Why have you directed plays other than American Laboratory Theatre productions?" His answer, preserved in *The Pit,* a single-issue Lab publication, betrays a mixture of his old idealism and a new pragmatism:

There is no such thing as art for art. Art is for the people from the people and of the people, and art must be studied amongst the people. It concerns every art. That luxury was always and is the guardian of the arts is a big mistake, and drawback for every art. I go and work on Broadway because I like to try myself out in the merciless and boiling conditions of the theatrical game. I like to see if I can fight with my art just as well as enjoy it. At the same time, I doubt if it is really possible to create much in Broadway's conditions. You can only more or less combine and reconstruct achievements gathered from all over the world, but to dictate to the world the art of the theatre, I presume Broadway is not yet able. And it is a tremendous pity because for the last 15 years whatever came to Broadway which was foreign (it matters not whether it was Moscow Art, Reinhardt, or Raquel Miller, or Copeau, or anybody else) I could show you step by step the things which were of the same value and of the same strength and sometimes of much brighter achievements, and they were found on Broadway. But the trouble is that they were drowned in chaotic disorder, in commercial separation, in merciless competition.

To conclude, Broadway is a *pit* full of everything that can come to the theatrical profession and one must be a little himself worthy of taking a place in it. One must have a cool head, hot heart and strong hands (not mentioning good vocabulary). That's why I personally find satisfaction in it. My work in the "Lab" usually is met with a sort of smile, even from both sides, from professional and from highbrows, but my laugh is the last one. As long as I know how to put over the "Song of the Vagabonds" or the "Song of the Three Musketeers," or the big ensemble scenes in "Miracle" to the perfect satisfaction of my employers and through them to the crowds, I know that I know my "game" and that I have a right (knowing the old theatre) to look for a new one; knowing what people want and looking for the things they may want tomorrow. At the same time, when I am scorned for doing "stylized work," I have the biggest laugh because never in my life did I like or do any stylization, which to my personal opinion, is not an art but dryness and exhaustion of artistic imagination. When it looks to everybody that I am doing stylization, it is only that I am trying to find economical and bright means of presenting the variety and richness of the elements of the theatre. . . . To make a theatre of tomorrow, one must know thoroughly the theatre of today. One must hold his hand on the pulse of today. That's why I go to Broadway and do my duty towards today there, but I live in the "lab" and profess my faith towards tomorrow here.[39]

His "faith towards tomorrow" would soon be badly shaken.

15

A Loss of Faith

Boleslavsky laid his plans for the 1928–29 Laboratory Theatre season in an atmosphere of change, excitement, and controversy. By the end of 1929, however, he had become so disillusioned that he left not only the Laboratory Theatre, but turned his back on Broadway as well, abandoning the live stage for Hollywood.

The controversy centered around the publication of *The Pit,* an eight page paper printed under the American Laboratory Theatre's name—but without prior approval of the Lab's board—and sold for a short time in the theatre's lobby:"Price 1 Dime." It was the brain-child of Charles A. Wagner, an aspiring journalist, who sold Boleslavsky on the idea; together, they were jointly responsible for both its publication and its contents. At issue were a brief item of humor titled, "Concerning One James Reynolds, Esquire," and a long, thoughtful essay by Frances Fergusson, "A Playreader's Viewpoint."

On the surface the piece concerning Reynolds was innocuous enough, and must have been merely puzzling to most casual readers. Reynolds and his friends—including Robert Edmond Jones—however, were outraged by what they understood to be a suggestion that Reynolds was homosexual. At one point Reynolds threatened to sue.[1] Boleslavsky's long-standing friendship with Reynolds and his newly formed alliance with Jones were both in jeopardy.

Boleslavsky reacted strongly to this situation. In a letter to Herbert Stockton, he accepted full responsibility—with Wagner—for the contents of *The Pit.* Regarding the question of offending Reynolds, he wrote: "I felt very badly—so badly that I was on the verge of writing to you and asking you to eliminate my work, except to the school, and release me from my duty towards the Theatre. But after a while I calmed down. . . . " He argued that no offence should be taken where none was intended: "Only shallow-minded and perverse and dirty minds can find in it what they are looking for." His considerable discomfort with the subject of homosexuality (he had once discovered a Lab student's homosexual tendencies and promptly made an appointment for him to see a psychiatrist) is reflected in the convoluted logic of his final statement on the subject: "You, as a lawyer, must understand that there is only one straight meaning in the Reynolds article and only the person who wants to can attach to it absolutely incredible and silly nonsense, which does not concern anybody and is nobody's business, even if it exists."[2]

Evidently Boleslavsky subsequently talked personally with Reynolds, and probably Jones as well, and wounded feelings were soothed. In any case, the issue soon died down, and Jones's new alliance with the Laboratory Theatre held firm.

The other controversy involving *The Pit* centered around Fergusson's article. For some time, Fergusson had been agitating for change and reform at the Lab because he was disturbed by the apparent absence of a coherent artistic policy in Boleslavsky's choice of plays. In his article, Fergusson described Boleslavsky, along with Stanislavsky, Craig, and Reinhardt, as the product of "the great 19th Century Romantic Tradition":

> Because of Mr. Boleslavsky's upbringing in this tradition he has a depth, a consistency and a reality which is denied to us American [sic]. His value to us is incalculable. They are forces in relation to which we can perhaps define ourselves, become self-conscious. What is the Romantic Tradition and where must we, as American and members of a succeeding generation, depart from it?

The great accomplishment of the "Romantic Tradition," in Fergusson's view, was its mastery of "form"; its great failure was that "it did not blaze the way to the creation of really new and living forms, because these depend on living subjects, and subjects were entirely discounted in the worship of form." Fergusson urged Boleslavsky and the Lab to move beyond an obsession with form and become equally concerned with content: "The dramatist, as the mouthpiece of the best thought and taste of the time, should rule the theatre." Specifically, he believed the Lab should produce only plays from the seventeenth century and by modern American writers. He believed that if Boleslavsky and the most promising American playwrights became "interested in each other," each would benefit.[3]

The Stocktons and others took exception to Fergusson, not because of the ideas he presented, nor even the implied criticism that Boleslavsky was incapable of adequately articulating his artistic vision, but rather that an issue affecting the Lab's internal operation had been exposed to public view and discussion. They objected even more strongly to another passage in the article regarding the "millionaires" who might dislike the course Fergusson recommended, which they took as an insult to the Lab's financial supporters.

In answering Herbert Stockton's complaints about the article, Boleslavsky reminded him that this was a revised and softened version of a memo that had previously circulated within the Lab, in which "Fregusson called me . . . inarticuate and almost ignorant." Despite such criticism, Boleslavsky felt the article was constructive: "That's where I personally got my idea of next season's repertory and that's why I did not hesitate to put in the magazine this article. . . . " As for Fergusson's comment about the "millionaires", Boleslavsky dismissed it as unimportant.[4]

Fergusson's article evidently served to remind Boleslavsky of his original vision for the Lab: to discover American methods, to probe the American spirit, to sink his roots into American soil. Somehow, among the expediencies of raising money, earning a living, producing plays, and dividing his time between art and commerce, the "American" had been lost from the American Laboratory Theatre. Now Boleslavsky was fired with renewed vision. John Mason Brown was invited to serve as the Lab's playreader and literary arbiter. At Boleslavsky's urging, Brown approached such writers as Paul Green, Philip Barry, Sidney Howard, Waldo Frank, and John Van Druten; Padraic Colum offered one of his new plays.

Robert Edmond Jones agreed to serve as artistic adviser for all productions and was told: "Mr. Boleslavsky wants to practically give you the Theatre as a vehicle for your ideas, with which he is so completely in sympathy." Partly for reasons of economy, Jones agreed to design a permanent unit setting featuring a double proscenium and an array of screens and set units that could be varied according to the demands of each play; it was expected that other designers—including Donald Oenslager, Boris Aronson, Jo Mielziner, and Rumanian-born Jonel Jorgulesco of the Boston Repertory Theatre—would agree to work in conjunction with Jones. The acting company was to be "augmented by strengthening and stabilizing talents . . . to give it the age it needs, talents recruited from such organizations as the Neighborhood Playhouse where the same ideal is flourished."[5]

Boleslavsky had come to believe: "We must have an author of our own. . . . Our theatre must become a theatre of native drama. To my mind, that's the only way." A great many plays were discussed and considered. It was agreed that the season would open with Bronson Howard's *Saratoga*, and include a new work incorporating pantomime, music, and motion pictures to be written by John Mason Brown and Douglas Moore: *The Saga of Jesse James.* Two other new plays would be produced—both to be new works, and both by American authors. *Somep'n Like Wings* and *Lonely West* by Lynn Riggs were prime candidates. By April 17, Boleslavsky had already begun tentative rehearsals for Riggs's works and made a startling discovery:

> There is something tremendously strong and vital and not at all morbid in them. They are tragic in some places but you know that the strong stuff is always good in the theatre. It matters not whether it is funny or tragic. What particularly impressed me in rehearsing was that all our actors discovered in them absolutely new strength and vitality, animation and richness of color, which I connect with the kind of language they have to use in that play. It is the native language of their own and I personally think that until now they all played, though in English, in a foreign language, but the moment they started to speak American, there is absolutely new animation and energy in it for them. They feel like fishes in water and I am sure we will be able to get something new and maybe really important from Riggs' plays.

In keeping with the change and ferment in Boleslavsky's thinking, he also pondered taking a bold step: "With the abnormal conditions of theatrical life in New York, you have to show every performance to the critics, which is an absurd and unjust idea. . . . I would suggest that no critics be invited next year."[6]

The critics did not attend performances at the Laboratory Theatre during the 1928–29 season, but they were absent for reasons Boleslavsky had not forseen. The fund-raising campaign initiated by the John Price Jones Corporation had not proved successful. On 1 June 1928, the Stocktons announced that the Lab was on the brink of insolvency and would have to close within a matter of weeks unless something could be done to save it. Sufficient money was raised to keep the school open for the coming year, but the Lab's "American" season was cancelled.

When the school opened in the fall, enrollment was considerably below the anticipated level. During the course of the year, five experimental productions were given for invited friends of the theatre at "Sunday night entertainments."[7] Boleslavsky was rarely seen at the Lab, though he made infrequent appearances at the school and conducted a few classes.

Not surprisingly, Boleslavsky had laid plans for the new Broadway season as well. By March of 1928, he was talking with Channing Pollock about possibly directing Pollock's "verbal cartoon," *Mr. Moneypenny,* which the playwright was producing himself. Surprisingly, Pollock and Boleslavsky had been brought together by Miriam Stockton.[8]

Boleslavsky read the play and on March 24 wrote to Pollock about it. Boleslavsky was interested, but had serious misgivings. He found the play interesting in form and content, but predicted that its "very cruel truth" would win little favor: "It seems to me that the general attitude will be very hostile. At the same time, I cannot restrain myself for admiring your courage and your plain words. I think it's a great thing for you to write a play like this and still a bigger thing to have the courage to produce it." Boleslavsky described the play's form as a blending of "absolutely real" characters with "purely artificial theatrical form," and called it a "splendid idea"—"the latest achievement of the most radical wing in present German and Russian literature." This combination of "native theatricality with native reality" would pose considerable technical difficulties, however; their solution would require a "strong, vital and practical" designer and rehearsal conditions that went beyond the usual Broadway practice. For the play to succeed, it would be necessary to find "very enthusiastic" and "modern" actors who understood that "this whole production is one big football team, that it is not individual performance that can carry this play" but a unified, ensemble effort.[9]

On April 17, Boleslavsky wrote to Robert Edmond Jones regarding the plans he was then formulating for the Lab, but including his growing doubts about directing *Mr. Moneypenny:*

> Mr. Pollock sent me a short note, telling me that you won't have time to do "Moneypenny" and that you didn't like the plays with a purpose. Your refusal to do "Moneypenny" is quite a blow for me. As I told you, I would do that play if you would do it and I meant it. Now, I am in a position where my talk with Pollock went too far and you don't want to do it. I really am in the air! I wish you would tell me whether I should do it. Is it so hopelessly bad in spite of all the ideas it has, that it should not be done in the theatre? I am so afraid to connect myself with the kind of cheap and trivial stuff and I am afraid that's the reason that you don't like the play. But on the other hand, you seldom find such a theatrical opportunity and material as is in this play, but here probably I am making a mistake because the word "theatre" is for me what a red rug [*sic*] is for the bull. The moment I see, hear or smell "theatre," I forget everything else.[10]

Jones eventually changed his mind and agreed to design the production. By the end of April, Boleslavsky had contracted to direct *Mr. Moneypenny* for $500 a week during rehearsals and $50 each week the play ran.[11]

Mr. Moneypenny, the tale of John Jones's rise to riches and unhappiness as a consequence of his pact with a modern Mephistopheles, opened at the Liberty Theatre on 17 October 1928. Donald Meek played Jones, and Evan Heflin (who later made a name for himself in films as

Van Heflin) made his stage debut as his son. Hale Hamilton played the title role, and Margaret Wycherly and Ruth Nugent acted important parts. The play's theme, expressed in "a mixture of allegory, fantasy, satire and comic-strip exaggeration, encased in an elaborate and fast-moving production,"[12] was generally dismissed by the critics as being self-evident, hackneyed, or preachy. As Robert Garland put it:

> The piece . . . is a curious and kaleidoscopic jumble of familiar quotations, familiar situations and the equally familiar belief that, even where money is concerned, you can get too much of a good thing. It takes three acts, ten scenes, a jazz band, an adding machine, a time clock, a dictaphone, a mechanical piano and a hundred distracted mummers to prove that all is not gold that glitters.[13]

If the reviewers were generally unimpressed with *Mr. Money-penny's* message, most were moved to write vivid and suggestive descriptions of the manner of its expression. Two are particularly rich in detail and seemingly perceptive analysis. Arthur B. Waters saw *Mr. Moneypenny* while it was being tried out at Philadelphia's Garric Theatre; he found the story and dialogue to be banal, cheap, and tepid, and compared it to "that glorified musical comedy, *Everywoman,* Morris Gest's *Experience,* and Pollock's earlier play, *The Fool,*" and felt that *Mr. Moneypenny* was distinguished from those plays primarily by the fact that it was "staged with far more discernment and taste": "Here is, indeed, a provocative study in impressionism, from first to last, needing only the bones and sinews of a worthwhile theme, worthily expounded, to mark it as another significant milestone in the art of the theatre." He continues:

> From the first scene, a grim, depressing bank vault, with doors that give the impression of immense weight and shadows that foretell the entrance of characters with wavering mystery, to the very end of the play, an impressive tableau that is somberly allegorical of something or other, "Mr. Moneypenny" is of constant appeal to the eye.
>
> The brokers' office, with its automatons, its chanting chorus of "millions, billions, millions," and its constant shoveling of filthy lucre by means of brooms and troughs, and even vacuum cleaners, into a huge safe, stands as an interesting achievement by itself. So does the nightclub scene, dimly lit, peopled by scantily clad performers, showing in the rear the vague outlines of the inevitable jazz band, enlivened now and again by staccato voices, mostly drunken, from the half-obscure tables.
>
> Mr. Jones has created some admirable effects; Mr. Boleslavsky has given a master's touch to the proceedings. Between them, however, they cannot obliterate the hackneyed exposition of an age-old theme.[14]

Describing the play after its New York opening, Robert Littell speaks of "a multitude of fantastic, symbolic, expressionistic scenes, flashes of light, gigantic shadows, voices in the dark . . . a mock wedding . . . a huge, mad gold interior. . . . '' He continues:

> Many of these scenes are marvels of imagination, of lighting, of crowd movement, and if we went to the theatre with our eyes alone we could truthfully report that "Mr. Moneypenny" was vast, groping, nightmarish and full of elaborate and sometimes extraordinarily effective pictures.
>
> But our ears bring us quickly back to earth, to the incredibly flat and familiar earth upon which Mr. Pollock is walking back and forth, back and forth. . . .
>
> As for Mr. Boleslavsky, upon whom fell the collossal labor of stylizing an endless string of not particularly true truisms, I think he managed to underline once again what had already been underlined three times. The performance clicked along with intricate, mobile smoothness. It could not have been better for its purpose. . . . It completely lacked humor, and so remained entirely faithful to the play. It had scale and magnificence and a kind of dark something which would be hard to name. It was worth while—if it is worth while hiring a sculptor to carve $2 + 2 = 4$ on the side of a mountain.[15]

If many of the roles were dehumanized "automatons," or, as Littell put it, "puppets repeating catchwords," that effect—reminiscent of the mechanized background characters of *Lâcheté*—was evidently both intentional and consistent with the style of Pollock's script. As one critic put it: "There is one scene in this piece in which the unhappy John Jones exhausts himself on a sort of treadmill, which is done in a masterly fashion. . . . But these symbolistic plays scarcely allow the actors to act, since the details of the decoration express all that the author has to say. . . . ''[16] Evidently by intention, the "automatons" were played without inner feelings or emotions; whether the characters—John Jones, his son, his wife, Mr. Moneypenny, and so on—were likewise lacking in humanity is not clear from the reviewers' remarks, but Donald Meek, in the central role, evidently humanized his character. One critic felt that he was the only "individual" in the cast: I mention the human qualities of Donald Meek. However they were injected into the happenings last night, not by the reality of Pollock, but by the sincerity of Meek's true characterization."[17]

Mr. Moneypenny continued at the Liberty for a time and then was transferred to Youmans Cosmopolitan Theatre at Columbus Circle; the play closed after sixty-one performances.

Despite the hostile reception accorded *Mr. Moneypenny* by the reviewers, Boleslavsky found reason to celebrate not long after the play's opening: on 29 October 1928 he became a naturalized American citizen.[18]

Boleslavsky's next stage assignment was an unusual one. George C. Tyler had persuaded Gordon Craig to design Shakespeare's *Macbeth*, with Douglas Ross directing. Craig sent sketches for the settings and costumes from Germany and asked that Boleslavsky assist in translating the designs into scenic embodiment. In September, Craig wrote:

> Boleslavsky! The more I say the more difficult for you—and embarrassing. The less I say the better you'll do it—for you know my likes and dislikes and when you don't you'll get heaps of ideas of your own. So go ahead and don't bother your head with "Am I doing as Gordon Craig likes"—I SHALL like it. I am so happy you are doing this.

Craig then described in detail certain scenic and atmospheric effects that were of particular importance to him, and ended: "Look at the original drawings if in doubt. They say much more than I could write. So I won't say any more. Only bless you, and be as bold as you like."[19] Boleslavsky designed the lighting himself, as well as watching over the visual aspects of the production, which opened at the Knickerbocker Theatre in New York on 19 November 1928.

The previous spring, Charles Wagner asked Boleslavsky for *The Pit:* "Do you think that Gordon Craig is a healthy influence on the theatre of the present?" Boleslavsky responded:

> There is no bigger man in the theatre than Gordon Craig. Shame! Shame! Shame! to America, that he did not come here yet, that he was not given opportunity in this country at least to tell what he thinks. He is the next man after Shakespeare in the theatre . . . and will probably have to wait as Shakespeare until a couple of hundred years after he is dead and some German professor discovers him for the English-speaking world. . . . There isn't a performance around the world lately with a slightest intention of being serious, where Craig's influence would not be manifested. Unfortunately very often, this influence is seriously and thoroughly corrupted.

Wagner also had asked Boleslavsky his nominations for the "five greatest names in the history of the theatre." Boleslavsky responded:

> I do not want to go so far away as into the world. I want to stick to Broadway and the 40's and I will cast for you an ideal performance with five people, including the audience. Well, I would ask Shakespeare to write a play; I would ask Gordon Craig to design the scenery and supervise the production; I would ask George M. Cohan to produce it; and I would ask Laurette Taylor to act it and I ask myself to sit in the audience for as many consecutive nights as this noble company would consent to play it.[20]

Boleslavsky had been in personal contact with Craig only during preparations for the Moscow Art Theatre production of *Hamlet* in 1911. Lighting *Macbeth* according to Craig's sketches and written descriptions was the closest he ever came to working again with the man he admired so greatly.

While working on *Macbeth,* Boleslavsky was also rehearsing David Boehm's *The Queen of Sheba,* starring Greta Nissen in the title role. The production opened in Atlantic City on 26 November 1928, but closed before reaching New York.

Immediately after that, Boleslavsky began directing what was to be his last New York production. The play was *Judas,* a retelling of the Biblical story from the point of view of a Brutus-like betrayer. It was written by Walter Ferris and Basil Rathbone, with Rathbone in the title role, and produced by William A. Brady, Jr., and Dwight Deere Wiman. Boleslavsky directed and designed the costumes; Jo Mielziner designed the settings. William Courtleigh, Jennie Eustace, Lyons Wickland, William D. Post, William Challee, and Doan Borup appeared in important roles.

Judas opened at the Longacre Theatre on 24 January 1929 to disastrous reviews. Arthur Pollock found Rathbone's good looks, Mielziner's scenery, and Boleslavsky's staging to be the chief distinctions of the evening, but the play, he felt, was composed of "words of almost no importance" though spoken with "fierce earnestness."[21] Brooks Atkinson felt that the play was an excuse for the actors

> to cast off the shackles of realistic drama and to revel in attitudinizing and posturing under the protection of a sacred theme. . . . And instead of taking on a reflected grandeur from such themes, mediocre plays seem more egregious than usual, and the roar and rant of the acting sound particularly hollow. The shriek of the wind machine, the whirr of the electric fan, the glare of electric light that symbolizes the radiant Master, the singing and harp accompaniment offstage reduce the theatre to a bag of tinker's tricks.[22]

Almost without exception, the critics dismissed *Judas* as a static exercise, devoid of real action, stultifying and sophomoric in its overall effort. Savaged by the critics, and under fire from some religious leaders as well, *Judas* closed after only twelve performances.[23]

The optimism with which Boleslavsky began working in America had by now been transformed into opportunism, growing pragmatism, and even cynicism. In Francis Fergusson's estimate:

> When Boleslavsky first started the Lab—or was induced to begin it—he had no idea what theatre was like in this country. He thought if he could make a little group that

was well-trained, governed by good taste, and so forth, that it would succeed. But his actors tended to drift away, because of course the Lab couldn't pay very much salary. That gradually got under his skin.

He did quite a bit of directing in other places. . . . He was a man of tremendous energy; he would be rehearsing a couple of Broadway plays at the same time he was directing at the Lab. He didn't like Broadway. He hated it. He objected to everything: to the general taste, to the terrible system of rehearsals, which were sloppy and meager. But he needed the dough, that was just it. . . . He soon began wondering whether the Laboratory Theatre was ever going to be possible.

It gradually dawned on him in the course of the three years or so that I knew him, that that's what it was like in this country, and that the chance of making anything "stick" was very slight. He also found that a good many actors, although they were eager to be trained by him, didn't have the ability to get what he was talking about. Some of them did—a few did. And there are a few still around today who were made by him actually. But a lot of them, including some he was very fond of, didn't "get" his system.[24]

The 1928–29 season had been a difficult one for Boleslavsky. The Lab had produced no plays. One of his productions, *The Queen of Sheba,* had folded before it ever reached "The Great White Way," and his two productions which did open on Broadway, *Mr. Moneypenny* and *Judas,* had been scorned by the critics and public alike. At some point during this year, he wrote his old friend, Monakhov, who had championed his cause when *The Torn Cape* had been threatened with censorship in St. Petersburg:

One can devote himself to art only in Russia. Theatrical art exists only there. Here in America I have learned to fight to live, fight for money, fight for a place in life. . . . But when I think about art, about the present state of the art, I inevitably think only of Russia, for only there does it exist and only there is it possible.[25]

Other artists could empathize with Boleslavsky's situation. In 1927, Jacques Copeau, who had also known disappointments in New York, delivered a series of lectures at the Laboratory Theatre; on the eve of his return to France, he paid tribute to Boleslavsky's work at the Lab, describing it as "the most fundamental and consequential thing I have observed during my stay":

It deserves the firm support of every man and woman who sees in the near future a great spiritual development which has already made itself manifest in this country.

The theatre, as always, is the mirror of our civilization. Too much attention cannot be paid to it.

It is a great relief to find an organization, altruistic, artistic and full-visioned, training American young people in the theatre, and, at the same time, preserving for them their ideals and ennobling the dignity of their profession.

Let us pray that it will receive every support and be borne to full maturity.
It has begun right and it is fundamentally sound.
I expect to see it a great success when I return again to America.[26]

In an undated letter written to Elizabeth Bigelow from Genova in 1928, Gordon Craig had warned Boleslavsky that his own experience in London had convinced him that "unless we join the 'Daily Mail-Society-Bible-class' groups, we are simply 'not known.' " Craig offered advice and encouragement:

I fear that New York is growing like Paris and London. It's no use complaining, it's the cities that have a first claim to cry out. . . .

If I were you I would shift your Laboratory Theatre to some unknown town. But I am not you so I must not make foolish suggestions.

But put it this way, none of the wide awake men and women should risk loss of life by suffocation in either Paris, London or New York or Chicago, or any big dull selfish city.

. . . All this is private talk with you and Mr. Boleslavsky. I wish I could see him—there are in Europe and America some 15 or 20 men who ought to get together and go round the world under my flag and B. could help get them together. I know half the men—I'm afraid that there are but 2 Englishmen among that 20.

Tell B. that I may shortly be having a theatre of my own here—as a workshop. It is talked about more or less seriously. It is there that 20 friends could assemble, prepare and then start out.

I should probably stay here & prepare the wine and cakes for the annual home coming. I have less and less liking for the racket of victories—but B. and the others if I could persuade them to link up would be able to relish all those victories—and theirs would really be all the good work. I could be useful and give things a touch.[27]

Boleslavsky did not join Craig, of course. Rather he gave up on New York and left for Hollywood on 3 April 1929. Shortly before leaving, he divorced Natasha Boleslavsky and married Norma Drury, a pretty woman with dark eyes and hair, who was some years younger than he. Drury had grown up in Worcester, Massachusetts. There, in 1915, she had once played at a reception honoring visiting opera star Margaret Matzenauer, who had described her then as "the greatest child pianist" she had heard during her visit to America.[28] This promise of greatness eluded her, though she developed into an accomplished musician and sometimes performed on the concert stage. She and Boleslavsky met during rehearsals for *Mr. Moneypenny,* when Drury was hired to play in the small orchestra for that production. In 1929, she became the third Mrs. Boleslavsky, after Maria Yefremova and Natasha Shimkevich Platonova—or the fourth, if in fact Boleslavsky had married the Polish girl known only as "Panna Julia" in Odessa. Later, in Hollywood, Drury played in studio orchestras and is said to have arranged music for films; she also acted at least one small role at RKO.[29]

Boleslavsky left New York under contract with Pathé to direct a single picture, *The Awful Truth,* starring Ina Clair,[30] and planned to return to New York after that assignment. Or at least he allowed the Lab's board to believe that he would return soon. The board offered Boleslavsky a revised contract under which he would guarantee exclusive work at the Lab for a period of two and one-half months. Boleslavsky declined the offer.[31] On 5 September 1929 Fergusson wrote to Miriam Stockton:

> I suspect that Boley is preparing something characteristic to knock us down with; something nice like a four-year contract on the coast, for instance. I wrote Madame Ouspenskaya a very urgent letter about ten days ago, and have had no reply. I fear she may have heard something bad from Boley, and may be making sure before she speaks. Bill Post yesterday reported that somebody on Broadway told him Boley was signed up for a year in California. Walter Ellsberg telegraphed Boley asking whether he should go west to join him. The answer, as follows, came today: VERY LITTLE CHANCE HERE. YOU MIGHT HAVE TO WAIT SIX MONTHS. IF I WILL GET A PICTURE ENTIRELY BY MYSELF, WILL TRY TO GET YOU IN. REGARDS. BOLEY. This sounds to me as though he had no intention of coming back here, what do you think?[32]

Fergusson was right; Boleslavsky by now had decided against returning to New York. The theatre he had helped found lasted only one more year. During the season of 1929–30, the Lab produced plays directed by Fergusson and Maria Germanova, who had been hired at Boleslavsky's recommendation. Formerly the head of the so-called Prague Group of the Moscow Art Theatre, Germanova used the Lab as a vehicle to star herself in her favorite roles; she spent money profligately; she was highly critical of the Lab's school, its actors, and its general operation. Before the year was out both Ouspenskaya and Fergusson were ready to resign. The Lab was in serious trouble when the Wall Street Crash came. By the summer of 1930, the Laboratory Theatre had ceased to exist.

In 1933, following the publication of *Acting: The First Six Lessons,* Fergusson reflected on the path Boleslavsky had chosen for himself:

> One may see how Mr. Boleslavsky, who is in his every breath or gesture a pure being of the theatre, could take no other course. And one may still hold that the best Mr. Boleslavsky has to offer will never take in the commercial theatre. . . . Who would try for a Broadway success through a laborious training when it is so obvious that success is usually achieved there through other methods? The only possible reason for studying Mr. Boleslavsky with care is to acquire skill in drama, acting or perhaps poetry. At present these good things are very rare and very lost on the American stage.[33]

16

The Last Years: An Epilogue

Boleslavsky's refusal to return to New York and the Laboratory Theatre was not the result of quick success in Hollywood. Pathé demoted him from director of *The Awful Truth* and he was replaced by Marshall Neilan; Boleslavsky was made a minor assistant and put in charge of staging the film's spectacle sequences. After working in a minor capacity on two or three unimportant pictures, he left Pathé and vainly sought work elsewhere.

At about the time he left New York, Boleslavsky resumed writing the series of lessons on acting he had begun in 1923 for *Theatre Arts Magazine*. The second lesson was printed in July 1929, and the third appeared in July 1931. In that third lesson, Boleslavsky wrote what might be taken as a defense of his "defection" to Hollywood. The talking cinema, he said, represented "the discovery of a great and final instrument of drama . . . the instrument that gives to the theatre the precision and scientific serenity which all the arts have had. . . . " He saw great potential value in the talking cinema:

> It is the preservation of the art of the actor—the art of the theatre. Spoken drama equally with written drama. Do you realize that with the invention of spontaneous recording of the image, movement and voice, and consequently the personality of and soul of the actor, the last missing link in the chain of the arts disappears, and the theatre is no more a passing affair, but an eternal record?[1]

After leaving Pathé, Boleslavsky directed or collaborated on minor films for Columbia and RKO; it was with RKO that he made the first film which won him a small measure of attention, *The Gay Diplomat* (1931), featuring Ivan Lebedeff, Genevieve Tobin, and Betty Compson. After a "personal feud with the RKO boss"[2] Boleslavsky left the studio and did not make another picture for over a year.

During that time, in collaboration with the novelist Helen Woodward, he wrote and published *Way of the Lancer*. It received enthusiastic critical notices when it appeared in February of 1932, and before the year was out, *Lances Down* was printed. A third "lancer" novel was projected, but never written.[3]

Elaborate, complex negotiations to sell the film rights to *Way of the Lancer* (at one point Samuel Goldwyn bought a 30-day option and set Sidney Howard to work on an adaptation) finally collapsed, and on 3 June 1932, Boleslavsky wrote his editor: "If you would be in this business as I am, you would realize that it is just part of the game, that you get those things on every side and that you have to be ready to face them. Or look for the nearest hook, a coil of rope and a handy harp."[4]

On the strength of his literary reputation, however, Boleslavsky was hired by M-G-M as a screen writer, and he was working in that capacity when he got his first important film assignment. Producer Irving Thalberg signed Boleslavsky to replace Charles Brabin, the British director, in directing *Rasputin and the Empress,* which co-starred Ethel, John, and Lionel Barrymore in their only screen performance together. Ethel Barrymore, who knew Boleslavsky from New York, had insisted on the change. Released in December of 1932, the picture did much to establish Boleslavsky's reputation as a film director.

Over the next four years, Boleslavsky directed an average of three pictures a year; at the time of his death, on 17 January 1937, he was completing his fifteenth major film.

In 1933, Boleslavsky directed *Storm at Daybreak,* adapted from a play by the Hungarian author, Sandor Hynyady, featuring Kay Francis, Nils Asther, and Walter Huston in a love triangle set in Serbia at the outbreak of the World War; and *Beauty for Sale,* a screen treatment of Faith Baldwin's novel, with Madge Evans, Alice Brady, Otto Kruger, Una Merkel, Hedda Hopper, and Phillips Holmes in major roles.

In 1934, Boleslavsky directed four feature films: a romantic chase drama, *Fugitive Lovers,* with Robert Montgomery and Madge Evans; a screen version of Sidney Kingsley's *Men in White,* starring Clark Gable and Myrna Loy, with Jean Hersholt, Elizabeth Allan, and Otto Kruger in featured roles; *Operator 13,* a spy story set in the American Civil War, starring Marion Davies and Gary Cooper; and *The Painted Veil,* based on W. Somerset Maugham's novel, starring Greta Garbo, Herbert Marshall, and George Brent in a love triangle set in China during a time of plague.

In 1935, Boleslavsky directed four films: *Clive of India,* an historical drama starring Ronald Colman, Loretta Young, and Colin Clive, with C. Aubrey Smith, Cesar Romero, Leo G. Carroll, and Mischa Auer in featured roles; an adaption of Victor Hugo's *Les Misérables,* starring

Fredric March and Charles Laughton, supported by Rochelle Hudson, John Beal, and Sir Cedric Hardwicke; *O'Shaughnessy's Boy,* with Wallace Beery as a circus animal trainer and Jackie Cooper as his son; *Metropolitan,* a musical film, starring Lawrence Tibbett, Virginia Bruce, Alice Brady, and Cesar Romero.

That year marked an important event in Boleslavsky's personal life: he and Norma Drury Boleslavsky had a son. He wrote his old friend Ryszard Ordyński in Warsaw:

> We have a son named Jan and this fulfills my life. All that I do is for Norma and "Janek," the devil can take me. I have become such an American that I'm amazed, but I subscribe to Polish periodicals and continually dream about the doings of Polish film. . . .
>
> I am interested by what is being done on the Polish stage and in Polish film. I am gratified by every piece of information. Write me all the news and give each of them my heartiest embrace. In particular, remember me to Schiller and Jaracz.[5]

(Jan Boleslavsky was pursuing a film career when he died on 1 November, 1962 at age 27.)

The year 1936 was marked by three "firsts" for Boleslavsky. He filmed *Three Godfathers* (a re-make of a silent picture by John Ford), starring Chester Morris, Lewis Stone, and Walter Brennan—Boleslavsky's first and only western. He followed it with his first thorough-going comedy, *Theodora Goes Wild,* starring Irene Dunne and Melvyn Douglas, with featured parts acted by Thomas Mitchell, Thurston Hall, Rosalind Keith, and Spring Byington. Next came Boleslavsky's first technicolor picture, *The Garden of Allah,* starring Marlene Dietrich and Charles Boyer, and featuring Basil Rathbone, C. Aubrey Smith, Tilly Losch, Joseph Schildkraut, and John Carradine; it was produced by David O. Selznick, who a few years later would cite Boleslavsky's use of color as the ideal to be followed in his *Gone With The Wind.*

Boleslavsky's last picture was a re-make of the film comedy, *The Last of Mrs. Cheyney,* based on the Frederick Lonsdale play. The picture starred Joan Crawford, William Powell, and Robert Montgomery.

Near the end of the filming, Boleslavsky returned home from the studio complaining that he felt unusually tired. After dinner, he went to bed early, troubled by what he thought was severe indigestion. The following morning he awoke late and remained in bed. Norma sat with him, knitting while they talked quietly. Boleslavsky was siezed by sudden severe pain. A doctor was summoned, but by the time he arrived Richard Valentinovich Boleslavsky was dead. The date was 17 January 1937; in less than a month Boleslavsky would have been 49. The press reported that Boleslavsky died of a heart attack; one report attributed it to complications from a wound received during the World War.

Funeral services were held on January 19 at St. Augustine's Church in Culver City. Boleslavsky was buried in private Catholic services at Calvary Cemetery, Forest Lawn Memorial Park, Glendale, California. The cast of *Mrs. Cheyney* attended. On January 24, Russian friends held memorial services. *The Last of Mrs. Cheyney* was completed by George Fitzmaurice and released on 19 February 1937; Boleslavsky was given sole directorial credit.

Boleslavsky's films were nominated for Academy Awards in several categories: notable among these were *Les Misérables,* nominated for best picture of 1935, and Irene Dunne, nominated in 1936 for best actress for her performance in the title role of *Theodora Goes Wild.* Also in 1936, a Special Award for color cinematography was given to W. Howard Greene and Harold Rosson, for their work on *Garden of Allah.*

In March of 1937, Edith J. R. Issacs wrote: "The death of Richard Boleslawsky on January 17 has deprived *Theatre Arts* of one of its most devoted friends and co-workers. . . . It was his responsive and sympathetic personality that brought him close to the theatre's people."[6] In a published letter, Russell Janney wrote: "The untimely death of Richard Boleslavski . . . removed, I sincerely believe, the coming master genius among the newer film directors."[7] Eric H. Rideout, the British film historian, wrote:

> There are . . . two directors whose European atmosphere has never been excelled. One of them, Eric Von Stroheim, has not directed a picture for several years, the other, Richard Boleslawski, has just died.

Rideout found values in Boleslavsky's films that American film critics either missed or denied:

> We mourn the loss of a fine director, who leaves behind him, if we have the sense to preserve them, a fitting memorial in his films. They were never superficial. Always he appeared to be using a particular story, however slight, to express a theme of general application.[8]

In one of his lessons on acting, Boleslavsky had written from Hollywood: "The only thing you have to do is to march abreast of the times and do your best—as an artist." Seemingly in justification of his move to Hollywood, he added that the "idea" of making just one good film is worth all the "hundreds of bad ones."[9] After his death, an obituary in the *New York Times* noted that Boleslavsky's *Les Misérables* "bore the unmistakable marks of a film classic."[10]

There was one final irony in Boleslavsky's life. Only months before his death, he sent a letter to Vera Soloviova, who had recently arrived in the United States. He would soon be going to Poland, he wrote, and hoped to see her in New York when he was there en route to Warsaw. Had Boleslavsky intended to return to Warsaw for only a visit, or, disenchanted with Hollywood, did he plan to live in the country of his birth? Soloviova has lost the letter and remembers nothing more about its message. In any case, Boleslavsky died before he could make the trip.

In founding the American Laboratory Theatre, Boleslavsky had said that every "laboratory" should point the way toward the future and eventually cede its place to a new generation of theatre artists. This aim, at least, was fulfilled. In November 1930, Harold Clurman began holding regular talks, trying to rouse interest in starting a new theatre; many of the ideals and beliefs he espoused echoed words previously spoken by Boleslavsky. Later, as a director and writer on subject of directing, Clurman would practice and expound ideas he had learned from Boleslavsky.

On 8 June 1931, twenty-eight actors, including several who had trained and acted at the Laboratory Theatre, and three directors—Clurman, Lee Strasberg, and Cheryl Crawford—went to Brookfield, Connecticut. There Strasberg drilled the actors according to his understanding of methods learned from Boleslavsky and Ouspenskaya; at the same time, he directed them in Paul Green's *House of Connelly*, which opened in September 1931. The Group Theatre, the most direct offspring of Boleslavsky's American Laboratory Theatre, was born.

Conclusions

For Americans, the most significant aspect of Richard Boleslavsky's life was most certainly his teaching and directing at the Laboratory Theatre from 1923 until 1929. During the Lab's seven years of operation (including its final season, when Boleslavsky was in Hollywood), some five hundred students studied there, some for only a few months, some for two or three years. All of them gained a degree of understanding of the methods first developed by Stanislavsky, ideas introduced in America by Boleslavsky and Ouspenskaya at the Laboratory Theatre.

The former Lab students I have talked with, as well as those interviewed by Ronald Willis for his study of the Laboratory Theatre, are all but unanimous in saying that their study at the Lab, however brief or lengthy, changed forever their perception of acting and theatre. Lee Strasberg has already been quoted: the lessons he learned at the Lab have been fundamental to all his subsequent work with actors. Harold Clurman acknowledges that "watching Boleslavsky work and listening to some of the things he said while working . . . certainly had an influence on me, elightened me and stimulated me. . . . Boleslavsky contributed to my understanding of direction, as he did to some extent to that of Lee Strasberg."[1] Francis Fergusson also considers Boleslavsky's influence basic to his career: "I was looking around for a sense of direction, and he gave it to me. . . . He led me to Aristotle. He certainly got me started on the way I've gone ever since."[2] Stella Adler, who studied first at the Lab and then with Stanislavsky, explains that her Lab training "had the biggest impact on me ":

> [At the Lab] I reached the point in my own life where whatever talent I have was augmented by craft. It was much easier for me after that. And then I realized that it is impossible to work without craft—impossible. Without it you have no starting point. My whole career I really owe to the Laboratory Theatre. I think that's true of everybody who studied there.[3]

Almost every former Lab student I have met has echoed the words of Strasberg, Clurman, Fergusson, and Adler.

Boleslavsky's students have spread his message throughout America. After leaving the Lab, many of them pursued careers as actors, directors, writers, critics, producers and theatre organizers. They have worked on the professional stage and in community and university theatres, as well as film and television. As Stella Adler puts it:

> Boleslavsky was important in that he was the first person who brought over the Stanislavsky technique of acting. He is important also in that he influenced some of the major people working in the theatre and carrying on those traditions (or not carrying on those traditions—distorting those traditions) and all the directors who came out of that, including Harold Clurman, Lee Strasberg, and the people who went to Hollywood. Boleslavsky influenced a great many people, including myself, who are the spokesmen for Stanislavsky in this country, who have influenced the whole of the theatre and all of the movie industry. And it was Boleslavsky who did it.[4]

Boleslavsky's students do not always agree on the meaning of the technique he presented at the Lab, but almost all of them agree that he included all the essential elements of the Stanislavsky system. Lee Strasberg remembers that when Stanislavsky's first published presentation of the elements, *An Actor Prepares,* appeared in 1936 it contained no surprises: "We already knew all that."[5] Asked if he found anything new in Stanislavsky's books, Harold Clurman answers: "No, I just found out that Stanislavsky is not a good writer. *An Actor Prepares* helped to organize the thing, but he's not a good writer and it's not the best presentation that can be made of the System."[6] Similarly, Francis Fergusson says: "I felt that Boley had worked it out much more consistently than Stanislavsky. Stanislavsky's books were all quite different. He was groping," while Boleslavsky offered "a very cogent, thorough picture of a technique of acting."[7]

Boleslavsky's students agree on the importance of his work in America and on the completeness of the system as he presented it. Most of them agree, too, as to Boleslavsky's essential ideas.

Some, however, differ sharply over a crucial aspect of his message. This disagreement first appeared in the early years of the Group Theatre, and the issues are most sharply defined by reviewing briefly the events leading up to the controversy in the Group, which came to a head in 1934.

After studying for three or four months at the Laboratory Theatre in 1924, Lee Strasberg left the Lab and found work as an actor at the Theatre Guild. At about the same time, he began applying Lab principles by directing amateur groups. Harold Clurman, who had worked under Boleslavsky's direction at about the same time Strasberg was at the Lab, joined the Theatre Guild in 1925. Strasberg and Clurman met and became fast friends.

Two events important in Clurman's artistic life occurred in 1926. First, he observed Strasberg rehearsing the amateur actors at the Chrystie Street Settlement: "He was working in a manner that struck me as altogether original. I did not know it then: he was following a method that he had been taught at the American Laboratory Theatre. I watched with keen interest." The other important event: Clurman enrolled in Boleslavsky's course for stage directors at the Lab.[8] At the Lab he met Stella Adler, a member of the acting company, whom he later married.

Soon, Clurman and Strasberg became eager to form their own theatre company, one which would employ the methods of acting taught at the Laboratory Theatre while seeking to convey the "life of our times" through the theatre.[9] Joined by Cheryl Crawford (who was never associated with the Lab), they worked at first under the auspices of the Theatre Guild, but broke away as the independent Group Theatre in 1931. The acting company of this new organization included former Lab actors Stella Adler, Eunice Stoddard, Ruth Nelson, Grover Burgess, John Garfield, and perhaps others, as well.

In the beginning, Strasberg was the Group's principal director. His methods, as described by Clurman, laid particular stress on two elements he had learned at the Lab, improvisation and affective memory. It was the use of the latter which drew the most attention and ultimately led to the greatest controversy. As Clurman writes:

> In this "exercise" the actor was asked to recall the details of an event from his own past. The recollection of these details would stir the actors with some of the feeling involved in the original experience, thus producing "mood." These "exercises" were used to set the mechanism of the actor's emotion rolling, so to speak. When the actor was in the grip of this mood—although that is not what we called it, nor was it the purpose of the exercise to capture it directly—the actor was better prepared to do the scene calling for the particular mood that the exercise had evoked. . . . But whatever its validity or error, the fact is that this procedure was used by us for the first four years of our work, and it unquestionably produced results—all kinds.[10]

From the very start, Stella Adler objected to Strasberg's emphasis. Her objections soon developed into disagreement, and disagreement soon became argument. By the summer of 1934, her opposition to Strasberg's approach brought the two into open conflict. That summer Strasberg went to Moscow, where he was particularly fascinated by the work of Meyerhold and that being done at the Vakhtangov theatre. Adler and Clurman travelled instead to Paris where they met Stanislavsky, who was there recuperating from an illness.

Adler told Stanislavsky that since learning his system she had lost all creative joy in acting. Moreover, she added, she did not like affective memory at all: "I said I thought it was sick." At Stanislavsky's invitation, she remained to study with him while Clurman went on to Moscow for a short visit. After some five weeks' study with Stanislavsky, Adler returned to the United States and announced to the other members of the Group Theatre what she had learned. As Clurman recounts:

> To put it bluntly, she had discovered that our use of the Stanislavsky system had been incorrect. An undue emphasis on the "exercises" of affective memory had warped our work with the actor. Strasberg's first reaction to this declaration was the charge that Stanislavsky had gone back on himself. Later, however, he decided to take advantage of the suggestions furnished by Stella's report, and to use what he could of the "innovations" in Stanislavsky's method. Stella herself began to give classes that summer.[11]

Briefly, that is the chronology of events that led up to a controversy that continues unabated up to the present day.[12] The central issue: the use and relative importance of affective memory in the actor's work.

Strasberg's position is unequivocal. In his view, "Emotional memory is a part of a process without which acting does not take place." Action is an important part of the actor's analytic work, but he is emphatic: "It does not lead to emotion. It leads to a certain reality, but not to emotion."[13]

Adler is equally adamant. She thinks Strasberg's emphasis is destructive. "Too many of his students have come to me ready for an institution."[14] Her own approach?

> In teaching I do not require a student ever to go to the emotion itself or ask the student to use emotion as a source. . . . All the emotion is contained in the action. The action can be a personal or an imaginative one. . . . To go back to a feeling or emotion of one's own experience I believe to be unhealthy. It tends to separate you from the play, from the action of the play, from the circumstances of the play, and from the author's intention. All this has to be embodied in the action.[15]

Both the issue and the respective positions staked out by the combatants are clear. Less clear is how two students of the same teacher could arrive at such antithetical positions. One might suppose that Adler had never been happy with the system as it was taught at the Lab, yet that was not the case. Adler says she had been more than satisfied with Boleslavsky's methods: "Boleslavsky was very, very graphic—external—in his emphasis as a director. I don't think the Group Theatre was. It was very internal. It tried very much to work emotionally first and left the outside bare. Boleslavsky didn't do that. He made it very visual, he was colorful." Moreover, she considers her private study with Stanislavsky in 1934 as a renewal, rather than a revision of the things she had already learned at the Laboratory Theatre.[16]

Stanislavsky's account of his work with Adler supports her recollection:

> They say my method is being introduced in America, yet suddenly this talented actress who has studied my system "withers away" before everyone's eyes. I had to take her on, if only to restore the reputation of my system. I wasted a whole month on it. It turned out that everything she had learnt was right. She had been shown and had studied everything in the school. "Do you know about the through-line action and the task?" "Yes," she said, "they told me something about that, but I did not understand it." Yet that was the crux of the whole system. So we started to proceed along this line. . . . When she had learnt this, she acted so brilliantly that we absolutely "howled" with delight. Only an understanding of the through action and tasks can completely remake a person. Without this understanding everything is merely exercises on the system.[17]

The weight of opinion is clearly against Strasberg's approach. Boleslavsky concluded that dramatic action is the actor's fundamental "emotion-maker," as he made clear in his 1927 article, if not earlier. Stanislavsky came to the same conclusion, though he later shifted his emphasis again and stressed the "method of physical actions." Adler understood Boleslavsky's message, though she evidently failed to fully appreciate the value of dramatic action until Stanislavsky went over it with her again.

Most other Lab students agree with Adler's view, or at least take a position much like hers. Francis Fergusson gained his insight into Boleslavsky's ideas during the course of his study at the Lab from 1926 to 1930:

> In my opinion the notion of "action" is the most basic and potentially the most valuable, part of the Moscow Art Theatre technique. . . . "Action" was certainly the word we heard must frequently . . . from Boleslavski in his rehearsals and informal talks, from Madame in her classes in the technique of acting. . . . [18]

As for Strasberg's approach, Fergusson says:

> It's very hard to talk about action and to know it well enough so that it can be used as a technique of acting. I remember when Strasberg was around the Laboratory

Theatre, around Boley's classes and rehearsals and so forth. I don't think he understood what Boleslavsky meant by it. Then he got involved in more or less Freudian ways of understanding the human animal, and he began to use emotion as the whole thing. I don't really know much about his work except indirectly from some of his students, but my impression is that he used only Boleslavsky's method of acquiring emotion and didn't understand the role of the intellect in guiding and forming. . . . [19]

Another Lab actor, Donald Keyes, also remembers that Boleslavsky was "always using the word action." In rehearsals, Keyes explains, Boleslavsky never asked the actors to use affective memory or to approach an emotion directly. Rather, he used dramatic action to bring the actor into the correct mood and to stimulate his emotions:

"Action"—"spine"—"beat"—those were the words he used most in rehearsals. I don't think he ever criticized an actor's mood or ever suggested the mood of the character at all. I think he thought that would come out of the action—out of the spine—out of working toward the objective. . . . We used the phrase "memory of emotion" sometimes. This was something we tried to recapture, but there was very little work on emotion. I don't think in rehearsal I ever heard Boley call for an emotion. He never said, "You must be more angry, or more happy." I don't think he ever used emotional terms. It was always translated into terms of the objective or the spine of the immediate action. [20]

Blanch Tancock points out that Boleslavsky had not eliminated the use of affective memory, but that it was never presented as the sole, or even the best means of rousing the actor's emotional life. She explains that in developing the "inner characterization" of a role, the Lab actors were taught to find the "inner line of truth, the below-the-surface truth of feeling, of emotion, fears, desires, of possessiveness, of aggressiveness, of sudden impulse, and of calculated intention."

This is where Boley taught us how to use our affective memory, how to deepen the level and truth of our emotional identification with the part. Emotion was also triggered and sustained through the interplay of action and connection when the actors entered into and re-created the life, not just the lines of their part. [21]

Harold Clurman considered affective memory "Stanislavsky's great discovery as the instrument to generate emotion" but he came to believe that "action is the fundamental of acting, and without that the rest will not serve." Action and imagination, he says, are the two "generating things" in the actor's technique. "Action is the center of the whole technique. They all say that now. Of course, you have to have more than action. . . . No one thing is sufficient, but action is the center." [22]

Further testimony from Boleslavsky's students could be added, but the point is clear. Strasberg stands virtually alone in his interpretation of the system as it was presented at the Lab. Very few actors from the Lab go along with Strasberg's approach; most think it is misguided. Ruth Nelson and Eunice Stoddard, both of whom were members at the Lab and then acted at the Group Theatre, tactfully avoid the question. Nelson admits discreetly that after the first few months of the Group's first summer, she asked to be excused from Strasberg's exercises: "I found him too trying."

Reflecting on the differences between working at the Laboratory Theatre and the Group, Nelson says:

> I would say the whole atmosphere of the Group was so theoretical, and this was totally the opposite of my experience with Boleslavsky, which was total love. It was very, very hard for me to adjust, although I was totally sold on the idea of the Group Theatre. I was in the first production and the last, and nothing could have dragged me away. . . . But it was very difficult for me, much as I loved it. It was very difficult for me to accept, because I felt Strasberg's approach so analytical—very trying to work with, very difficult.

When the argument over the "method" arose she tried to stay out of it and avoided discussions as much as possible. "By that time I had accepted the method, of course, but I never took it as seriously as many of the darlings did, you see." Still, she remembers that dramatic action was the secret of Boleslavsky's work with her in *Martine*. She adds: "You see, this can fool you so—the 'method', 'affective memory,' and all these things. . . . God knows, there are so many ways. Stanislavsky used it as a living thing, and not as 'the book.' And that's the way Boleslavsky used it." Boleslavsky's secret? "He worked with *me*, not with theories, not with ideas he had in his head." His was the most important influence on her artistic life, "Because, for me at any rate, you learn best with love. And in Boleslavsky there was tremendous love."[23]

There are, I believe, two explanations for Strasberg's misunderstanding of Boleslavsky's essential teaching. In the first place, Strasberg entered the Lab at a time when Boleslavsky's own thinking was in transition. In 1924, Boleslavsky evidently placed greater stress on emotional memory than he did only a year or two later. Even so, Strasberg failed to grasp at least one important aspect of Boleslavsky's doctrine: the actor's emotions can be roused and engaged by a number of means: affective memory is neither the only, nor necessarily the best route to the actor's inner life.

Further, Strasberg paid inadequate attention to the ways Boleslav-

sky applied theory to practical work. Strasberg never acted under Boleslavsky's direction. When asked about Boleslavsky's directorial methods,
Strasberg answers that he does not remember much about them. Strasberg signed up for Boleslavsky's 1926 directing class, as did Harold
Clurman and Francis Fergusson. Clurman does not recall that Strasberg
attended and adds that in any case Strasberg was set in his own methods
by that time. Fergusson remembers vaguely that Strasberg came a time
or two but then stopped coming. Asked about that class, Strasberg
answers: "We discussed the principles of directing. Frankly, I don't
remember too much. On me, it didn't make too much of an impression. . . . I imagine that he must have explained 'spine' and so forth—
the analytic part of the System."[24] Had Strasberg paid greater attention
to Boleslavsky's practical application of the theory perhaps he would
have come away with a fuller understanding of, and a greater appreciation of dramatic action.

The second reason for Strasberg's misplaced emphasis, I believe, is
that he came to the Lab with a strong predisposition to a particular
approach. As he once explained in a talk at the Actors Studio:

> I never went to college; I didn't finish high school. But by the time I came to the
> American Laboratory Theatre, which was the first time I came into real contact with
> the technical work we do here, I had already arrived at the essential principles. I say
> that only to show that such a thing is possible. I had read the lives of the actors. I
> had read all the books about acting. The only thing I didn't know was how the hell
> you do it. I already knew everything, except I didn't know what I really knew.
>
> At that time Boleslavsky said in his first talk, "There are two kinds of acting. One
> believes that the actor can actually experience on the stage. The other believes that
> the actor only indicates what the character experiences, but does not himself really
> experience. We posit a theatre of real experience. The essential thing in such experi-
> ence is that the actor learns to know and to do, not through mental knowledge, but
> by sensory knowledge." Suddenly, I knew, "That's it! that's it!" That was the
> answer I had been searching for. The point is that I had already read Freud and
> already knew the things that go on in a human being without consciousness. I had
> already picked up everything Boleslavsky said, but he showed me what it meant.[25]

Strasberg came to the Laboratory Theatre looking for a specific thing,
and he went away having found the thing he wanted to find. All the rest
he deemed of relatively less importance.

Another Lab member, Arthur Sircom, describes Strasberg's visits:

> Lee Strasberg, Harold Clurman and Philip Loeb all came each week to Boleslavsky's
> lectures. They entered in single file, serious, funereal, marched down the aisle and
> into their seats and sat there. They never moved—they listened—stoney faced.
> (Loeb twitched often with a sense of humor, the only one with *any* humor.) And

when the lecture was over they exited in solemn single file. They read also about Stanislavsky; they delved deeply into books—and started the Group Theatre as the last word on everyone and everything Russian!

I started in Theatre in New York in the same play, *Processional,* for the Theatre Guild, with Strasberg, Clurman, Sandy Meisner, etc. Oh, it was quite a crew! The Method people . . . certainly got a great deal from Boley. They read into his lectures what they wished.[26]

Judging from Sircom's account, Strasberg might have profited from another lesson Boleslavsky taught through his example: that work in the theatre should be a thing of joy and love, and not an exercise in solemnity or pain or self-torment.

Boleslavsky had one final message that everyone connected with the theatre might do well to remember: "How do you expect to learn your craft if you don't analyze what has been already achieved? Then forget about it all and go after your own achievements." He added: "The only real rules in art are the rules that we discover for ourselves."[27] In the end it mattered little to Boleslavsky himself who was "right" or "wrong" in disputes over theory, for theory was less important to him than the practical artistic accomplishments that flow from it. His theatrical heirs must be judged finally by the results born of the ideas they have promulgated.

Appendix

Filmography

Mimo zhizni (Passing Life By). 1914. 4 reels, 1,258 m. "Golden Russia" Series. Director: Yakov Protazanov. Photographer: A. Levitsky. Premiere: 28 February 1914.
CAST: V. Maksimov (Yurevsky, a poet), Ye. Naydenova (Nina), R. Boleslavsky (Volin, an artist).

Tanets vampira (Dance of the Vampires). 1914. 85m. "Golden Russia" Series. Director: Yakov Protazanov. Photographer: A. Levitsky, Premiere: 22 March 1914.
CAST: V. Lasky, R. Boleslavsky.

Podvig kazaka Kuz'my Kryuchkova (Exploits of the Cossack Kuzma Kryuchkov). Producer: Kinoinstsenirovka. 2 reels, 850 m. "Golden Russia" Series. Director: V. Gardin. Photographer: V. Levitsky. Premiere: 12 October 1914.
CAST: R. Boleslavsky (Cossack Kryuchkov).

Tsar Ivan Vasilievich Grozny (Tsar Ivan the Terrible). Producer: "Sharez" (Shalyapin-Reznikov). Adapted from Rimsky Korsakov's opera, *Pskovityanka*. Photographer: A. Winkler. Scenic Designer: V. Yegorov. Premiere: 20 October 1915.
CAST: F. Shalyapin (Ivan the Terrible), Volk-Krachkovskaya (Olga), N. Saltykov (Tucha), G. Chernova (Vera Sheloga), Ye. Korsak (Perfilevna), P. Bazilevsky (Boris Godunov), R. Boleslavsky (Prince Vyazemsky), B. Sushkevich (Malyuta), M. Zharov, V. Karin.

Mara Kramskaya (Zhritsa svobodnoy lyubvi) [*A Woman of Easy Virtue*]. 6 reels. Director: V. Izumrudov (Garlitsky). Producer: R. Persky. Scenario: O. Gzovskaya and R. Persky. Photographer: G. Lemberg. Scenic Designer: M. Werner. Premiere: 24 November 1915.
CAST: O. Gzovskaya (Mara Kramskaya), I. Lazarev (Pavel Aleksandrovich Kramsky, her father), Armenina (Polina Petrovna, her mother), G. Khmara (Nikolai Ivanovich Neverov), A. Geyrot (Boris Sergeyevich, Prince Protas'yev), Ye. Rayevskaya (Princess Varvara Semenovna, his wife), S. Popov (Grigori Ivanovich Voloshin), R. Boleslavsky (Vladimir Nikolayevich Panov, a pianist), S. Popova (Shatova, a ballerina), M. Kemper (Nina Mikhailovna Burova, friend of Mara), B. Rutkovskaya (Mlle Julie, companion to Mara), A, Bondarev, A. Stakhovich, V. Gotovtsev.

Domik na Volge (Little House on the Volga). 4 reels, 1,400 m. Director and photographer: Władysław Starewicz. Producer: N. Kagana. Premiere: 2 October 1917.

CAST: R. Boleslavsky (Volgen), Ye. Porfir'yeva, L. Deykun, V. Gotovtsev, D. Zeland, A. Vasil'kova.

Lyubov'—nenavist'—smert' (Love—Hate—Death). 7 reels. Director: Ivan Perestiani. Producer: Biofilm. Scenarist: A. Smoldovsky. Photographer: Grigori Giver. Scenic designer: V. Rakovsky. Premiere: 1918.
CAST: Zoya Karabanova, Perestiani, R. Boleslavsky.

Die Gezeichneten (Love One Another). Also known as *Elsker Hvandre* and *Pogrom*. Director and scenarist: Carl Dreyer. Based on the novel by Aage Madelung. Producer: Otto Schmidt. Production: Primusfilm, Berlin. Photographer: Friedrich Weinmann. Art Director: Jens G. Lind. Historical Advisers: Vikto Aden, Prof. Krol. Assistant to the director: Richard Boleslavsky. Premiere: 7 February 1922, Copenhagen.
CAST: Polina Piekovska (Hanna-Liebe), Vladimir Gaidarov (Jakov Segal), Torleif Reiss (Aleksander "Sasha" Sokolov), Richard Boleslavsky (Fedja), Duwan (The Merchant Suckoswerski), Johannes Meyer (Klimov, alias Rylovitch, alias Father Roman), Adele Reuter-Eichberg (Hanna's mother), Emmy Wyde, Friedrich Kühne, Hugo Döblin.

Films Directed by Boleslavsky to 1921

Ty yeshchë ne umeyesh' lyubit' (You Still Cannot Love). 3 reels. Director: R. Boleslavsky. Producer: A. Pechkovsky. Photographer: A. Pechkovsky. Premiere: 1915.
CAST: N. Kozlyaninova, M. Kireyevskaya, R. Boleslavsky.

Tri vstrechi (Three Meetings). 4 reels. Director: R. Boleslavsky. Producer: T/D "Russ." Photographer: Yakovlev. Premiere: 1915.
CAST: G. Khmara (Strumilov, a student), Beatriche Blazhevich (Olga Ukhvatova), N. Boleslavskaya (Mother), D. Zeland (Baron), Ye. Kestler (Emma Shpits), A. Bondarev, P. Basilevsky, A. Michurin, Yu. Osterva, Grigor'eva.

Sem'ya Polenovykh (The Family Polenov). 3 reels, 1,100 m. Director: R. Boleslavsky. Producer: "Kinolenta." Premiere: 13 June 1917.
CAST: R. Boleslavsky (Polenov), M. Kireyevskaya (Nina, his stepdaughter), N. Kozlyaninova (Nina as a child). (See *Ty yeshchë ne umeyesh' lyubit'* above.)

Ne razum, a strasti pravyat mirom (Not Reason But Passion Rules the World). Also known as *Otravlennoye serdtse (The Poisonous Heart)* or *Skorbnaya povest' yunykh (A Mournful Tale of Youth)*. 4 reels. 1,400 m. Director: R. Boleslavsky. Producer: "Russ." Photographer: Ivan Frolov. Premiere: 8 August 1917.
CAST: A. Chargonin (Pavel Sel'tsov, an artist), V. Charova (Lydia Ramenskaya), Ye. Bel'skaya-Chaleyeva (Ol'ga Gribunina), S. Ayarov (Pomorsky), N. Toranitsky, N. Orlov, P. Romanov, E. Kyl'ganek, Pomerantsev, Nikitina, Belov.

Khleb (Bread). 1,300 m. Directors: R. Boleslavsky and B. Sushkevich. Producer: Mos-Kino-Committee. Scenarist: V. Dobrovolsky (Fedorovich). Photographer: N. Rudakov. Premiere: 1918.
CAST: Leonid Leonidov, Olga Baklanova, Richard Boleslavsky, Eugene Vakhtangov.

Bohaterstwo Polskiego Skauta (Bravery of the Polish Scout). Director: Richard Boleslavsky. Producer: Sfinks. Photographer: Zbigniew Gniazdowski. Scenic Designer: Józef Galewski. Premiere: 3 November 1920, Stylowy, Warsaw.
CAST: Kazimierz Junosza-Stępowski (Janicki), Władysław Macherski (Scout Janek Zwidlicz), Laura Duninówna (his mother), Edmund Gasiński, Jadwiga Smosarska (Hanka), Feliks Norski, A. Chmielewski.

Cud nad Wisła (Miracle on the Vistula). Director: Richard Boleslavsky. Producer: Orientfilm. Scenarist: Adam Zagórski. Photographer: Zbigniew Gniazdowski. Scenic Designers: E. Librowiczowa, Borowski, Jozef Galewski. Premiere: 16 March 1921, Palace, Warsaw.
CAST: Honorata Leszczyńska, Anna Belina, Jadwiga Smosarska, Wincenty Rapacki Sr., Edmund Gasiński, Władysław Grabowski, Stefan Jaracz, Jerzy Leszczyński, Leonard Bończa-Stępiński, Kazimierz Junosza-Stępowski.

Films Directed by Boleslavsky in Hollywood

In 1929 Boleslavsky worked in a minor capacity on *The Awful Truth* (Director: Marshall Neilan); *Paris Bound* (Director: Edward H. Griffith); and *This Thing Called Love* (Director: Paul L. Stein) for Pathé Studio.

The Last of the Lone Wolf (Columbia). Producer: Harry Cohn. Screenplay: John T. Neville. Continuity: Dorothy Howell. Dialogue: James Wittaker. Adapted from a novel by Louis Joseph Vance. Assistant Directors: C. C. Coleman, Stuart Walker. Premiere: September 1930.
CAST: Bert Lytell (Michael Lanyard), Patsy Ruth Miller (Stephanie, the lady-in-waiting).

The Gay Diplomat (RKO-Radio). Screenplay: Benn W. Levy. NY Premiere: 9 October 1931, Warner.
CAST: Ivan Lebedeff (Captain Orloff), Genvieve Tobin (Diana Dorchy), Betty Compson (Baroness Corri), Ilka Chase (Bliniss), Purnell Pratt (Colonel Gorim), Rita La Roy (Natalie), Colin Campbell (Gamble), Edward Martindel (Ambassador), Arthur Edmund Carew (The Suave Man).

Rasputin and the Empress (MGM). Screenplay: Charles MacArthur. Producer: Irving Thalberg. NY Premiere: 23 December 1932, Astor.
CAST: John Barrymore (Prince Chegodieff), Ethel Barrymore (The Czarina), Lionel Barrymore (Rasputin), Ralph Morgan (The Czar), Diana Wynyard (Princess Natasha), Tad Alexander (The Czarevitch), C. Henry Gordon (Grand Duke Igor), Edward Arnold (Doctor Remezov).

Storm at Daybreak (MGM). Adapted from Sandor Hynyady's Hungarian play, *Feketeszaru Csereszyne*. Music: Dr. William Axt. Lyrics: Gus Kahn. NY Premiere: 21 July 1933, Capitol.
CAST: Kay Francis (Irina), Nils Asther (Geza), Walter Huston (Dushan), Phillips Holmes (Csaholyl), Eugene Pallette (Janos), C. Henry Gordon (Panto), Louise Closser Hale (Militza), Jean Parker (Danitza).

Fugitive Lovers (MGM). Based on a story by Ferdinand Reyher and Frank Wead. NY Premiere: 12 January 1934, Capitol and Loew's Metropolitan.

CAST: Robert Montgomery (Paul Porter), Madge Evans (Letty Morris), Ted Healy (Hector Withington Jr.), Nat Pendleton (Legs Coffee), C. Henry Gordon (Daly), Ruth Selwyn (Babe Callahan).

Men in White (MGM). Screenplay: Waldemar Young. Adapted from the play by Sidney Kingsley. Photography: Frank Sullivan. (Released 28 March 1934.) NY Premiere: 8 June 1934, Capitol.
CAST: Clark Gable (Dr. George Ferguson), Myrna Loy (Laura Hudson), Jean Hersholt (Dr. Hochberg), Elizabeth Allan (Barbara Dennin), Otto Kruger (Dr. Levine), C. Henry Gordon (Dr. Cunningham), Russell Hardie (Dr. Michaelson), Wallace Ford (Shorty), Henry B. Walthall (Dr. McCabe), Russell Hopton (Pete), Samuel S. Hinds (Dr. Gordon), Frank Puglia (Dr. Vitale), Chalzel (Dr. Wren), Donald Douglas (Mac).

Operator 13 (MGM-Cosmopolitan). Producer: Lucien Hubbard. Screenplay: Harry Thew, Zelda Sears, Eve Green. From the story by Robert W. Chambers. Photography: George Folsey. Art Director: Cedric Gibbons. Associate Art Directors: Arnold Gillespie, Edwin B. Willis. Costumer: Adrian. Editor: Frank Sullivan. Music: Dr. William Axt. Songs and Lyrics: Walter Donaldson and Gus Kahn. NY Premiere: 22 June 1934, Capitol and Loew's Metropolitan.
CAST: Marion Davies (Gail Loveless), Gary Cooper (Captain Jack Gailliard), Jean Parker (Eleanor), Katharine Alexander (Pauline), Ted Healy (Doctor Hitchcock), Russell Hardie (Littledale), Henry Wadsworth (John Pelham), Douglass Dumbrille (General Stuart), Willard Robertson (Captain Channing), Fuzzy Knight (Sweeney), Sidney Toler (Major Allen), Robert McWade (Colonel Sharpe), Marjorie Gateson (Mrs. Shackleford), Wade Boteller (Gaston), Walter Long (Operator 55), Hattie McDaniel (Cook), The Four Mills Brothers.

The Painted Veil (MGM). Screenplay: John Meehan, Salka Viertel, Edith Fitzgerald. From the novel by Somerset Maugham. Producer: Hunt Stromberg. NY Premiere: 8 December 1934, Capitol.
CAST: Greta Garbo (Katrin), Herbert Marshall (Walter Fane), George Brent (Jack Townsend), Warner Oland (General Yu), Jean Hersholt (Herr Koerber), Bodil Rosing (Frau Koerber), Katherine Alexander (Mrs. Townsend), Cecilia Parker (Olga), Soo Yong (Amah), Forrester Harvey (Waddington).

Clive of India (Twentieth Century). Written and adapted by W. P. Lipscomb and R. J. Minney from their London play. Music: Alfred Newman. Released by United Artists. NY Premiere: 17 January 1935, Rivoli.
CAST: Ronald Colman (Robert Clive), Loretta Young (Margaret Maskelyne), Colin Clive (Captain Johnstone), Francis Lister (Edmund Maskelyne), C. Aubrey Smith (Prime Minister), Cesar Romero (Mir Jaffar), Montague Love (Governor Pigot), Lumsden Hare (Sergeant Clark), Ferdinand Munier (Admiral Watson), Gilbert Emery (Mr. Sullivan), Leo G. Carroll (Mr. Manning), Etienne Girardot (Mr. Warburton), Robert Greig (Mr. Pemberton), Ian Wolfe (Mr. Kent), Herbert Bunston (First Director), Mischa Auer (Suraj Ud Dowlah), Ferdinand Gottschalk (Old member), Wyndham Standing (Colonel Townsend), Doris Lloyd (Mrs. Nixon), Edward Cooper (Clive's butler), Ann Shaw (Lady Lindley), Vernon Downing (Mr. Stringer), Neville Clark (Mr. Vincent), Peter Shaw (Mr. Miller), Pat Somerset (Lieutenant Walsh), Elly Malyon (Mrs. Clifford), Keith Kenneth (Second director), Desmond Roberts (Third director), Joseph Tozer (Sir Frith), Connie Leon (Ayah), Leonard Mudie (General Burgoyne), Phillip Dare (Captain George),

Charles Evans (Surveyor), Vesey O'Davern (Assistant surveyor), Lila Lance (Mango Seller).

Les Misérables (Twentieth Century). An adaptation of Victor Hugo's novel. Screenplay: W. P. Lipscomb. Produced by Darryl Zanuck. Released through United Artists. NY Premiere: 21 April 1935, Rivoli.
CAST: Fredric March (Jean Valjean), Charles Laughton (Javert), Cedric Hardwicke (Bishop Bienvenu), Rochelle Hudson (Big Cosette), Marilynne Knowlden (Little Cosette), Frances Drake (Eponine), John Beal (Marius), Jessie Ralph (Madame Magloire), Florence Eldridge (Fantine), Ferdinand Gottschalk (Thenardier), Jane Kerr (Madame Thernadier), Elley Malyon (Mother Superior), Vernon Downing (Brissac), Lyons Wickland (Lamarque), John Carradine (Enjoiras), Charles Haefeli (Brevet), Leonid Kinskey (Genflou), John Bleifer (Chenildieu), Harry Semels (Cochepaille), Mary Forbes (Madame Baptiseme), Florence Roberts (Toussaint), Lorin Raker (Valsin), Perry Ivins (M. Devereux), Thomas Mills (L' Estrange), Lowell Drew (Duval), Davidson Clark (Marcin), Ian McClaren (Head Gardener).

O'Shaughnessy's Boy (MGM). Based on a story by Harvey Gates and Malcolm Stuart Boylan. Screenplay: Leonard Praskins, Wanda Tuchock, and Otis Garrett. Music: Dr. William Axt. Producer: Philip Goldstone. NY Premiere: 4 October 1935, Capitol.
CAST: Wallace Beery (Windy), Jackie Cooper (Stubby), Spanky McFarland (Stubby as a child), Henry Stephenson (Major Winslow), Sarah Haden (Martha), Leoma Maricle (Cora), Willard Robertson (Hastings), Clarence Muse (Jeff), Ben Hendricks (Franz), Wade Boteler (Callahan), Jack Daley (Mack), Oscar Apfel (Lawyer), Granville Bates (Doctor).

Metropolitan (Twentieth Century-Fox). Based on a story by Bess Meredyth. Screenplay: Bess Meredyth and George Marion Jr. Producer: Darryl F. Zanuck. NY Premiere: 17 October 1935, Radio City Music Hall.
CAST: Lawrence Tibbett (Thomas Renwick), Virginia Bruce (Anne Merrill), Alice Brady (Ghita Galin), Cesar Romero (Niki Baroni), Thurston Hall (T. Simon Hunter), Luis Alberni (Ugo Pizzi), George Marion Sr. (Perontelli), Adrian Rosley (Mr. Tolentino), Christian Rub (Weidel), Ruth Donnelly (Marina), Franklyn Ardell (Marco), Etienne Girardot (Nello), Jessie Ralph (Charwoman).

Three Godfathers (MGM). Screenplay: Edward E. Paramore Jr. and Manuel Seff. Adapted from a story by Peter B. Kyne. Producer: Joseph L. Manckiewicz. NY Premiere: 6 March 1936, Rialto.
CAST: Chester Morris (Bob), Lewis Stone ("Doc"), Walter Brennan (Gus), Irene Hervey (Molly), Sidney Toler (Professor Snaps), Dorothy Tree (Blackie), Roger Imhof (Sheriff), Willard Robertson (Rev. McLane), Robert Livingston (Frank), John Sheehan (Ed), Joseph Marlevaky (Pedro), Victor Potel ("Buck Tooth"), Helen Brown (Mrs. Marshall), Harvey Clark (Marcus Treen), Virginia Brissac (Mrs. McLane), Jean Kirchner (Baby).

Theodora Goes Wild (Columbia). Screenplay: Sidney Buchman. From a story by Mary McCarthy. Photographer: Joseph Walker. NY Premiere: 12 November 1936.
CAST: Irene Dunne (Theodora Lynn), Melvyn Douglas (Michael Grant), Thomas Mitchell (Jed Waterbury), Thurston Hall (Arthur Stevenson), Rosalind Keith (Adelaide Perry), Spring Byington (Rebecca Perry), Elisabeth Risdon (Aunt Mary), Margaret McWade (Aunt

Elsie), Nana Bryant (Ethel Stevenson), Henry Kolker (Jonathan Grant), Leona Maricle (Agnes Grant), Robert Greig (Uncle John), Frederick Burton (Governor Wyatt).

The Garden of Allah (Selznick-International). Screenplay: W. P. Lipscomb, Lynn Riggs. From the novel by Robert Hichens. Photographer: W. Howard Greene. Photographic Advisor: Harold Rosson. Music: Max Steiner. Production Designer: Lansing C. Holden. Assistant Director: Eric Stacey. Producer: David O. Selznick. NY Premiere: 19 November 1936, Radio City Music Hall.
CAST: Marlene Dietrich (Domini Enfilden), Charles Boyer (Boris Androvsky), Basil Rathbone (Count Anteoni), C. Aubrey Smith (Father Roubier), Tilly Losch (Irena), Joseph Schildkraut (Batouch), John Carradine (sand diviner), Alan Marshall (De Trevignan), Lucille Watson (Mother Superior), Henry Brandon (Hadj).

The Last of Mrs. Cheyney (MGM). Screenplay: Leon Gordon, Samson Raphaelson, Monckton Hoffe. Based on the play by Frederick Lonsdale. Producer: Lawrence Weingarten. NY Premiere: 18 February 1937.
CAST: Joan Crawford (Fay Cheyney), William Powell (Charles), Robert Montgomery (Arthur), Frank Morgan (Lord Kelton), Jessie Ralph (Duchess), Nigel Bruce (Willie), Colleen Clare (Joan), Benita Hume (Kitty), Ralph Forbes (Cousin John), Aileen Pringle (Maria), Melville Cooper (William), Leonard Carey (Ames), Sara Haden (Anna), Lumsden Hare (Inspector Witherspoon), Wallis Clark (George), Barnet Parker (Purser).

Notes

The following abbreviations are used for works or sources frequently cited in the notes:

Bobbs Merrill   Bobbs-Merrill Collection. "Author's Questionnaire" filed by Richard Boleslavsky (1932); correspondence and miscellaneous records, 1931–36. Lilly Library, Indiana University.

Creative Theatre   Richard Boleslavsky. "The Creative Theatre." Transcribed and edited by Michael Barroy. Mimeographed irregular pagination; sequential page numbers used, n.d. [1923], The Library and Musuem of the Performing Arts, Lincoln Center.

Down   Richard Boleslavsky. *Lances Down* (Indianapolis, 1932).

Lab Files   American Laboratory Theatre Files. Possession of Ronald A. Willis (given to him by Anne Stockton Goodwin). University of Kansas, Lawrence. Copies provided by Willis in the possession of the author.

Willis Collection   Ronald A. Willis. Collection of correspondence, interviews, and other materials relating to the American Laboratory Theatre.

Six Lessons   Richard Boleslavsky. *Acting: The First Six Lessons* (New York, 1933).

Way   Richard Boleslavsky. *Way of the Lancer* (Indianapolis, 1932).

Chapter 1

1. Woodward to Boleslavsky, n. d. [Feb., 1932], *Willis Collection.*

2. Boleslavsky to Woodward, Feb. 18, 1932, *Willis Collection.*

3. Natasha Boleslavsky, interview (Dec. 13, 1971); and Jean Srzednicki, interview (Sept. 24, 1973).

4. Natasha Boleslavsky; and *Słownik Biograficzny Teatru Polskiego 1765–1965*. (Warsaw, 1973), p. 53.

5. *Way,* pp. 231–32.

6. Ibid., p. 233.

7. Ibid., p. 101.

8. Richard Boleslavski, "Pro Domo Sua," *Wings* 6, no. 3 (March, 1932), p. 3.

9. Tadeus Hiż, "Ryszard Bolesławski w Rosji," *Scena Polska* 14 (1937), p. 47.

10. Ibid., p. 48.

11. Ibid., p. 47. Hiż seems sure that Boleslavsky was in the "sixth" class, (roughly equivalent to the eleventh grade in the American system, although the students were younger), but is uncertain of the date, which he gives as "either 1905 or 1906." Either date is improbable. I have adjusted the year to accord with the probable date of Boleslavsky's study in the sixth class. Boleslavsky finished his year at the University of Odessa in 1906 (see "Author's Questionnaire," *Bobbs-Merrill*); other dates are calculated by working back from this year and assuming there was no break in his school attendance.

12. Natasha Boleslavsky; see B. V. Verneke, "History of the Russian Theatre," translated by Boris Brasol (1951; repr. New York, 1971), p. 384.

13. Hiż, p. 47.

14. See "Author's Questionnaire," *Bobbs-Merrill.*

15. Hiż, p. 47.

16. Vera Soloviova, interview, Dec. 1, 1975.

17. *Way,* p. 71.

18. Natasha Boleslavsky.

19. Richard Boleslavsky, unpublished American Laboratory Theatre lecture 1925, possession of the author.

20. Michael T. Florinsky, *Russia: A Short History* (London, 1969), p. 355.

21. *Way,* p. 232.

22. *Down,* p. 239.

23. Boleslavsky to Woodward, Jan. 28, 1932, *Willis Collection.*

24. Boleslavsky to Woodward, Feb. 18, 1932, *Willis Collection.*

25. *Down,* pp. 78–79.

26. Boleslavsky to Woodward, May 16, 1932, *Willis Collection.*

27. Boleslavsky to George Shively, Sept. 19, 1932, *Bobbs-Merrill.*

28. Hiż, pp. 48–49.

29. Natasha Boleslavsky; photograph in her scrapbook.

30. See *Creative Theatre,* p. 12.

31. Helen Woodward, "Richard Boleslavski," *Wings* 6, no. 3 (March, 1932), pp. 6; 26.

32. *Creative Theatre,* pp. 15–16.

33. Natasha Boleslavsky.

34. *Down,* p. 38.

35. Ibid., pp. 239–240.

Chapter 2

1. Tadeus Hiż, "Ryszard Bolesławski w Rosji," *Scena Polska* vol. 14 (1937), p. 47.

2. Vera Soloviova, letter to the author, Nov. 12, 1975.

3. *Down,* pp. 61–62.

4. Ibid., p. 39.

5. Ibid., pp. 51–52.

6. Hiż, "Ryszard Bolesławski," p. 48.

7. *Down,* p. 52.

8. See Vladimir Nemirovitch-Dantchenko, *My Life in the Russian Theatre* (New York, 1968), pp. 43–46.

9. Hiż, "Ryszard Bolesławski," p. 51.

10. *Down,* p. 53.

11. Ibid., p. 52.

12. *Down,* p. 58. *Moskovskii Khudozhestvennyi Teatr v illyustratsiyakh i dokumentakh 1898–1938* (Moscow, 1938) is an authoritative source for documenting casts at the MAT during this period; unless otherwise noted, all roles attributed to Boleslavsky at the MAT have been verified here (it credits him with a total of twenty-one roles). His part in *The Blue Bird,* essentially that of a stage hand, is one of those exceptions; the omission does not invalidate Boleslavsky's claim, but rather testifies to the insignificance of the part.

13. I. Vinogradskaya, ed. *Zhizn' i tvorchestvo K. S. Stanislavskogo,* vol. II (Moscow, 1971), p. 168.

14. Constantin Stanislavsky, *My Life in Art,* trans. J. J. Robbins (Boston, 1938), p. 463, hereinafter, *My Life* (Boston).

15. Ibid., pp. 474–75; cf. Konstantin Stanislavsky, *My Life in Art,* trans. G. Ivanov-Mumjiev (Moscow, n.d.), pp. 360–61, hereinafter, *My Life* (Moscow); see also David Magarshack, *Stanislavsky: A Life* (New York, 1951), pp. 282; 305; 330.

16. *My Life* (Boston), pp. 480–81; 497. Cf. *My Life* (Moscow), p. 359; see also Magarshack, *Stanislavsky,* pp. 289; 293.

17. Magarshack, *Stanislavsky,* pp. 310–11.

18. Ibid.

19. *My Life* (Moscow), p. 378; cf. *My Life* (Boston), pp. 542–43.

20. Magarshack, *Stanislavsky*, p. 305.

21. Vinogradskaya, *Zhizn' i tvorchestvo*, vol. II, pp. 206–7.

22. Magarshack, *Stanislavsky*, pp. 305–6.

23. Vinogradskaya, *Zhizn' i tvorchestvo*, vol. II, pp. 206–7.

24. Ibid., p. 208.

25. P. Ya., " 'Mesyats v derevne' Turgeneva. Khudozhestvennyi teatr. Igra," *Utro Rossii*, no. 54-21 (Dec. 10, 1909), p. 5.

26. A. Koiransky, " 'Mesyats v derevne' Turgeneva," *Utro Rossii*, no. 55-22 (Dec. 11, 1909), p. 6.

27. N. Efros, "Moskovskie teatry," *Yezhegodnik Imperatorskikh teatrov*, VI-VII (1910), pp. 113–14.

28. Nikolai Efros, *Moskovskii Khudozhestvennyi Teatr* (Moscow-Petersburg, 1924), p. 382.

29. Eugenie Leontovich, interview, July 28, 1972.

30. Hiż, "Ryszard Bolesławski," p. 48.

Chapter 3

1. Natasha Boleslavsky, interview, Dec. 13, 1971.

2. Ryszard Ordyński, *Z mojej włóczęgi* (Kraków, 1956), p. 104.

3. Constantin Stanislavsky, *My Life in Art*, trans. J. J. Robbins (Boston, 1924), p. 531, hereinafter, *My Life* (Boston).

4. P. A. Markov, *Pravda Teatra* (Moscow, 1965), p. 253.

5. David Magarshack, *Stanislavsky: A Life* (New York, 1951), pp. 242–43; and Magarshack, "Introduction," *Stanislavsky on the Art of the Stage* (New York, 1961), p. 79.

6. *My Life* (Boston), pp. 531–32.

7. Sergei Melik-Zakharov and Shoel Bogatyrev, eds., *K. Stanislavsky, 1863–1963*, trans. Vic Schneierson (Moscow, 1963), p. 250.

8. Natasha Boleslavsky interview.

9. Many writers use the terms "memory of emotion" and "affective memory" interchangeably; Boleslavsky, at least in his later work, did not.

10. *Creative Theatre*, p. 56.

11. Ibid., p. 23.

12. *Six Lessons*, p. 22.

13. *Creative Theatre*, p. 46.

14. *Six Lessons*, p. 84.

15. Markov, *Pravda teatra,* p. 264.

16. Ibid., pp. 256–57.

17. William Lonnie Kuhlke, "Vakhtangov's Legacy" (Ph. D. diss., State University of Iowa, 1965), p. 251.

18. *My Life* (Boston), pp. 535–37.

19. Vera Soloviova, letter to the author, Nov. 12, 1975.

20. Donald Keyes, interviews, Dec. 24, 1974; Jan. 14, 1975.

21. Markov, *Pravda Teatra,* p. 254.

22. Magarshack, "Introduction," p. 79.

23. *Down,* p. 55. Boleslavsky generally provides only first names; Natasha Boleslavsky helped with identifications.

24. N. D. Valkov, *Teatral'nye vechera* (Moscow, 1966), pp. 17–18. Valkov reports that he began studying privately with Boleslavsky, whom he describes as one of the Adashev School's teachers, at Boleslavsky's "cosy apartment on Arbat," shortly after the public success of *The Good Hope.*

25. Boleslavsky, "Author's Questionnaire," *Bobbs-Merrill;* for details of model shop, see *My Life* (Boston), pp. 510–12.

26. Serafima Birman, *Put' aktrisy* (Moscow, 1959), p. 87.

27. Soloviova, letter, Nov. 12, 1975.

28. *Down,* p. 203. Oliver Sayler, *Russian Theatre Under the Revolution* (Boston, 1920), p. 84, does not include Boleslavsky's name as one of the Studio's leaders. Boleslavsky had returned from the war only a few months before Sayler's visit; likely, he was elected after that time. In any case, there is no strong reason to dispute Boleslavsky's claim.

29. Magarshack, *Stanislavsky,* p. 333.

30. *Down,* p. 63.

31. Valkov, *Teatral'nye vechera,* p. 18; Natasha Boleslavsky.

32. Lydia Deykun, quoted in Ye. Polyakova and V. Ye. Vilenkina, *Leopold Antonovich Sulerzhitsky* (Moscow, 1970), p. 596.

33. Playbill, *The Good Hope.*

34. Giantsintova, "S. V. Giantsintova," *O Stanislavskom: sbornik vospominanii 1863–1938,* ed. L. Ye. Gurevich, N. D. Valkov, and Ye. N. Semyanovsky (Moscow, 1948), pp. 366–67.

35. *Down,* p. 65.

36. Soloviova, letter, Nov. 12, 1975.

37. Stanislavsky, *My Life in Art,* trans. G. Ivanov-Mumjiev (Moscow, n. d.), p. 407, hereinafter *My Life* (Moscow).

38. Giantsintova, *O Stanislavskom,* pp. 366–67.

39. *My Life* (Moscow), pp. 407–8; cf. *My Life* (Boston), p. 352. In the summer of 1898, the newly formed MAT rehearsed in a barn in Pushkino to prepare their formal opening in Moscow.

40. Giantsintova, *O Stanislavskom,* p. 367.

41. *Down,* p. 64.

42. *My Life* (Boston), p. 532, cf. *My Life* (Moscow), p. 408.

43. Quoted in Marc Slonim, *Russian Theatre* (New York, 1962), p. 200.

44. Ibid.

45. Nikolai Efros, *Moskovskii Khudozhestvennyi Teatr* (Moscow-Petersburg, 1924), p. 400.

46. *Down,* p. 65.

47. Untitled newspaper clipping, n.d., in Vera Soloviova's scrapbook, The Library and Museum of the Performing Arts, Lincoln Center.

48. I. Vinogradskaya, ed., *Zhizn' i tvorchestvo K. S. Stanislavskogo,* vol. II (Moscow, 1971), p. 520.

49. Efros, *MKhT;* and I. B. Berezark, *Boris Sushkevich* (Leningrad-Moscow, 1967), p. 17.

50. S. Ya., "Teatr i muzyka: spektakl' studii," *Russkoye Slovo* (Moscow). Clipping from Soloviova's scrapbook, dated only 1913. The critic's description of the physical theatre establishes that it was written after the Studio's move.

51. *My Life* (Moscow), p. 408.

52. Markov, *Pravda teatra,* p. 272.

53. Soloviova, interview.

54. Slonim, *Russian Theatre,* p. 200.

55. Abstracted from Markov, *Pravda Teatra,* pp. 271–72.

56. Boleslavsky, "Stanislavsky—The Man and His Methods," *Theatre Magazine* 37 (April, 1923), p. 74.

Chapter 4

1. All roles credited to Boleslavsky at the MAT in this chapter are documented in *Moskovskii Khudozhestvennyi Teatr v illyustratsiyakh i dokumentakh 1898–1938* (Moscow, 1938). One small role not credited here, an officer in *The Three Sisters,* might be added, for Boleslavsky was rehearsing that part in February, 1909, and may have played it as well; see I. Vinogradskaya, ed., *Zhizn' i tvorchestvo K. S. Stanislavskogo,* vol. II, p. 163.

2. Elizabeth Reynolds Hapgood, "A Chronology of the Life of Vladimir Nemirovitch-Dantchenko," Dantchenko, *My Life in the Russian Theatre* (New York, 1968), p. 362.

3. Nikolai Efros, *Moskovskii Khudozhestvennyi Teatr* (Moscow-Petersburg, 1924), p. 382.

4. Tadeus Hiż, "Ryszard Bolesławski w Rosji," *Scena Polska* vol. 14 (1937), p. 49.

5. Marc Slonim, *Russian Theatre* (New York, 1962), p. 182.

6. V. Bryusov, "Gamlet v Moskovskom Khudozhestvennom teatre," *Yezhegodnik Imperatorskikh Teatrov*, vol. II (1912), p. 57.

7. A. Koiransky, "Gamlet," *Utro Rossii*, no. 296 (Dec. 24, 1911), p. 2.

8. Denis Bablet, *Edward Gordon Craig*, trans. Daphne Woodward (New York, 1966), p. 146.

9. Boleslavsky to Gordon Craig, June 9, 1927, *Lab Files*.

10. A. Koiransky, "Molyer na tsene Khudozhestvennoga teatra," *Utro Rossii*, no. 72 (March 28, 1913), p. 4.

11. Yak. Lvov, "Dva Molyera," *Obozrenie teatrov*, quoted in I. Vinogradskaya, ed., *Zhizn' i tvorchestvo K. S. Stanislavskogo*, vol. II (Moscow, 1971), p. 379.

12. A. Koiransky, "Gol'doni na tsene Khudozhestven. teatra (Khozyaika gostinitsy)," *Utro Rossii*, no. 28 (Feb. 4, 1914), p. 6.

13. Edward Braun, *Meyerhold on Theatre* (New York, 1969), p. 177.

14. Slonim, *Russian Theatre*, p. 200; Boris Sushkevich, "Vstrechi s Vakhtangovym," *Yevgenii Vakhtangov, Materialy i stat'i* (Moscow, 1959), pp. 366–67; Vera Soloviova, interview, Dec. 1, 1975.

15. Vakhtangov, *Materialy i stat'i*, p. 39.

16. Ibid., p. 38.

17. Ibid, pp. 38–39.

18. Ibid, pp. 39–40.

19. David Magarshack, *Stanislavsky: A Life* (New York, 1951), p. 334.

20. A. Koiransky, "'Prazdnik mira.' Studiya Khudozhestvennogo teatra," *Utro Rossii*, no. 265 (Nov. 16, 1913), p. 6.

21. William Lonnie Kuhlke "Vakhtangov's Legacy," (Ph.D. diss., University of Iowa, 1965), pp. 30; 71.

22. Magarshack, *Stanislavsky*, p. 334.

Chapter 5

1. Natasha Boleslavsky, interview.

2. Ibid., and Vera Soloviova, interview, Dec. 1, 1975.

3. Ven. Vishnevsky, ed., *Khudozhestvennye fil'my dorevolutsionnoi Rossii* (Moscow, 1945), provides most of the details about the films in which Boleslavsky acted or directed; see Filmography for fuller listing.

4. Jay Leyda, *Kino* (New York, 1960), p. 63.

5. Ibid., p. 76.

6. David Magarshack, *Stanislavsky: A Life* (New York, 1951), pp. 410–11.

7. Vishnevsky, *Khudozhestvennye fil'my*, p. 45.

8. Paul Gray, "A Critical Chronology," *Stanislavski and America*, ed. Erika Munk (Greenwich, Conn., 1967), p. 142.

9. Marc Slonim, *Russian Theatre* (New York, 1962), p. 202.

10. *Down*, pp. 239–40.

11. P. A. Markov, *Pravda teatra* (Moscow, 1965), pp. 272–73.

12. Ibid.

13. Ibid., p. 273, quoting an anonymous critic.

14. A. Koiransky, " 'Osenniye skripki.' (Khudozhestvennyi teatr)," *Utro Rossii*, no. 12 (March 14, 1915), p. 5.

15. Ibid.

16. Slonim, *Russian Theatre*, p. 139.

17. Leyda, *Kino*, pp. 77–78.

18. Ibid., p. 50.

19. Ibid., pp. 78; 146.

20. Yevgenii Vakhtangov, *Materialy i stat'i* (Moscow, 1959), p. 42.

Chapter 6

1. *Way*, p. 232.

2. Ibid.

3. "Author's Questionnaire," *Bobbs-Merrill;* Tadeus Hiż, "Ryszard Bolesławski w Rosji," *Scena Polska*, vol. 14 (1937), p. 51; and N. von Arnold, letter to the author, March 21, 1975 (Arnold trained at Tver a year ahead of Boleslavsky).

4. *Way*, p. 13.

5. Ibid., pp. 101; 107.

6. Ibid., pp. 235–36.

7. Ibid., p. 244.

8. Ibid., p. 299.

9. *Down*, p. 66.

10. Boleslavsky to Woodward, Feb. 18, 1932, *Willis Collection*.

11. Richard Boleslavsky, "Pro Domo Sua," *Wings*, 6, 3 (March, 1932), 13–14.

12. *Moskovskii Khudozhestvennyi Teatr v illyustratsiyakh i dokumentakh 1898–1938* (Mos-

cow, 1938), confirms the roles, but does not provide the dates Boleslavsky first played them. Hiż, "Ryszard Bolesławski," p. 49, reports that Boleslavsky also acted in *Uncle Vanya, The Cherry Orchard, The Inspector General,* and the part of Fortinbras in a St. Petersburg production of *Hamlet;* he does not date these performances and no authenticating sources have been found.

13. *Down,* pp. 62–63.

14. N. Efros, *Moskovskii Khudozhestvennyi Teatr, 1898–1923* (Moscow-Petersburg, 1924), pp. 406–7, hereinafter Efros, *MKhT.*

15. *Down,* pp. 68–69.

16. Ibid., p. 82.

17. Ibid., p. 151.

18. Serge Orlovsky, "Moscow Theatres, 1917–1941," *Soviet Theatres, 1917–1941,* ed. Martha Bradshaw (New York, 1954), p. 4.

19. *Down,* pp. 316–17.

20. Ibid., pp. 152–54.

21. William Lonnie Kuhlke, "Vakhtangov's Legacy" (Ph.D. diss., University of Iowa, 1965), pp. 67–68.

22. Orlovsky, "Moscow Theatres," p. 4.

23. Boleslavsky includes *Twelfth Night* among the directorial credits he listed on the Questionnaire he filed with Bobbs-Merrill in 1932. As a rule, he erred on the side of omission rather than making false claims.

24. Oliver Sayler, *The Russian Theatre Under the Revolution* (Boston, 1920), p. 17.

25. Marc Slonim, *Russian Theatre* (Cleveland, 1961), p. 203.

26. Huntley Carter, *The New Theatre and Cinema of Soviet Russia* (London, 1924), pp. 218–19.

27. P. A. Markov, *Pravda Teatra* (Moscow, 1965), p. 284.

28. Efros, *MKhT,* p. 407.

29. *Down,* p. 60.

30. Jay Leyda, *Kino* (New York, 1973), p. 132.

31. Natasha Boleslavsky, interview, Dec. 13, 1971.

32. Aleksander Blok, *Zapisnye knizhki, 1901–1920* (Moscow, 1965), p. 459.

33. Monakhov, *Povest' o zhizni* (Leningrad-Moscow, 1961), pp. 172–73.

34. Monakhov, quoted in *Sovetskii teatr: Dokumenty i materialy: Russkii Sovetskii teatr 1917–1921* : (Moscow, 1968), p. 257,hereinafter *Sovetskii teatr.*

35. Monakhov, *Povest' o zhizni* , p. 172.

36. N. I. Komarovskaya, "Gody druzhby," in M.F. Andreyeva, *Vospominaniya o Marii Fedorovne Andreyevoi,* p. 521.

37. Blok to Andreyeva, September 24, 1919, in Andreyeva, pp. 319–20.

38. Bolesław Taborski, *Polish Plays in English Translation: A Bibliography* (New York: 1968), p. 17.

39. Ibid.

40. Irena Schiller, "Balladyna; w I Studio MChAT," *Pamiętnik Teatralny,* vol. 8, 1–23 (Warsaw, 1959), p. 349.

41. Ibid., p. 359.

42. Sergei Melik-Zakharov, Shoel Bogatyrev, and Nikolai Solntsev, ed. *K. Stanislavsky 1863–1963,* trans. Vic Schneierson (Moscow, n. d.), p. 203.

43. A. Diky, *Povest' o teatralnoi yunosti* (Moscow, 1957), p. 292.

44. Notes from Stanislavsky's daybook ("Vypiski iz zapisnoi knigi K. S. Stanislavskogo 1919–1920 g."), found in the Museum of the Art Theatre (KS No. 834), repr. in Schiller, "Balladyna" pp. 367–70. In most instances, these notes merely contain such basic information as the date, the number of the rehearsal, the scene(s) to be rehearsed, and—in some cases—the actors present, suggesting that Stanislavsky attended rehearsals only as an observer. For the fourth rehearsal (November 15), however, Stanislavsky noted Boleslavsky's absence (not explained) and made extensive notes, indicating that he conducted the rehearsal; some of these relate to the specific rehearsal and others seem pertinent to the overall plan of production; in at least one case, Stanislavsky evidently questioned Boleslavsky's scenic plan. After this rehearsal, Stanislavsky's notes revert to brief entries and grow gradually less frequent. The last is dated Dec. 29, 1919.

45. A. Ar., "Studiya Khudozhestvenogo Teatra 'Balladyna,' " *Vestnik Teatra,* no. 57 (1920), p. 9; quoted in Schiller, "Balladyna," p. 360.

46. B. M., "K postanovke 'Balladyna,' " *Vestnik Teatra,* no. 55 (1920), p. 10; quoted in Schiller, "Balladyna," pp. 361–62.

47. Schiller, "Balladyna," p. 363. The direction of *Balladyna* has been variously attributed. Efros, MKhT, pp. 407–8, credits the staging to Boleslavsky, Sushkevich, and Vakhtangov. Markov, *Pravda Teatra,* p. 284 and Slonim, *Russian Theatre,* p. 295, attributes it solely to Boleslavsky. Schiller, "Balladyna," p. 354, reports that a handwritten program found in the MAT Museum archives credits Boleslavsky as *régisseur* and lists no other collaborators. A printed program, n.d., lists Boleslavsky as the equivalent of *metteur en scène* and credits Serafima Birman as *régisseur.* Birman, *Put' aktrisy* (Moscow, 1962), p. 149, says that she assisted Boleslavsky but that he claimed full credit for the production when he was asked about it by Danchenko in her presence.

This tangle of attribution has been solved to the author's satisfaction by Schiller who writes (p. 354): "According to all existing documents the main responsibility rested on Bolesławski." As supporting proof she offers a 1959 interview with Vakhtangov's widow and Lyubov Vendrovskaya (an expert on his career), both of whom deny his participation in the production; Hope Bromley, (Sushkevich's wife), insisted in an interview that Sushkevich's only contribution to *Balladyna* had been as an actor.

48. Bromley to I. Schiller, Feb. 22, 1920, quoted in Schiller, "Balladyna,"p. 362. Bromley

directed Gabriel D'Annunzio's *The Daughter of Yorio* at the First Studio in 1918; it was not a success. Boleslavsky may have played the part of the young shepherd; Natasha Boleslavsky remembers that he did, but Vera Soloviova, who won praise in the leading part, does not remember him in the role.

49. L. M. Leonidov, *Stat'i i vospominaniya o L. M. Leonidove* (Moscow, 1960), p. 292.

50. Markov, *Pravda Teatra,* p. 270–72. Markov acknowledges that *The Good Hope* set the pattern followed by subsequent Studio production, both scenically and in the acting, until about 1918, but he denies credit for charting this course to Boleslavsky; rather, he claims that Sulerzhitsky was in fact the "main" director of the Studio's first five productions, and that he "corrected" the mistakes of the directors of record. There is ample testimony of studio actors to contradict this claim. In addition to accounts by Deykun and Giantsintova, already cited, there is Alexander Diky, *Povest' o teatral'noi yunosti,* pp. 213–14: "Leopold Antonovich often came to us, watched our rehearsals, made some short comments but tried to give us and our young director, Richard, full independence. Konstantin Sergeevich himself said that he would come to see the whole play when everything was ready—all the decorations, lighting, and sound."

51. Efros, *MKhT,* p. 400. Efros excludes *The Festival of Peace* from this judgment, describing it as Vakhtangov's "first, though still very timid attempt at directing"; in his opinion, the future director of *Eric XIV, The Dybbuk,* and *Turandot* could in no way be divined in this first effort.

52. See Slonim, *Russian Theatre,* pp. 202–3.

53. Boris Sushkevich, "Vstrechi s Vakhtangovym," *Ye. B. Vakhtangov, materialy i stat'i* (Moscow, 1959), pp. 366–67.

54. *Sovetskii teatr,* p. 257.

55. Leon Schiller, "Gdy Bolesławski przyjechał do Warszawy," *Scena Polska,* vol. 14 (1937), pp. 76; 79.

56. Vera Soloviova, letter to the author, Nov. 12, 1975.

57. I. Schiller, "Balladyna," p. 356.

58. Bromley to I. Schiller, Feb. 20, 1959, quoted in Schiller, "Balladyna," p. 356.

59. Schiller, "Balladyna," p. 357.

60. Richard Boleslawsky, "The Laboratory Theatre," *Theatre Arts Magazine,* 7, 2 (July, 1923), p. 244.

61. *Sovetskii teatr,* p. 257.

62. Kuhlke, "Vakhtangov's Legacy," pp. 38–39; see also pp. 27; 54–55.

63. Vakhtangov was working regularly with the First and Second Studios of the MAT, at his own studio, and the Habima Theatre, as well as acting at the MAT; in addition to these regular commitments, he was involved with ten other groups in one capacity or another.

64. I. Schiller, "Balladyna," pp. 367–70.

65. Ibid., p. 353.

66. Nikolai Gorchakov, *The Vakhtangov School of Stage Art*, trans. G. Ivanov-Mumjiev (Moscow, n. d.), pp. 85–86.

67. Efros, *MKhT*, pp. 407–8.

68. Natasha Boleslavsky.

69. *Sovetskii teatr*, p. 257.

Chapter 7

1. *Down*, p. 316.

2. Ibid., pp. 320–21.

3. Ibid., p. 316.

4. Ibid., p. 39.

5. Boleslavsky to Helen Woodward, Feb. 18, 1932, *Willis Collection*.

6. Natasha Boleslavsky, interview, Dec. 13, 1971.

7. Ibid.

8. Nikolai Efros, *Moskovskii Khudozhestvennyi Teatr, 1898–1923* (Moscow-Petersburg, 1924), p. 406.

9. Leon Schiller, "Gdy Boleslawski przyjechal do Warszawy," *Scena Polska* 14 (1937), p. 73.

10. *Słownik Biograficzny Teatru Polskiego 1765–1965* (Warsaw, 1973), p. 53

11. Tadeusz Hiż, "Ryszard Bolesławski w Rosji," *Scena Polska* 14 (1937), p. 51.

12. Sergei Melik-Zakharov, Shoel Bogatyrev, and Nikolai Solntsev, eds., *K. Stanislavsky 1863–1963* (Moscow, n.d.), pp. 203; 198–99.

13. See Roman Szydłowski, *The Theatre in Poland* (Warsaw, 1972), p.29; and *Teatr Polski w Warszawie 1913–1923* (Warsaw, n.d.), pp. 15–16; hereinafter *Teatr Polski*.

14. Ven. Vishnevsky, *Khudozhestvennye filmy dorevolutsionnoi Rossii* (Moscow, 1945), p. 80; see also "Filmography" below.

15. Schiller, "Gdy Bolesławski," p. 73.

16. Ibid.; and *Teatr Polski*, p. 61.

17. Unless otherwise noted, productions credited to Boleslavsky are verified in *Teatr Polski*, which provides premiere dates, casts lists, and number of performances; this source also documents productions at the Teatr Mały, but has fewer details about them.

18. *Teatr Polski*, p. 122.

19. Ibid., p. 123.

20. Ibid.

21. Natasha Boleslavsky has since contributed her copy of *Mandragora* to the music collection, The Library and Museum of the Performing Arts, Lincoln Center.

22. *Teatr Polski,* p. 113.

23. *Słownik Biograficzny,* p. 53.

24. Schiller, "Gdy Bolesławski," p. 73.

25. Ryszard Ordyński, *Z mojej włóczęgi* (Krakow, 1956), pp. 113–14.

26. Schiller, "Gdy Bolesławski," p. 85.

27. *Way,* p. 279.

28. Hiż, "Ryszard Bolesławski," p. 51.

29. Jerzy Chociłowski, ed., *Contemporary Polish Cinematography* (Warsaw, 1962), p. 9.

30. Jerzy Teoplitz, ed., *Historia filmu polskiego,* vol. I (Warsaw, 1966), pp. 131–32.

31. Lev V. Kuleshov, "The Origins of Montage," *Cinema in Revolution,* ed. Luda and Jean Schnitzer and Marcel Martin, trans. David Robinson (New York, 1973), p. 71.

32. Kazimierz Czachowski, "Roztworowski [sic]—Polish Tragic Dramatist: 1877–1938," *The Slavonic Review,* 17, 51 (April, 1939), p. 687.

33. *Teatr Polski,* pp. 107–110.

34. Walter René Fuerst and Samuel J. Hume, *Twentieth-Century Stage Decoration,* vol. I (New York, 1967), p. 75.

35. *Teatr Polski,* p. 112.

36. Ordynski, *Z mojej włóczęgi, p. 104.*

37. *Teatr Polski,* p. 61.

38. "Sezon 1920/21," *Teatr Polski,* p. 177.

39. Natasha Boleslavsky, interview.

40. Teatr Polski, p. 20.

41. *Creative Theatre,* p. 14.

42. *Teatr Polski,* p. 110.

43. Schiller, "Gdy Bolesławski," p. 89.

44. *Teatr Polski* gives the titles and number of performances for productions at its studio theatre, but does not give opening dates. The first of Boleslavsky's productions at the Mały, *The Deluge,* may in fact have preceded *Ruy Blas,* but *Kiki* almost certainly came after it.

45. *Teatr Polski,* p. 61.

46. Schiller, "Gdy Bolesławski," p. 90; and *Teatr Polski,* p. 61.

47. Hiż, "Ryszard Bolesławski," p. 51.

48. Schiller, "Gdy Bolesławski," p. 90.

49. Ordyński, *Z mojej włóczęgi,* p. 104.

50. *Słownik Biograficzny,* p. 53.

51. Szydlowski, *Theatre in Poland,* p. 31.
52. Schiller, "Gdy Bolesławski," p. 90.
53. Ibid.
54. Ibid., pp. 83–84.
55. Ibid., pp. 88–89.
56. Ibid., pp. 53–54.
57. Szydłowski, *Theatre in Poland,* p. 78.
58. Edward Csato, *The Polish Theatre* (Warsaw, 1963), p. 43.
59. Ibid., p. 51.
60. Leon Schiller, "Gdy Bolesławski," p. 54.

Chapter 8

1. *Way,* p. 257.
2. Ryszard Ordyński, *Z mojej włóczęgi* (Kraków, 1956), p. 104.
3. Claus Just, "Stanislawski und das deutschsprachige Theater. Daten, Texte und Interpretationen bis 1940," (Erlangen-Nürnberg, 1970), p. 293; hereinafter Just.
4. *Artisty Moskovskago Khudozhestvennago Teatra za rubezhom'* (Prague, 1922), pp. 8–10; hereinafter *Artisty MKhT.*
5. Natasha Boleslavsky, interview.
6. Just, pp. 295.
7. *Artisty MKhT,* pp. 54–55. Makovsky's article is dated: "Prague, October, 1921."
8. Ibid., photo page following p. 50; and Olga Leonardovna Knipper-Chekhova, *Chast' vtoraya—perepiska,* vol. II (Moscow, n.d.), pp. 126–27.
9. Natasha Boleslavsky, interview.
10. Knipper-Chekhova, *Chast' vtoraya,* pp. 126–27.
11. Just, p. 297.
12. *Artisty MKhT,* pp. 54–55.
13. Emil Kläger, *Neue Freie Presse* (Oct. 30, 1921), quoted in Just, p. 296.
14. Alfred Klaar, *Vossiche Zeitung* (Feb. 30, 1921), quoted in Just, p. 295.
15. Herbert Ihring, *Der Tag* (Feb. 11, 1921), quoted in Just, p. 295.
16. Just, p. 263.
17. Kachalov to Nemirovich-Danchenko, Dec. 30, 1921, *Sovetskii teatr: Dokumenty i materialy* (Leningrad, 1968), p. 134.
18. Just, p. 292. Questioned by Berlin critics, Stanislavsky offered this as a justification of the MAT's "conservative repertoire."

19. Kachalov to Nemirovich-Danchenko, *Sovetskii teatr,* pp. 134–135.

20. Knipper-Chekhova, *Chast' vtoraya,* pp. 126–27.

21. Vera Soloviova, interview, Dec. 1, 1975.

22. Ilya Ehrenberg, *Memoirs: 1921–1941,* trans. Tatania Shevunina with Yvonne Kapp (Cleveland-New York, 1963), p. 18.

23. Natasha Boleslavsky, interview; and Richard Boleslavsky, "Author's Questionnaire," *Bobbs-Merrill.*

24. The plot summary is indebted to Ebbe Neergaards, *Dreyer* (Copenhagen, 1963), pp. 33–34, and Tom Milne, *The Cinema of Carl Dreyer* (New York, 1971), pp. 57–58.

25. Neergaards, *Dreyer,* p. 33.

26. Andre Levinson, *Bakst* (Benjamin Blom, 1971), pp. 228–29.

27. "Kousnezoff Russian Troupe at Booth Oct. 3," *New York Times,* Sept. 21, 1922.

28. Charles Darnton, "The New Plays," *New York Evening World,* Sept. 6, 1922.

29. " 'Revue Russe' Has Premiere," *New York Sun,* Oct. 6, 1922.

30. "Maria Kousnezoff's 'Revue Russe,' " *New York Daily Mail,* Oct. 6, 1922.

31. Eugenie Leontovich, interview, July 28, 1972.

32. Opening dates for Boleslavsky's U.S. productions are from newspaper reviews and the appropriate volume of the *Best Plays* series, edited by Burns Mantle.

33 Various sources report that Boleslavsky was hired to "assist" Stanislavsky. The nature of his work is described by Natasha Boleslavsky, who was among those hired for the crowd scenes.

34. I Vinogradskaya, ed., *Zhizn' i tvorchestvo K.S. Stanislavskogo,* vol. III (Moscow, 1973), p. 345.

35. *Christian Science Monitor,* Jan. 10, 1923, quoted in Christine Edwards, *The Stanislavsky Heritage* (New York, 1965), p. 229.

36. Edwards, p. 330.

37. Unidentified clipping, files, The Library and Museum of the Performing Arts, Lincoln Center.

38. Playbills of the MAT's U.S. tour, The Library and Museum of the Performing Arts, Lincoln Center.

39. Richard Boleslawsky, "Stanislavsky—The Man and His Methods," *Theatre Magazine* 38, 4 (April, 1923), 27; 74; 80.

40. Miriam K. Stockton, "Report and Synopsis of Growth of The American Laboratory Theatre from June 1, 1920–June 1, 1928," *Lab Files.*

41. Brochure, American Laboratory Theatre, 1928–1929, p. 2, *Lab Files.*

42. Ronald A. Willis, "The American Laboratory Theatre, 1923–1930" (Ph.D. diss., University of Iowa, 1968), p. 2.

43. Richard Boleslawsky, "The Laboratory Theatre," *Theatre Arts Magazine* 7 (July, 1923), pp. 249–50.

Chapter 9

1. Richard Boleslawsky, "The Laboratory Theatre," *Theatre Arts Magazine,* 7, 2 (July, 1923), 245.

2. Roi Henri Fricken, "An Experiment in Play Production," *Theatre Magazine,* 46 (Oct., 1927), 41; 65.

3. "The Laboratory Theatre," pp. 245–46.

4. Richard Boleslavsky, "The Education and Fundamentals in the Development of the Actor as a Technician," *Proceedings of the Conference on the Drama In American Universities and Little Theatres* (Carnegie Institute of Technology, 1925), 51.

5. Ibid., p. 55.

6. "The Laboratory Theatre," p. 246.

7. Ibid., p. 250.

8. *Creative Theatre,* pp. 25–26.

9. Fricken, p. 65.

10. "The Laboratory Theatre," pp. 247–48.

11. Playbill, *The Shewing-Up of Blanco Posnet* and *The Player Queen,* Neighborhood Playhouse, 1923.

12. "A Neighborhood Playhouse," *New York Sun,* October 17, 1923.

13. Alice Lewisohn Crowley, *The Neighborhood Playhouse* (New York, 1959), pp. 169–71.

14. Ronald A. Willis, "The American Laboratory Theatre, 1923–1930" (Ph.D. diss., University of Iowa, 1968), p. 40.

15. Miriam K. Stockton, "Report and Synopsis of Growth of the Laboratory Theatre from June 1, 1920–June 1, 1928," p. 7, *Lab Files;* hereinafter: MKS "Report and Synopsis."

16. Shirley White to her sister, Jan. 6, 1924. White joined the Lab about this time and wrote several letters to her sister over the next several months. Portions of those letters dealing with Lab Theatre matters were tape recorded for Ronald A. Willis by Blanch Tancock; Willis provided a copy of the tape to the author. Accordingly, the spelling and punctuation of quoted portions of White's letters are the author's.

17. MKS "Report and Synopsis," p. 8, *Lab Files.*

18. Richard Boleslawsky, "An Artist of the Theatre," *Theatre Arts Magazine,* 8, 8 (Aug., 1924), 572–73.

19. Willis, diss., pp. 20–23; also, interviews with various Lab students, especially Francis Fergusson, November 10, 1975; and interview with Natasha Boleslavsky.

20. "Portrait," *Theatre Arts Monthly,* 9, 4 (April, 1925), 239.

21. Arthur Hornblow, "Mr. Hornblow Goes to the Play," *Theatre Magazine,* 39, 276 (March, 1924), 15.

22. Alexander Woollcott, " 'The Miracle' at Full Strength," *New York Sun,* Aug. 19, 1924.

23. E.W.O., " 'The Miracle' Has Lost No Interest," *New York World,* Aug. 25, 1924.

24. White letters, Jan. 6; 16; 26; 1924, *Willis Collection.*

25. Giles Edgerton, "The Laboratory Theatre: A New Stage Ideal," *Arts and Decoration,* 11 (May, 1924), 30.

26. White letter, April 5, 1924, *Willis Collection.*

27. Willis, diss., pp. 67–69.

28. Ibid., pp. 70–71.

29. Herbert K. Stockton, "Treasurer's Report to Shareholders of the Laboratory Theatre Trust," June 1, 1925, pp. 1–2.

30. MKS, "Report and Synopsis," pp. 10–11.

31. Ibid.

32. White letter, Jan. 26, 1924, *Willis Collection.*

33. Lee Strasberg, interview, Oct. 11, 1975.

Chapter 10

1. Lee Strasberg, interview, Oct. 11, 1975. Strasberg is familiar with the transcript of the lectures and considers them much more complete than *Acting: The First Six Lessons:* "It is more or less what we heard at the Lab in one form or another."

2. *Creative Theatre,* p. 2.

3. Ibid., p. 10.

4. Ibid., p. 7.

5. Ibid., p. 9.

6. Ibid., p. 10.

7. Richard Boleslavsky, "Fundamentals of Acting," *Theatre Arts Magazine,* 11, 2 (Feb., 1927), p. 121.

8. Ibid., p. 122.

9. *Creative Theatre,* pp. 23–24.

10. Ibid., p. 8.

11. Ibid., pp. 14–15.

12. Richard Boleslavsky, "Six Questions to Richard Boleslavsky," *The Pit* (April, 1928), p. 2.

13. *Creative Theatre,* p. 10.

14. Ibid., pp. 12–13.

15. "Fundamentals," pp. 122–23.

16. Ibid.

17. Ibid., pp. 125–26.

18. Ibid.

19. Ibid., p. 127.

20. *Creative Theatre*, p. 22.

21. Ibid., pp. 36–37.

22. Ibid., pp. 38–39.

23. Ibid., p. 36.

24. Ibid., pp. 38–39.

25. Ibid., p. 40.

26. Ibid., pp. 36–37.

27. Ibid., p. 37.

28. Ibid., p. 41.

29. Ibid., pp. 26–27.

30. Ibid., pp. 24–26.

31. Ibid., pp. 28–33.

32. Ibid., pp. 16–19.

33. Ibid., pp. 41–43.

34. Ibid., p. 22.

35. Ibid., pp. 22; 52.

36. *Six Lessons*, p. 15.

37. "Fundamentals," p. 128.

38. Ibid.

39. *Creative Theatre*, pp. 50–51.

40. *Six Lessons*, p. 20.

41. *Creative Theatre*, p. 52; *Six Lessons*, p. 22.

42. *Creative Theatre*, pp. 54–59.

43. Boleslavsky cites the title of Ribot's book as *Problèmes de Psychologie Affective* (*Six Lessons*, p. 36); other sources give it as *Psychologie des Sentiments*. It was published in 1896 and translated into Russian in 1898 by F. Pavlenkov.

44. *Creative Theater*, p. 64.

45. Ibid., pp. 69–70.

46. Ibid.

47. Ibid., p. 69.

48. Ibid., pp. 70–71.

49. Ibid., pp. 73–74.

50. Richard Boleslavsky, "Stanislavsky—The Man and his Methods," *Theatre Magazine,* 37 (April, 1923), p. 80.

Chapter 11

1. Richard Boleslawsky, "The Laboratory Theatre and Its Realization in America," unpublished article, n.d., [ca. 1923], *Lab Files.*

2. Abstracted from Ronald A. Willis, "The American Laboratory Theatre, 1923–1930" (Ph.D. diss., University of Iowa, 1968), and brochures and catalogues, American Laboratory Theatre.

3. Ronald A. Willis, "The American Lab Theatre," *Tulane Drama Review,* 9, 1 (Fall, 1964), 113.

4. Lee Strasberg, interview, Oct. 11, 1975.

5. Donald Keyes, interview, Dec. 24, 1974.

6. Francis Fergusson, interview, Nov. 10, 1975.

7. For other specific examples of exercises in Ouspenskaya's class, see Willis, diss., pp. 320–24.

8. Strasberg, interview.

9. Fergusson, interview.

10. Elizabeth Gresham, letters to the author, April 5, March 13, 1979.

11. Harold Clurman, *The Fervent Years* (New York, 1966), pp. 6–7.

12. Harold Clurman, interview, Nov. 5, 1975.

13. Alexander Woollcott, "'The Saint' at Greenwich Village," *New York Sun,* Oct. 13, 1924.

14. " 'The Saint' Reveals Lofty Aim and Beauty," *New York Times,* Oct. 13, 1924.

15. Willis, diss., pp. 60–61.

16. Herbert K. Stockton to Edgar A. Levy, Jan. 8, 1925, *Lab Files;* and Willis, diss., p. 81.

17. Blanch Tancock, tape recording, March, 1964, *Willis Collection.*

18. Boleslavsky to Amelie Rives, June 5, 1926, *Lab Files.*

19. Rachel Crowthers, letter to the Dramatic Editor dated April 27, 1925, "In the Dramatic Mailbag," *New York Times,* May 3, 1925.

20. Stella Adler, interview, Oct. 21, 1975.

21. Letter addressed to Stella Adler, Jan. 22, 1926, *Lab Files*.

22. Elizabeth Bigelow to Stella Adler, April 2, May 1, 1926, *Lab Files*.

23. MKS "Report and Synopsis," p. 14.

24. "Actors Build Their Own Theatre," unpublished article, *Lab Files*.

25. Richard Boleslavsky, unpublished Lab Theatre Lecture n.d., [ca. 1925], possession of the author, courtesy of Stella Adler.

26. Donald Keyes, interview.

27. Blanch Tancock, tape, *Willis Collection*.

28. Gilbert W. Gabriel, "Review of 'The Sea-Woman's Cloak,' " *New York Sun,* Nov. 6, 1925; New York correspondent of *Paris Times,* quoted in Lab playbill for *Twelfth Night*.

29. J. Brooks Atkinson, "What the Actors Will," *New York Times,* Oct. 16, 1925.

30. "The Sea Woman's Cloak," *New York Drama Calendar,* Nov. 16, 1925; " 'Sea Woman's Cloak' Charms at Laboratory Theatre," *Billboard,* Dec. 19, 1925.

31. "In 'The Sea Woman's Cloak,' " *New York Sun,* Nov. 6, 1925.

32. Willis, diss., p. 112.

33. R. W. Jr., "Actors in 'Scarlet Letter,' Compete With Background," *New York Tribune,* Jan. 6, 1926.

34. J. Brooks Atkinson, " 'The Scarlet Letter' As Drama," *New York Times,* Jan. 8, 1926.

35. Gilbert W. Gabriel, "The Play of 'The Scarlet Letter,' " *New York Sun,* Jan. 8, 1926.

36. Lee Strasberg, interview.

37. Blanch Tancock tape, *Willis Collection*.

38. Special Correspondent, "The Scarlet Letter," *The Stage* [London] (Jan. 28, 1926), p. 22.

39. Alexander Samalman, "Amelie Rives' Play Presented," *New York Telegraph,* Jan. 4, 1926.

40. Lee Strasberg, interview.

41. Crowthers, letter.

42. Atkinson, *Times,* Jan. 8, 1926.

Chapter 12

1. *Six Lessons,* p. 40.

2. Ibid., pp. 42–43.

3. Boleslavsky, unpublished Lab Theatre Lecture 8, ca. 1925, possession of the author.

4. Harold Clurman, interview, Nov. 5, 1975.

5. Boleslavsky, unpublished Lab Theatre Lecture 6, ca. 1925, possession of the author.

6. Ibid.

7. Boleslavsky, unpublished Lab Lecture 8, ca. 1925, possession of the author.

8. Richard Boleslavsky, "Fundamentals of Acting," *Theatre Arts Magazine* 11, 2 (Feb., 1927), pp. 128–29.

9. *Six Lessons,* p. 60.

10. Ibid., p. 63.

11. Ibid., pp. 60; 62.

12. Ibid., pp. 60–61.

13. Ibid., pp. 56–57.

14. Ibid., p. 35.

15. Ibid., p. 46.

16. Ibid., pp. 54–55.

17. David Magarshack, *Stanislavsky: A Life* (New York, 1951), p. 380.

Chapter 13

1. Russell Janney to Drama Editor, Jan. 20, 1937, "From the Drama Editor's Mailbag," *New York Herald Tribune,* Jan. 31, 1937; and "The History of 'The Vagabond King,'" rep. from *New York Times,* playbill for *The Vagabond King.*

2. Stephen Rathbun, " 'The Vagabond King' at Casino," *New York Sun,* Sept. 22, 1925.

3. " 'The Vagabond King' Lavish and Tuneful," *New York Times,* Sept. 22, 1925.

4. Janney to Drama Editor, Jan. 20, 1937.

5. Clipping (Detroit) *Free Press,* Feb. 20, 1926, *Lab Files.*

6. "History," *Vagabond King* playbill.

7. Janney to Drama Editor, Jan. 20, 1937.

8. Ibid.

9. J. Brooks Atkinson, "The Play," *New York Times,* Dec. 19, 1925.

10. John Mason Brown, "The Director Takes a Hand," *Theatre Arts Monthly,* 10, 2 (Feb., 1926), 76.

11. Ibid.

12. "Shakespeare's Modern Comedy," *New York Sun,* Jan. 13, 1926.

13. Jane Cowl, quoted in Lab Theatre playbill for *Twelfth Night* (1925).

14. Atkinson, *New York Times,* Dec. 19, 1925.

15. Alexander Woollcott, "The Stage," *New York World,* Dec. 19, 1925.

16. Atkinson, *New York Times,* Dec. 19, 1925.

17. Natasha Boleslavsky, interview.

18. For details, see Ronald A. Willis, "The American Laboratory Theatre, 1923–1930" (Ph.D. diss., University of Iowa, 1968), pp. 134–35.

19. Boleslavsky to Herbert K. Stockton, June 6, 1926, *Lab Files.*

20. Willis, diss., p. 142.

21. E. W. Osborn, " 'The Straw Hat,' " *New York Evening World,* Oct. 16, 1926.

22. Boleslavsky to Henry Allen Moe (John Simon Guggenheim Memorial Foundation), Jan. 17, 1927, *Lab Files;* and Blanch Tancock, tape recording, March, 1964, *Willis Collection.*

23. "New American Play is Quite Fantastic," *New York Times,* Dec. 12, 1926; B.S., "Laboratory Theatre Adds New Wilder Play to Repertory," *New York Herald Tribune,* Dec. 12, 1926; L.M., "The Play," *New York Evening Post,* Dec. 13, 1926.

24. John Anderson, "The Play," *New York Post,* Jan. 5, 1927; " The Play," *New York Times,* Jan. 6, 1927; "'Ballyhoo' Depicts Tent Show Life," *Wall Street Journal,* Jan. 5, 1927; Percy Hammond, "The Theatres," *New York Herald Tribune,* Jan. 5, 1927.

25. Alexander Woollcott, "The Stage," *New York World,* Jan. 5, 1927.

26. *Creative Theatre,* pp. 6; 24.

27. Francis Fergusson, interview.

28. Harold Clurman, interview, Nov. 5, 1975.

29. Boleslavsky to H. Stockton, June 6, 1926.

30. Willis, diss., p. 138.

31. Tancock tape, *Willis Collection.*

32. Fergusson interview.

33. Tancock tape, *Willis Collection.*

34. Nathan Zatkin, " 'Granite' Opens at Lab. Theatre," *New York Telegraph,* Feb. 13, 1927.

35. J. Brooks Atkinson, "The Play: What the Sea Spews Up," *New York Times,* Feb. 13, 1927.

36. R. Dana Skinner, "Granite," *Commonweal,* March 9, 1927.

37. Percy Hammond, " 'Granite,' an Interesting Play by Clemence Dane, Presented Perfectly by the Laboratory Theatre," *New York Herald Tribune,* Feb. 12, 1927.

38. Elizabeth Bigelow to Richard Boleslavsky, February 25, 1927, *Lab Files.*

39. *Lab Files.*

40. Tancock tape, *Willis Collection.*

41. Boleslavsky to Elizabeth Bigelow, n.d. [ca. March 10, 1927], *Lab Files.*

42. Bigelow to Boleslavsky, March 11, 1927; Boleslavsky to Bigelow, March 15, 1927, *Lab Files*.

43. Janney letter, Jan. 20, 1927.

44. "The Vagabond King," *The Play Pictorial* (London), 51 (July–Dec. 1927), viii.

45. Miriam Stockton to Boleslavsky, n. d. [ca. July, 1927], *Lab Files*.

Chapter 14

1. Boleslavsky to New York State Revenue Service, Dec. 13, 1928, *Lab Files*.

2. Boleslavsky to Basil Sidney, May 20, 1927; Boleslavsky to Russell Janney, May 25, 1927; Boleslavsky to Rollo Peters, July 13, 1927; Elizabeth Bigelow to Boleslavsky, July 15, 1927 *Lab Files*.

3. Robert Edgar Long to Boleslavsky, May 14, 1927; Boleslavsky to Long, May 17, 1927 *Lab Files*.

4. Boleslavsky to Gordon Craig, June 9, 1927, *Lab Files*.

5. Playbill for *A Midsummer Night's Dream;* Boleslavsky to Douglas Moore, June 9, 1927, *Lab Files*.

6. B.S. " 'Midsummer Night's Dream' in Open Air Draws 2,000 Crowd," *New York Herald Tribune,* June 27, 1927.

7. Daniel Frohman to Ruth Vivian, Aug. 5, 1927, *Lab Files*.

8. Boleslavsky to Miriam Stockton, July 23, 1927, *Lab Files*.

9. Ronald A. Willis, "The American Laboratory Theatre, 1923–1930," Ph.D. diss, University of Iowa, 1968, p. 185.

10. See Willis, pp. 187–95 for details.

11. Boleslavsky to Herbert K. Stockton, Oct. 7; Oct. 12, 1927, *Lab Files*.

12. Elizabeth Bigelow to Boleslavsky, Sept. 23, 1927, *Lab Files*.

13. Stella Adler to Boleslavsky, n. d. [ca. Sept, 1927]; Boleslavsky to Adler, September 9, 1927.

14. Boleslavsky to George Auerbach, Oct. 6, 1927, *Lab Files*.

15. Grover Burgess to Bigelow, n. d. [ca. Dec., 1927]; Boleslavsky to Bigelow, Dec. 16, 1927, *Lab Files*.

16. Boleslavsky to Herbert Stockton, Oct. 12, 1927; Stockton to Boleslavsky, Oct. 18, 1927, *Lab Files*.

17. Constance McLean to Boleslavsky, Nov. 19, 1927, *Lab Files*.

18. Miriam Stockton to Boleslavsky, Nov. 29, 1927, *Lab Files*.

19. Miriam Stockton to Boleslavsky, Dec. 5, 1927, *Lab Files*.

20. Miriam Stockton to Boleslavsky, Dec. 8, 1927, *Lab Files*.

21. "Laboratory Theatre Acts Norwegian Play," *New York Times,* Dec. 9, 1927.

22. Miriam Stockton to Boleslavsky, Dec. 15, 1927, *Lab Files.*

23. " 'The White Eagle' Is Lavishly Staged," *New York Times,* Dec. 27, 1927.

24. Boleslavsky to Russell Janney, Jan. 14, 1928; Boleslavsky to Clarence Luce, Jr., Jan. 20, 1928, *Lab Files.*

25. Gordon M. Leland, "Twelve Thousand," *Billboard,* March 24, 1928.

26. J. Brooks Atkinson, "The Play: Buffoonery Ill-Advised," *New York Times,* Feb. 24, 1928.

27. Percy Hammond, "The Theaters," *New York Herald Tribune,* Feb. 24, 1928.

28. John Anderson, "A French Satire of Medicine at American Laboratory," *New York Journal,* Feb. 25, 1928.

29. "Doctor Knock," *New York Sun,* Feb. 24, 1928.

30. Barclay V. McCarty, "Dr. Knock," *Billboard,* March 3, 1928.

31. Boleslavsky to John Anderson, Feb. 27, 1928, *Lab Files.*

32. Miriam K. Stockton to Elizabeth McCormick, Dec. 16, 1927, *Lab Files.*

33. Boleslavsky to Anderson, Feb. 27, 1928, *Lab Files.*

34. J.M.B., "The Suburbs of Columbia," unidentified clipping, March 6, 1928, *Lab Files.*

35. Ruth Nelson, interview, Jan. 2, 1976.

36. Leonard Hall, " 'Martine' Brings Out a Striking Young Actress," *New York Telegram,* April 5, 1928.

37. Robert Littell, "The Play," *New York Post,* April 5, 1928.

38. M.C.D., " 'Martine' at the Laboratory," *New York Graphic,* April 5, 1928.

39. Richard Boleslavsky, "Questions to Richard Boleslavsky," *The Pit* (April, 1928), 2.

Chapter 15

1. Elizabeth Bigelow to Boleslavsky, April 5, 1928, *Lab Files.*

2. Boleslavsky to Herbert K. Stockton, April 10, 1928, *Lab Files.*

3. Francis Fergusson, "A Playreader's Viewpoint," *The Pit* (April, 1928), pp. 6–7.

4. Boleslavsky to Herbert K. Stockton, April 10, 1928, *Lab Files.*

5. John Mason Brown, "The Coming Season," n.d. [1928]; Elizabeth Bigelow to Robert Edmond Jones, March 25, 1928, *Lab Files.*

6. Boleslavsky to Herbert K. Stockton, April 19, 1928, *Lab Files.*

7. Francis Fergusson to Miriam Stockton, Sept. 5, 1928, *Lab Files.*

8. Channing Pollock to Miriam Stockton, Oct. 28, 1928, *Lab Files.*

9. Boleslavsky to Channing Pollock, March 24, 1928, *Lab Files.*

10. Boleslavsky to Robert Edmond Jones, April 11, 1928, *Lab Files.*

11. Boleslavsky to Willie Edelsten, April 26, 1928, *Lab Files.*

12. " 'Mr. Moneypenny' An Allegorical Play," *New York Times,* Oct. 18, 1928.

13. Robert Garland, " 'Mr. Moneypenny' Opens With Big Cast at Liberty," *New York Evening Telegram,* Oct. 18, 1928.

14. Arthur B. Waters, "Pollock Leans to Impressionism in Drama at Garrick," *Pennsylvania Ledger,* Sept. 25, 1928.

15. Robert Littell, "The Play," *New York Evening Post,* Oct. 18, 1928.

16. St. John Ervine, "The New Play," *New York World,* Oct. 19, 1928.

17. Mitzi Kolisch, "The New Plays," *New York Morning Telegraph,* Oct. 18, 1928.

18. Ronald A. Willis, "The American Laboratory Theatre, 1923–1930," Ph.D. dissertation (University of Iowa, 1968), p. 266.

19. Gordon Craig to Boleslavsky, Sept. 21, 1928, repr. in playbill for *Macbeth.*

20. Richard Boleslavsky, "Questions to Richard Boleslavsky," *The Pit* (April, 1928), 2.

21. Arthur Pollock, "The Theatre," *Brooklyn Eagle,* Jan. 25, 1929.

22. Brooks Atkinson, "The Play," *New York Times,* Jan. 25, 1929.

23. Basil Rathbone, *In and Out of Character* (New York, 1962), p. 116.

24. Francis Fergusson, interview with the author, Nov. 10, 1975.

25. Quoted in N. F. Monakhov, *Povest' o zhizni* (Leningrad-Moscow, 1961), p. 173.

26. Quoted in American Lab brochure, 1928–1929, p. 1.

27. Gordon Craig to Elizabeth Bigelow, n.d. [ca. 1928], *Lab Files.*

28. Unidentified clipping, Dec. 1925, The Library and Museum of the Performing Arts, Lincoln Center.

29. Ruth Nelson, interview, Jan. 2, 1976.

30. Marion Crowne to Celeste Piriwitz, April 3, 1929, *Lab Files.*

31. Willis, p. 267.

32. Francis Fergusson to Miriam Stockton, Sept. 5, 1929, *Lab Files.*

33. Francis Fergusson, *The Human Image in Dramatic Literature* (Garden City, New York, 1957), pp. 110–11.

Chapter 16

1. *Six Lessons,* pp. 52–53.

2. Boleslavsky to George Shively, June 3, 1932, *Bobbs-Merrill.*

3. Boleslavsky to Shively, Dec. 21, 1934; May 8, 1935, and July 20, 1936, *Bobbs-Merrill.*

4. Boleslavsky to Shively, April 15, 16, 20; May 12, 16, 21, 25; June 3, 1934, *Bobbs-Merrill.*

5. Richard Ordyński, *Z mojej włóczęgi* (Kraków, 1956), pp. 104–6.

6. "The World and the Theatre," *Theatre Arts Monthly,* 21 (March, 1937), pp. 171–72.

7. Russell Janney, letter dated Jan. 20, 1937, "From the Drama Editor's Mailbag," *New York Herald Tribune,* Jan. 31, 1937.

8. Eric H. Rideout, *The American Film* (London, 1937), pp. 77–78.

9. *Six Lessons,* pp. 52–53.

10. "Boleslawski Dies; Film Director, 47," *New York Times,* Jan. 18, 1937.

Conclusions

1. Harold Clurman, interview, Nov. 5, 1975.

2. Francis Fergusson, interview, Nov. 10, 1975.

3. Stella Adler, interview, Oct. 21, 1975.

4. Ibid.

5. Lee Strasberg, interview, Oct. 11, 1975.

6. Clurman interview.

7. Fergusson interview.

8. Harold Clurman, *The Fervent Years* (New York, 1966), p. 14.

9. Ibid, p. 21.

10. Ibid., pp. 40–41.

11. Ibid., p. 130.

12. See Suzanne O'Malley, "Can the Method Survive the Madness?" *New York Times Magazine* (Oct. 7, 1979), pp. 32–40; 139–41.

13. Strasberg interview.

14. O'Malley, "Can the Method Survive?" p. 32.

15. Paul Gray, "The Reality of Doing," *Stanislavski and America* (Greenwich, Conn.: 1967), p. 208.

16. Adler interview.

17. Boris Filippov, *Actors Without Makeup* (Moscow, 1977), p. 59; cf. I. Vinogradskaya, ed. *Zhizn' i tvorchestvo K. S. Stanislavskogo,* vol. IV (Moscow, 1976), p. 368.

18. Francis Fergusson, "The Notion of 'Action,' " *Stanislavski and America,* pp. 85–86.

19. Fergusson interview.

20. Donald Keyes, interview, Dec. 24, 1974.

21. Blanch Tancock, tape recording, *Willis Collection.*

22. Clurman interview.

23. Ruth Nelson, interview.

24. Strasberg, interview.

25. Lee Strasberg, *Strasberg at the Actors Studio,* ed. Robert H. Hethmon (New York, 1968), pp. 144–45.

26. Arthur Sircom to Ronald A. Willis, Nov. 8, 1963, *Willis Collection.*

27. *Six Lessons,* pp. 45; 52.

Bibliography

What follows is a list of works containing significant references to Boleslavsky, bearing significantly on his career, or written by him. Newspaper and periodical reviews are not included; for these the reader is referred to the footnotes above. A separate listing of collections, interviews, and unpublished materials follows.

Andreyeva, Mariya Fedorovna. *Vospominaniya o Marii Fedorovne Andreyevoi*. Moscow: "Iskusstvo," 1960.

Berezark, I. B. *Boris Sushkevich*. Leningrad-Moscow: "Iskusstvo," 1967.

Birman, Serafima. *Put' aktrisy*. Moscow: Vserossiiskoe teatral'noe Obshchestvo,1962.

Blok, Aleksander. *Zapisnye knizhki 1901–1920*. Moscow: "Khudozhestvennaya literatura," 1965.

"Bolesławski, Ryszard." *Słownik Biograficzny Teatru Polskiego 1765–1965*. Warsaw: Państwowe Wydawnictwo Naukowe, 1973.

Boleslavski, Richard. "Pro Domo Sua." *Wings*. A publication of The Literary Guild. 6, 3 (March, 1932), pp. 12–14.

Boleslavski, Richard and Helen Woodward. *Lances Down*. Indianapolis: Bobbs-Merrill, 1932.

———. *Way of the Lancer*. Indianapolis: Bobbs-Merrill, 1932.

Boleslavsky, Richard. *Acting: The First Six Lessons*. New York: Theatre Arts Books, 1933.

———. "Collective Education in the Art of the Theatre." Catalogue, American Laboratory Theatre, 1925–26. The Library and Museum of the Performing Arts.

———. "The Education and Fundamentals in the Development of the Actor as a Technician." *Proceedings of the Conference on the Drama in American Universities and Little Theatres*. Carnegie Institute of Technology, 1925, pp. 51–61.

———. "The First Lesson in Acting: A Pseudo-Morality." *Theatre Arts Magazine*, 7 (October, 1923), pp. 284–92.

———. "A Second Lesson in Acting: A Pseudo-Morality." *Theatre Arts Monthly*, 13, 7 (July, 1929), pp. 498–505.

———. "A Third Lesson in Acting: A Pseudo-Morality." *Theatre Arts Monthly*, 15, 7 (July, 1931), pp. 608–12.

———. "A Fourth Lesson in Acting: A Pseudo-Morality." *Theatre Arts Monthly*, 16, 2 (Feb., 1932), pp. 121–28.

———. "A Fifth Lesson in Acting: A Pseudo-Morality." *Theatre Arts Monthly*, 16, 4 (April, 1932), pp. 294–98.

———. "A Sixth Lesson in Acting: A Pseudo-Morality." *Theatre Arts Monthly*, 16, 6 (June, 1932), pp. 477–83.

————. "Fundamentals of Acting." *Theatre Arts Monthly* 11, 2 (Feb., 1927), pp. 121–29.

————. *Komediespil; de seks første lektioner.* Ed. Ove Brusendorff. Copenhagen: Thanning & Appel, 1947.

————. "Color Photography." *Radio City Music Hall Weekly* 2, 5 (Nov. 12, 1936), p. 5.

————. "The Director's Viewpoint." *Photoplay Studies* 1, 2 (1935), pp. 5-6.

————. "An artist of the Theatre." *Theatre Arts Magazine,* 8 (Nov., 1924), pp. 572–73.

————. "The Laboratory Theatre." *Theatre Arts Magazine,* 7 (July, 1923), pp. 244–50.

————. "Stanislavsky—The Man and His Methods." *Theatre Magazine* 37 (April, 1923), 27; 74; 80.

"Boleslawski Dies; Film Director, 47." *The New York Times,* Jan. 18, 1937.

"Boleslawski Dies of Heart Attack; Movie Director." *The Brooklyn Daily Eagle,* Jan. 18, 1937.

"Boleslawski, Film Director, Dies Suddenly." *The New York American,* Jan. 18, 1937.

"Boleslawski, Film Director, Is Dead at 47." *The New York World-Telegram,* Jan. 18, 1937.

Bradshaw, Martha, ed. *Soviet Theatres: 1917–1941.* New York Research Program on the U.S.S.R., 1945.

Carter, Huntley. *The New Spirit in the Russian Theatre: 1917–1928.* New York: Arno Press, 1970.

Centkiewicz, St. "Teatr Amerykański." *Ameryka,* 2, 4 (April, 1924), pp. 20-21.

Chociłowski, Jerzy, ed. *Contemporary Polish Cinematography.* Warsaw: Polonia Publishing House, 1962.

Clurman, Harold. *The Fervent Years.* New York: Hill and Wang, 1957.

————. *Lies Like Truth.* New York: Macmillan, 1958.

————. *On Directing.* New York: Macmillan, 1972.

————. "The Principles of Interpretation," *Producing the Play.* Ed. John Gassner. New York: Dryden Press, 1941.

Cole, Toby, ed. *Acting: A Handbook of the Stanislavski Method.* Rev. ed. New York: Crown Publishers, 1955.

Cole, Toby and Helen Krich Chinoy, eds. *Directors on Directing: A Source Book of the Modern Theatre.* Rev. ed. Indianapolis and New York: Bobbs-Merrill, 1963.

Crowley, Alice Lewisohn. *The Neighborhood Playhouse.* New York: Theatre Arts Books, 1959.

Csato, Edward. *Leon Schiller.* Warszawie: Państwowy Instytut Wydawniczy, 1968.

————. *The Polish Theatre.* Warsaw: Polonia, 1963.

Diky, Aleksei. *Povest' o teatral'noi yunosti.* Moscow: "Iskusstvo," 1957.

————. *Stat'i, perepiska, vospominaniya.* Ed. N. G. Litvinenko and A. G. Guliyev. Moscow: "Iskusstvo," 1967.

Efros, Nikolai. *Moskovskii Khudozhestvennyi Teatr, 1898–1923.* Moscow-Leningrad: Gosudarstvennoe izdatelstvo, 1924.

Fergusson, Francis. *The Human Image in Dramatic Literature.* Garden City, N.Y.: Doubleday Anchor Books, 1957.

————. "The Notion of 'Action.' " *Stanislavski and America.* Ed. Erika Munk. Greenwich, Conn.: Fawcett, 1967.

Fricken, Roi Henri. "An Experiment in Play Production." *Theatre Magazine* 46 (Oct., 1927), pp. 41; 65.

Gaidarov, V. G. *V teatre i kino.* Leningrad-Moscow: "Iskusstvo," 1966.

Gorchakov, Nikolai Aleksandrovitch. *The Theatre in Soviet Russia.* Trans. Edgar Lehrman. New York: Columbia University Press, 1957.

Gorchakov, Nikolai M. *The Vakhtangov School of Stage Art.* Trans. G. Ivanof-Mumjiev. Ed. Phyl Griffith. Moscow: Foreign Languages Publishing House, n.d.

Gourfinkel, Nina. "The Actor Sets to Work on His Part—Vol. IV of The Works of Stanislavski." *Theatre World,* 8, 1 (Spring, 1959), pp. 10–22.

Gremov, V. *Mikhail Chekhov.* Moscow: "Iskusstvo," 1970.

Grey, Paul. "A Critical Chronology." *Stanislavski and America.* Ed. Erika Munk. Greenwich, Conn.: Fawcett, 1967.

Hiż, Tadeusz. "Ryszard Bolesławski w Rosji." *Scena Polska,* vol. 14 (1937), pp. 47–52.

Janney, Russell. "From the Drama Editor's Mailbag." *The New York Herald-Tribune,* Jan. 31, 1937.

Knipper-Chekhova, Olga Leonardovna. *Chast' vtoraya—perepiska.* Vol. II. Moscow: "Iskusstvo," n.d.

Krasiński, Edward. *Teatr Jaracza.* Warsaw: Państwowy Instytut Wydawniczy, 1970.

Leonidov, Leonid Mironovich. *Stat'i i vospominaniya o L. M. Leonidove.* Moscow: "Iskusstvo," 1960.

Leyda, Jay. *Kino: A History of the Russian and Soviet Film.* London: George Allen & Unwin, 1960.

Magarshack, David. "Introduction." *Stanislavsky on the Art of the Stage.* Trans. David Magarshack. Second ed. New York: Hill and Wang, 1961.

———. *Stanislavsky: A Life.* New York: Chanticleer, 1950.

Markov, P. A. "Pervaya studiya MKhT: Sulerzhitsky—Vakhtangov—Chekhov." *Moskovskii Khudozhestvennyi Teatr, vtoroi.* 1925; repr. *Pravda teatra: Stat'i.* Moscow: "Iskusstvo," 1965.

Melik-Zakharov, Shoel Bogatyrev, and Nikolai Solntsev, eds. *K. Stanislavsky: 1863–1963.* Trans. Vic Schneierson. Moscow: Progress Publishers, n.d.

Moskovskii Khudozhestvennyi Teatr v illyustratsiyakh i dokumentakh 1898–1938. Moscow: Izdanie Moskovskogo ordena Lenina khudozhestvennogo akademicheskogo teatra SSSR imeni M. Gor'kogo, 1938.

Monakhov, N. F. *Povest'o zhizni.* Leningrad-Moscow: "Iskusstvo," 1961.

Nemirovitch-Dantchenko, Vladimir. *Izbrannye pis'ma.* Vol. II. Moscow: "Iskusstvo," 1979.

———. *My Life in the Russian Theatre.* Trans. John Cournos. 1938; repr. New York: Theatre Arts Books, 1968.

Ordyński, Ryszard. "Bolesławski w Ameryce." *Scena Polska,* vol. 14 (1937), pp. 91–95.

———. *Z mojej włóczęgi.* 1939; repr. Krakow: Wydawmoctwo Literackie, 1956.

Polyakova, Ye. and V. Ye. Vilenkina. *Leopold Antonovich Sulerzhitsky.* Moscow: "Iskusstvo," 1970.

Rathbone, Basil. *In and Out of Character.* Garden City, New York: Doubleday, 1962.

"Richard Boleslawski." *The New York Sun,* Jan. 18, 1937.

"Richard Boleslawski." *Variety,* January 20, 1937.

"Richard Boleslawski, the Soldier-Director." *Cue* 8, 30 (May 25, 1935), pp. 3–4.

"Richard Boleslawski Dies at 47: Ex-Russian Actor, Film Director." *The New York Herald-Tribune,* Jan. 18,1937.

Rideout, Eric H. *The American Film.* London: The Mitre Press, 1937.

Rudnitsky, K., ed. *Istoriya sovetskogo dramaticheskogo teatra 1917–1920.* Vol. I. Moscow: "Nauka," 1966.

"Ś. p. Ryszard Bolesławski." *Czas* (Warsaw), Jan. 24, 1937, p. 11.

Savage, Richard. "A Theatre That is Different." *Theatre Magazine* 43 (March, 1926), pp.22; 66

Sayler, Oliver M. *The Russian Theatre Under the Revolution*. Boston: Little, Brown, 1920.

Schiller, Irena, "Balladyna' w I Studio MChAT." *Pamiętnik Teatralny*. 8, 1–23 (1959), pp. 346–75.

Stanisławski a teatr polski. Warszawa: Państwowy Instytut Wydàwniczy, 1965.

————. ed. "Ze wspomnień o 'Balladynie' w I Studio MChAT: Fragmenty stenogramu." *pamiętnik Teatralny*, 9, 1 (1960), pp. 346–53.

Schiller, Leon. "Gdy Bolesławski przyjechał do Warszawy." *Scena Polska*, 14 (1937), pp. 53–90.

Sibiryakov, N. N. *Stanislavski i zarubezhnyi teatr*. Moscow: "Iskusstvo," 1967.

Sovetskii teatr: Dokumenty i materialy: Russkii Sovetskii teatr 1917–1921. Ed. A. E. Dufit. Leningrad: "Iskusstvo," 1968.

Stanislavski, K. S. *My Life in Art*. Trans. J. J. Robbins. Boston: Little, Brown, 1924.

————. *My Life in Art*. Trans. G. Ivanov-Mumjiev. Moscow: Foreign Languages Publishing House, n.d.

————. *Pis'ma*. Vols. 7, 8. Moscow: "Iskusstvo," 1960; 1961.

————. *Stat'i, rechi, otkliki, zametki, vospominaniya 1917–1938*. vol. 6. Moscow: "Iskusstvo," 1959.

————. *Zhizn' i tvorchestvo K. S. Stanislavskogo*. Ed. I. Vinogradskaya. Vols. II, III, IV. Moscow: Vserossiiskoe teatral'noe obshchestvo, 1971, 1973, 1976.

Strasberg, Lee. "Acting and the Training of the Actor." *Producing the Play*. Ed. John Gassner. New York: Dryden Press, 1941.

————. "Strasberg at The Actors Studio: Tape-Recorded Sessions." Ed. Robert H. Hethmon. New York: Viking, 1968.

Szydłowski, Roman. *The Theatre in Poland*. Warsaw: Interpress, 1972.

Teatr Polski w Warszawie 1913–1923. Warsaw: Towarszystwo Wydawnicze "Ignis," n.d.

Toeplitz, Jerzy, ed. *Historia filmu polskiego*. Vol. I. Warsaw: Wydawnictwa Artystyczne i Filmowe, 1966.

————. *Historia sztuki filmowej*. Vols. I, IV. Warsaw: Wydawnictwa Artystyczne i Filmowe, 1969.

Vakhtangov, Yevgenii B. *Materialy i stat'i*. Moscow: Vserossiskoe teatral'noe obshchestvo, 1959.

Valkov, N. D. *Teatral'nye vechera*. Moscow: "Iskusstvo," 1966.

Vilenkin, F. *Kachalov*. Moscow: "Iskusstvo," 1962.

Vishnevsky, Ven. *Khudozhestvennye fil'my dorevolutsionnoi Rossii*. Moscow: Goskinoizdat, 1945.

Willis, Ronald A. "The American Lab Theatre." *Tulane Drama Review* 9, 1 (Fall, 1964), pp. 112–16.

Collections, Interviews, and Unpublished Sources

Adler, Stella. Interview (taped). October 21, 1975.

American Laboratory Theatre Files, 1923–1930. The files contain numerous letters; photographs; speeches; memos; playbills; catalogues; brochures; scrapbooks of clippings; legal documents; minutes of meetings; and miscellaneous items formerly belonging to the Lab. Possession of Ronald A. Willis (given him by Anne Stockton Goodwin), University of Kansas, Lawrence. Copies (provided by Willis) in the possession of the author.

American Laboratory Theatre playbills, catalogues, brochures, newsclippings, 1923–1929. The Library and Museum of the Performing Arts, Lincoln Center.

Arnold, N. N. von. Letter to the author, March 21, 1975.

Bobbs-Merrill Collection. "Author's Questionnaire," filed by Richard Boleslavsky 1932, correspondence, and miscellaneous records, 1931–1936.

Boleslavsky, Natasha. Interviews. Dec. 13, 1971 (taped); Jan. 12; Jan. 28, 1972; and numerous informal conversations.

———. Scrapbooks, photographs, personal memorabilia.

Boleslavsky, Richard. American Laboratory Theatre Lectures. Mimeographed, ca. 1925–1926. Copy provided to the author by Stella Adler.

———. "The Creative Theatre." Transcribed and ed. Michael Barroy. Mimeographed, ca. 1923. The Library and Museum of the Performing Arts, Lincoln Center.

Clurman, Harold. Interview (taped). Nov. 5, 1975.

Cromwell, Ruth Nelson. Interview (taped). Jan. 2, 1976.

Fergusson, Francis. Interview (taped). Nov. 10, 1975.

Gresham, Elizabeth Fenner. Letters to the author. Dec. 10, 1978; Jan. 3; March 13; April 5, 1979.

Hardy, Michael Carrington. "The Theatre Art of Richard Boleslavsky." Ph.D. dissertation, University of Michigan, 1971.

Just, Claus. "Stanislawski und das deutschsprachige Theater. Daten, Texte und Interpretationen bis 1940." Dissertation, Friedrich-Alexander universität, Erlangen-Nürnberg, 1970.

Keyes, Donald. Interviews (taped). Dec. 24, 1974; Jan. 14, 1975.

Kuhlke, William Lonnie. "Vakhtangov's Legacy." Ph.D. dissertation, State University of Iowa, 1965.

Leavitt, Max. Interview (taped). Dec. 19, 1971.

Leontovich, Eugenie. Interview (taped). July 28, 1972.

MacGregor, Robert M. Letter to the author, Jan. 26, 1972.

Mielziner, Jo. Telephone conversation. Nov. 10, 1975.

Moscow Art Theatre, playbills for the 1923–1924 American tour. The Library and Museum of the Performing Arts, Lincoln Center.

Roberts, Jerry W. "The Theatre Theory and Practice of Richard Boleslavsky." Ph.D. dissertation, Kent State University, 1977.

Scharfenberg, Jean. "Lee Strasberg. Teacher." Ph.D. dissertation. University of Wisconsin, 1963.

Soloviova, Vera. Letter to the author, Nov. 12, 1975. Interview (taped). Dec. 1, 1975.

Squire, Katharine. Interview (taped).

Srzednicki, Jean. Telephone conversation. Sept. 24, 1973.

Strasberg, Lee. Interview (taped). Oct. 11, 1975.

Willis, Ronald A. "The American Laboratory Theatre, 1923–1930." Ph.D. dissertation, University of Iowa, 1968.

———. Private collection of materials gathered in preparation of Ph.D. dissertation, including numerous interviews and correspondence with former Lab Theatre students or members; and Boleslavsky-Woodward correspondence. Copies provided to the author.

Index